Printed by CreateSpace, An Amazon.com Company

Graphic project and Typeset: Annalisa Scaccabarozzi
Editing and Publishing Coordination: Yun Zhang John
First published in June 2014

ISBN: 978-1497345577

THE SMOUHA CITY VENTURE

Alexandria 1923-1958

Richard Smouha
Cristina Pallini
Marie-Cécile Bruwier

Table of contents

Forewords

Richard Smouha

There is a point in the passage of time when one's ambitions and one's future take on less importance and one's past and its memories take over. Having now reached this point in my life, I have for the second time returned to the family files, but this time in a context very different from the first time in the early Nineties.

My original project of writing a family history as well as the recent volume of family histories from Egypt such as my cousin Jean Naggar's wonderful book *Sipping from the Nile* has inevitably remoulded my ideas.

So much has changed in this New World and at such speed that my thoughts and memories are much closer to the horizon of time requiring more specificity in the choice of any project. My point of departure was to discover to my dismay that, not only did my grandchildren know virtually nothing of our fairly significant family history; but even my children had comparatively little knowledge of it.

Then came the "Arab Springtime," and my brother Brian one day remarked on the importance of Joseph Smouha's creation of Smouha City. With that, the family story went on to the back burner… With this I have chosen a subject, which I consider the earliest on which my generation can comment with personal memories and anecdotes. I begin with what is the most important element in our family history, especially because I have been informed that no such work yet exists: the Smouha City story. Much of what follows is pure family legend and even many of the facts will require correction, but it is a historical version, which will give our descendants an idea of what Joseph Smouha accomplished and the man that he was.

In 1919, Joseph Smouha, in Egypt on mission for HM government, took the train from Cairo to Alexandria with his assistant Daniel Delbourgo, who became probably his closest friend and worked for him for over thirty years.

Even after retirement he would come to the office frequently for a chat with Joseph Smouha. Daniel was a Jew from Aden who according to the family, made mistakes in English that sent everyone into hysterics. They were looking at a city map of 1910 showing Lake Hadra, and Joseph Smouha asked: "How can this city grow?"

Cristina Pallini

Alexandrie entre deux mondes, Colonial Bridgehead, City of Memory: just three titles among the many on the legendary history of nineteenth and twentieth-century Alexandria, often extolled as "a transitory model of conviviality." Indeed, throughout the last thirty years, many scholars have explored the multicultural character of this city, often trying to unravel the relationship between its ever-changing social make-up and the distinguishing features of its built environment.The history of Smouha City is certainly an important piece of the mosaic.

The competition launched by Joseph Smouha in 1925 for "a modern city inspired by the best European examples" brought together a number of architects and town planners from different origins and backgrounds, which lead us to the heart of the debate then arising on urbanism. A number of photographic surveys carried out from 1996 to 2010, show an increasing densification of Smouha City, where many villas have been replaced by huge apartment buildings. Equipped with the central bus terminal, Sidi Gaber Station has become the main access to Alexandria. In 2009 the Ministry of Transportation together with the Egyptian National Railways launched a project aimed at reshaping the station, including a two-storey mall and a multi-level garage (850 parking spaces). In the meantime the famous racecourse has been subdivided to accommodate additional sporting facilities. A new "Smouha Club" has been built in Burg el-Arab. The history of Smouha City, whose modernist architecture marked a clear break with the eclectic townscape of nineteenth-century Alexandria, may have a relevance from many different standpoints: not only for those who are studying the "shared architectural and urban heritage" in the East Mediterranean, but also for those who are called upon to plan the future of Alexandria. Based on archival sources and discussions between the authors, this book is the first stage of further research needed in other public and private archives (i.e. the Archives of the Alexandria Municipality, the National Archives in Cairo, the National Archives in London). My contribution is based on research carried out at the following archives:

Richard Smouha's family archive, Geneva
Margarita Sakka's archive, Athens
Luisa Secchi Tarugi's family archive, Milan
Rodolfo Loria's family archive, Milan
Caccia Dominioni's archive, Nerviano
CEAlex, Alexandria
ELIA-MIET Photographic Archive, Athens
Archive of the Musée Social, Paris
Alinari photographic archive, Florence
Cité de l'Architecture et du Patrimoine, Paris
Institute d'Urbanisme, Paris
Musée d'Orsay Archive, Paris

Marie-Cécile Bruwier

Smouha, the oriental suburb of Alexandria to which Richard Smouha dedicates this book, was created about 90 years ago during the drainage and the drying out of Lake Hadra in the development of a modern urbanization.

The outstanding spirit of Joseph Smouha, Richard's grandfather, led him to create a town schedule and a garden city, which still bears his name.

How did this Alexandria district look like in antiquity? Various questions arise on the landscape renewal outside the ramparts of antique Alexandria, beyond the Sun Gate, near the road that leads to Canopus (today Abukir).

Was there, during the Græco-Roman period, a retention lake of the Nile waters, as thought by some?

The antique geographer Strabo evokes a district east of Alexandria named *Eleusis*, which he places at the water's edge (is it the lake or the canal connecting the Nile to Alexandria?).

Were festivals celebrated there to Demeter as in the case of its Greek homonym? There are references that cemeteries existed there in late antiquity; one of them, situated in the east necropolis, was called *Ta Boukolou*, a Greek word for "pastures." Former authors sometimes suggested a hostile landscape occupied by shepherds and where burglary was rife. At the same time, on the sea coast Saint Mark's *martyrium*, a grave and a church where the tormented corpse of the first Patriarch of the Coptic Church would have been preserved for some time.

The name of the suburb had various spellings (*Boukolia, Boucalis, Bucalis*) in the accounts of western travellers and pilgrims. Closer to the Canal is a district called *al-Hadrah*, a name which, over centuries, will deal with a larger area.

At the end of the 18th century, during the French Expedition (1798-1805), it was reported that the dike was cut, introducing a floor of salt water. After which, the Lake Hadra neighbourhood extended into the marshy fields.

At the end of the 19th century, next to Lake Hadra, fragments of a Colossal Couple in Egyptian style were rediscovered and uncovered.

In the early 20th century, two of the pieces ended up in the Musée royal de Mariemont and two others are now housed in the Græco-Roman Museum of Alexandria.

A related survey was launched in 1989, and led to investigating the archives in both Mariemont and Alexandria, as well as to consulting maps and accounts of earlier travellers and scholars who have mentioned, described, and located these fragments since the 18th century. An archaeological research in the field was conducted from 2008 until 2012.

Within the framework of this research, I was delighted to meet Richard Smouha and Cristina Pallini. Our numerous and friendly contacts convinced me to collaborate with happiness on this book.

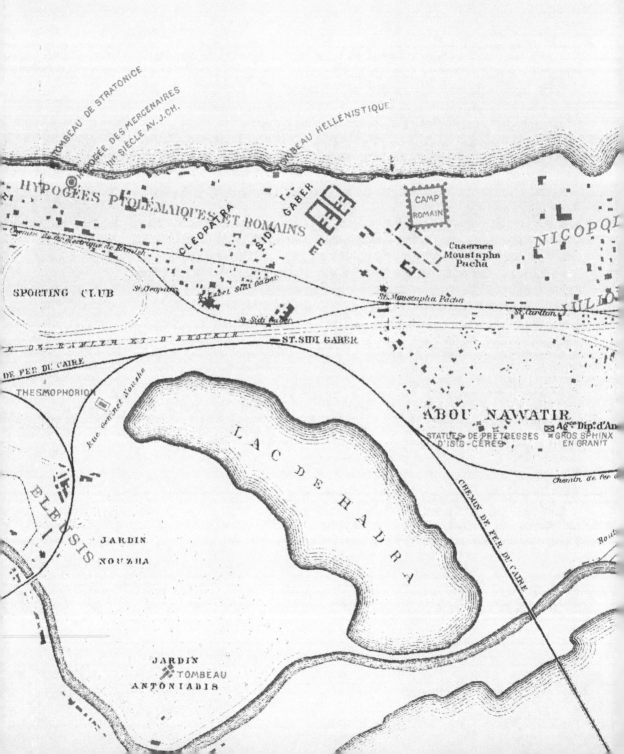

MÉDITERRANÉE

TOMBEAU DE STRATONICE

HYPOGÉE DES MERCENAIRES
IIᵐᵉ SIÈCLE AV. J.CH.

TOMBEAU HELLÉNISTIQUE

HYPOGÉES PTOLÉMAÏQUES ET ROMAINS

CLEOPATRA

GABER

SIDI

CAMP
ROMAIN

NICOPOI

Chemin de fer électrique de Ramleh

Casernes
Moustapha
Pacha

SPORTING CLUB

St Cléopâtre

St Mab: Sidi Gaber

St Moustapha Pacha

St Carlton

JULLO

St Sidi Gaber

St Sidi Gaber

DE RAMLEH ET D'ABOUKIR

DE FER DU CAIRE

THESMOPHORION

Rue Gamal Nouzha

ABOU NAWATIR

Agᶜᵉ Dipᵗ d'An

STATUES DE PRÊTRESSES
D'ISIS-CÉRÈS

GROS SPHINX
EN GRANIT

LAC DE HADRA

Chemin de fer d

ELEUSIS

JARDIN
NOUZHA

CHEMIN DE FER DU CAIRE

Rout

JARDIN
TOMBEAU
ANTONIADIS

Introduction

Richard Smouha

When one looks at a satellite map of Alexandria, the most distinctive feature that catches the eye is a large green oblong of land not far from the centre. It is the racecourse encircling the former golf course (now a sports ground).

My grandfather, a Jew from Baghdad, who went to Manchester and was sent to Egypt by the British government, conceived it, my father created it and I am writing its history, mainly for my children and grandchildren, but also for anyone who can find common ground with the wide variety of subjects covered.

I find that most people treat history as a static fact, a reality, "it must have been like that - it said so in *The Times*." For me, history is a constantly moving story, an interpretation which is never right, never wrong but always different if it is to be acceptable. History is basically taught as a science, based on well-documented facts and figures, confidently confirmed. I am not a historian but I am attempting to write a history some 60 to 90 years after the facts, I must emphasize that I consider history to be more of an art-form and that the real education of history should teach that while facts and figures may be absorbed, it is more important to know how to question the various aspects of what happened. Ask any police force about an accident that has 10 witnesses. Two wonderful books which bring this out in great detail are *Jesus the Man* by Professor Barbara Thiering and *Telling the Truth about History* by Appleby, Hunt and Jacob, and in particular, the importance of context in terms of the two infinities of time and space: when it happened, where it happened, in relation to the rest of the world at that time.

That is why the most difficult decision I had was with the first word of the title. Should it be "The", "A" or "My"? "My" was the easiest to discard as I believe there is sufficient objective documentation to justify something stronger. "A" was tempting and easily justified but not what I was looking for, especially as I had been informed that no other such history existed. So then, "The." I am not a historian and have never written a book. My justification is that I have covered a full timescale and a wide range of facts. Insufficient!

I finally decided on "The" with the promise that if ever there is a second edition every later relevant fact presented to me will be included. I must explain the exceptionally large number of photographs, drawings and maps in this history.

First, photography has only existed in a developed form over the last 90 years. This means that photographs appearing in books dealing with history, whether biographies, events or situations before this period, were more the exception than the rule, as photography did not really become widespread until after the Second World War and any story less than 50 years old is not history.

Second, old customs die hard. Most serious modern histories, for many reasons and especially if they are expected to be taken seriously, have few photographs and those are often grouped in small packages with no connection with the basic historical text. On the other hand, the magazine industry has grown exponentially during this period with the complete opposite structure and policy where the photograph is by far the major part of the presentation and the text is a small but necessary explanatory adjunct to the main message. I am laying myself open to criticism by claiming that serious writers feel slightly demeaned if they have to back up their descriptions and statements with photographs It implies in their eyes that they are incapable of getting their full message across with just the text.

Third, I have another and contrary point of view. I differentiate between text and photograph in the following manner: I believe that the text appeals to the equivalent of the ear/brain and the photo appeals to the eyes/senses. If this is true, then certainly in a large number of works of modern history the required result is not fully achieved.

Fourth, I have therefore attempted where I have text + photo, to complement one with the other and in certain cases expressly giving more importance to either the photo or the text.

Much has happened in and to the world in the last 60 to 90 years. It is not my intention to dwell on this. In most of this history I leave the reader to use memory and imagination to picture a world with few cars, almost no planes, primitive communications, no dials on the operator-controlled telephones, no television. It is so easy to forget these limitations of the old world. I will therefore only emphasize this when, for example, I have a personal memory where the difference between today and then, changes the impact of my anecdote.

1 Marie-Cécile Bruwier
Smouha District in Antiquity

1.1 From Alexandria to Mariemont, Fragments of the Colossal Dyad

This contribution aims at giving an explanation of what we know regarding the Smouha district in Ptolemaic and Roman times (between the 4th century B.C.E. to the 6th century C.E.).

Why the Musée royal de Mariemont (Belgium) undertakes archaeological excavations in this area?

The steps of the current research and the present results are developed here.

In the Alexandrian eastern suburb, close to the place named Lake Hadra in the 19th century, later drained and dried by Joseph Smouha (1878-1961), several parts of a colossal antique dyad were discovered: a female bust and two hands, which since 1912 are in the Musée royal de Mariemont;[1] and the head and the left leg of a male figure acquired by the Græco-Roman Museum of Alexandria before 1907.

The parts of the huge couple probably backed to a stela may represent a goddess (Isis, the ideal mother and wife as well as the patroness of nature and magic), a son-god (Horus, son of Isis), or a Ptolemaic queen, possibly Cleopatra VII and her core-gent Cæsarion, Cleopatra's son.

The questions raised by the fragments of the dyad have been discussed since their discovery, but for the first time in a scientific manner in 1949, 1950 and 1952 by egyptologist Prof. Baudouin Van de Walle (1901-1988), and later from 1989 onwards.

The couple's hands initiated the idea of a sistership between the Musée royal de Mariemont and the Græco-Roman Museum of Alexandria. It became reality in 2001 to study the colossal dyad and to explore and excavate the site which they came from.[2]

Based on ancient cartography, particularly the 1865 map of Mahmoud Bey Al Falaki, on Arab and European travel accounts and diaries, Dr. Sally-Ann Ashton (Senior Assistant Keeper at the Fitzwilliam Museum of Cambridge), Cécile Shaalan (Head of the Topographical Service of the Centre d'Études Alexandrines, CEAlex), and myself proposed to identify the site where the dyad comes from as lying between the current Lewa Mohamed Fawzi Moaaz Street and the Tutankhamun Street in Smouha, in the Alexandrian eastern suburb.

In 2004, a first geo-physical survey was conducted by Dr. Sally-Ann Ashton and geophysicians Paul & Neil Lindford. Positive anomalies were observed, needing improvement.

Later, from 2008 to 2012, excavations have been looking for the remains of a supposed Ptolemaic or Roman building embedded in the grounds of Smouha.

The Musée royal de Mariemont led the project under the authority of the Supreme Council of Antiquities and in partnership with the CEAlex (logistic, scientific and friendly support and co-operation).[3] The archaeological work was conducted by Field archaeologist Francis Choël (CEAlex).

Female Bust and two clenched hands from Alexandria to Mariemont

The research began with the exploration of the Musée royal de Mariemont archives to clarify how Albert Daninos (1843?-1925),[4] while in Egypt, proposed to sell both fragments of the presumed Cleopatra and Mark Antony, her consort, to the Belgian industrialist and collector Raoul Warocqué (1870-1917). On January 12, 1912, Daninos wrote:

"I hereby confirm to you the verbal discussion I had the pleasure to have with you on the subject of the digs of Heliopolis of which I obtained the concession and I expect to undertake in association with you after the acquisition that you wish to make of my head of Cleopatra in grey granite and the two clenched hands of Mark Antony and this famous queen.

The price of this head and the two hands being fifteen thousand francs, I shall allocate ten thousand, which with the other ten thousand that yourself would allocate, would form a total of twenty thousand francs. This sum would be used solely for the expenses of the excavations which I would direct with the aim of finding the Necropolis of Heliopolis."[5]

Rediscovery of the fragments of the colossal dyad

A. Daninos who "rediscovered" these fragments was "excavating" the site in 1892 as testified[6] by Giuseppe Botti (1853-1903),[7] the founder and the first Director of the Græco-Roman Museum.

"This temple lies within the property of the Daira of H.E. Ibrahim Pasha at Sidi Gaber. …

The peribolos of the temple can still be recognized from the digs organized in 1892 by H.E. Daninos Pasha and company. The temple was decorated with colossal statues in granite, made at the Ptolemaic Period. Part of a colossal group was discovered by Daninos Pasha. The colossal head of a second statue was discovered in 1896 by Abdallah Attya."[8]

The three meter-high bust, which may represent Isis or a Ptolemaic queen (Cleopatra VII as Isis?) and two clenched hands were bought by the Belgian collector Raoul Warocqué and were since 1912 housed in his castle. In 1917, he bequeathed his park, castle, and collections to the Belgian State. The Domain became the Musée royal de Mariemont. The two fragments of the male figure, the head and the left leg, belong to the Græco-Roman Museum of Alexandria. Nowadays, this Museum is under renovation and these two fragments are now stored in Kom al-Chougafa.

1.2 Ancient Cartography and Travellers' Accounts

The fragments of the colossal dyad were first noticed by Richard Pococke (1704-1765). The 18th century traveler wrote that the broken statues were lying in marshes near granite columns constituting a portico (?) and were preceded by at least six sphinxes

in *yellow marble* (marble, sandstone, or limestone?). This presence, as well as the nearby *colossi*, may suggest that the building, associated with the dyad, could have been preceded by an Egyptian-type *dromos* and associated pylon.

"About two miles nearer Alexandria, are ruins of an antient (sic) temple in the water: … there are pieces of columns in the water three feet diameter. I saw also three broken statues of Sphynxes, about seven feet long, and three other about four feet long, most of them of a yellow marble. I took particular notice of the statue of a woman of red granite, twelve feet long, and a block of marble four feet diameter, which seem'd to have been the head of a colossal statue, and many pieces about it appear'd to be fragments of the same statue; particularly the hands, which from the wrist to the knuckles measured eighteen inches. Near this building also are other ruins, part of which seems to have been a grand portico, there being about it many pieces of pillars of grey and red granite. To the south of these are many red granite pillars, which form the order they lie in, and the shape of the ground, seem to have belong'd to a round temple; most of them are fluted, and three feet three inches diameter. Several pieces of plain pillars lie together two feet diameter; I conjectured that they might belong to the portico, and that the fluted pillars were within the temple."[9]

Surprisingly, the scholars members of the famous French Expedition at the end of 18th century did not mention the fragments in the *Description de l'Égypte*.

Later in 1842, during the Prussian Expedition to Egypt and Nubia, egyptologist Karl-Richard Lepsius (1810-1884) examined the fragments of the colossal statues. He commissioned Johann Jakob Frey (1813-1865) to draw them. In the later published *Denkmäler aus Ägypten und Äthiopien*, he comments:

"Half an hour walk from the Rosetta gate, right of the road to Rosetta and Abukir, approximately 100 steps left of the irrigation canal of Ibrahim Pasha, lie two colossal statues in black granite: a Roman Emperor, at it seems, or a very late Ptolemaic King and his wife both represented in a colossal way. Their back had no inscription, their nose is unfortunately mutilated. The Emperor, who wears the crown [*hemhem*], over the headgear shows hearcurls under the cap [*nemes*], contrary to the Egyptian way."[10]

Joseph Bonomi (1796-1878) who was part of the Prussian Expedition saw the fragments and drew them. In a letter addressed to John Gardner Wilkinson (1797-1875), he acknowledged the fragments were "discovered" by Anthony Charles Harris (1790-1869), a collector who acquired a lot of ancient Egyptian papyri and artefacts.

As official supplier of the army, Harris was based in Alexandria for the last four decades of his life. Selima Harris, his natural daughter, offered her father's collection for sale in 1871, which was bought by the British Museum in 1872.

"Mr. Harris, our mutual friend, mentioned to me that you desired to have the measure of the fragments composing the statues

Colossal male head, Græco-Roman Museum of Alexandria, inv. 11275 (photo: Marie-Cécile Bruwier).

opposite
Proposal of reconstitution of the colossal couple, Drawing by Pierre Gilbert.
In *Les antiquités égyptiennes, grecques, étrusques, romaines et gallo-romaines du Musée de Mariemont*, Bruxelles, Éditions de la Librairie Encyclopédique, 1952, pl. 7.

Colossal female bust in the park of Mariemont, 1912.

Colossal female bust
Musée royal de Mariemont, inv. B . 505.1
©Musée royal de Mariemont (photo: Michel Lechien).

Limestone fragment with hieroglyphic signs (photo: Marie-Cécile Bruwier).

Clenched hands
Musée royal de Mariemont, inv. B . 505.2
©Musée royal de Mariemont (photo: Michel Lechien).

opposite
Leg of the male figure in Kom el-Chougafa.

(found, or belonging to him) situated in a field in a NEly direction about 20 minutes (donkey pace) from the Rosetta Gate, Alexandria. The statues are made of black granite."[11]

Underneath this text, on the left side of the letter, are five drawings by Bonomi representing: the male head of a "Ptolemy," showing a row of hair locks round the edge of the cap; the *hem-hem* crown; the left part of the king's chest; a portion of the lower body, covered by a loincloth; and part of the left leg. On the right half of the letter, Bonomi drew two pieces of the female part of the dyad: the head and bust with part of the back pilaster, and a leg. Later on, John Gardner Wilkinson wrote about the dyad:

"On leaving the Rosetta gate, the road runs for half a mile over the mounds of the ancient city, when it crosses the old wall, on which the French lines were raised, and descends into a plain, now partly cultivated by order of Ibrahim Pasha. Here, about 3/4 of a mile from the old wall, two granite statues were discovered by Mr. Harris, apparently of one of the Ptolemies, or of a Roman emperor, with his queen, in the Egyptian style. One has the form of Osiris, the other of Isis, or of Athor. Other granite blocks and remains of columns show that this was the site of some important building."[12]

Finally, the site was neglected. Travellers and archaeologists passing by just mention the fragments of the colossal statues and their unhealthy environment. In 1849-1850, Florence Nightingale (1820-1910) wrote:

"On our way home, we saw our first Egyptian monument, the colossal head and bust of a queen, as Isis (the rest of the body, at some distance), in granite, lying in a marsh, half covered with water; a companion Ptolemy, also broken, as Osiris, lying near, the features very beautiful, but blackened with the water; bulrushes growing about."[13]

Later in the 19th century, the Egyptian scholar Mahmoud Bey Al Falaki situated precisely the location of the ancient building:

"This temple is to be found approximately 180 metres to the north-west of a point situated on the prolongation of the Canopic road at 700 metres from the gate. It has four plethre wide and of a length of a stadium in parallel pointing in the direction of the longitudinal roads. Even today one can still see a number of bases in their original place, cornice of broken columns and entire fusts, the whole in red granite. But what attracts the attention of visitors are the two colossal statues, of which one can recognize Cleopatra despite being broken in three pieces as well as the other believed to be Anthony.[14]

The Colossal heads unearthed by Mr Harris 50 years ago, and rediscovered in 1895, may be visited by taking the train from the Ramleh Station at Alexandria to Sidi Gaber from which station they lie in an open marshy field about 500 yds. SW One head has the form of Osiris and the other of Isis. They are on the site of the ancient temple of Ceres and Proserpine. They are supposed to represent Cleopatra and Antony deified.*"[15]

1. They were acquired by Raoul Warocqué (1870-1917), a Belgian industrialist and a major collector who bequeathed his domain and collections to the Belgian State.

2. Thanks to Mr. Ahmed Abd el-Fattah, Dr. Mervat Seif el-Din, Dr. Mohamed Mustafa Abd al-Megid for their steady scholarly and friendly cooperation.

3. Thanks to Dr. Jean-Yves Empereur, Director of the CEAlex. The work has been made thanks to the support of the Ministry of French-speaking Community of Belgium (Fédération Wallonie-Bruxelles) and the Non-Profit Association *Les Amis de Mariemont* for their persevering support and trust.

4. Albert Daninos was born in Algiers maybe in 1843. In the mid 1860's he was appointed to the Louvre Museum under the direction of Adrien de Longpérier (1816-1882). After 1870, he was sent to Egypt to assist the French egyptologist Auguste Mariette (1821-1881). He has been digging especially in Meidum, Abukir, Alexandria. See *Who was Who in Egyptology* (fourth Revised Edition by Morris L. Bierbier), London, The Egypt Exploration Society, 2012, p. 142.

5. Letter addressed by Albert Daninos to Raoul Warocqué (January 12, 1912) – Musée royal de Mariemont, Archives de Raoul Warocqué (translated from French by R. Smouha.)

6. Translated from French by R. Smouha.

7. *Who was Who in Egyptology*, cit., p. 73.

8. Giuseppe Botti, *La côte Alexandrine dans l'Antiquité*, II, Cairo, 1898.

9. Richard Pococke, *A Description of the East, and some other Countries*, London, 1743-1745.

10. *Denkmäler aus Agypten und Athiopien*, Berlin, Ergänzungsband, 1913, pl. I a.b.

11. Joseph Bonomi to John Gardner Wilkinson, October 1842 (archived in Bodleian Library, Oxford within the *Wilkinson Archives*, Mss. XVII H. 39-41.

12. John Gardner Wilkinson, *Hand-book for travellers in Egypt; including descriptions of the course of the Nile to the second cataract, Alexandria, Cairo, the pyramids, and Thebes, the overland transit to India, the peninsula of Mount Sinai, the oases, & c. Being a new edition, corrected and condensed, of "Modern Egypt and Thebes"*, London, 1847.

13. Florence Nightingali, *Letters from Egypt. A Journey on the Nile 1849-1850,* ed. by A. Sattin, London, 1987, p. 25.

14. Mahmoud Bey Al Falaki, *Mémoire sur l'Antique Alexandrie, ses faubourgs et environs découverts par les fouilles, les sondages, nivellements et autres recherches*, Copenhague, 1872, p. 65-67.

15. H.-R. Hall, *Handbook for Egypt and the Sudan*, London, 1907.

2 Richard Smouha
Alexandria Background

2.1 Lake Hadra Roman Spa

The myth of Alexandria is linked mainly to its role as a Græco-Roman capital. There is much evidence that the Romans prized this area greatly. The fresh sea breezes would sweep over the ridge of higher land along the seashore to the north and then having become cooler, the air descended across the lake keeping the temperature agreeable even in the height of summer. The draining of the lake uncovered one of their spas and many artefacts were rescued. Where have they ended up? In museums? Even recently, in 2004, a geophysical survey was carried out by N. and P. Linford over the suspected site of the remains of the sanctuary temple complex in the Smouha district. The relevance of the antiquities of the site were its geographical proximity to Alexandria; the attractiveness of its topography; and its isolation from surrounding land and water.

I have however given some importance to the following extract from the Report by N. and P. Linford:[1]

"Alexandria is largely built on a limestone ridge. However in the Smouha district a substantial thickness of lacustrine deposits (some 2-4 metres deep) overlies the bedrock due to the presence of Lakes Hadra and Hydra in this area. The depth of these deposits was acknowledged as a potential problem, however as remains were reported to still be visible on the surface in 1872, it was considered unlikely that they would in the last 150 years have become covered by a substantial depth of overburden."

In fact, according to family legend, the area had only been in this pre-drainage state since the battle of the Nile in 1798 between the English fleet under Admiral Sir Horatio Nelson and the French, already in position with their dragoons in an advantageous position on land. Nelson landed some troops before the battle which cut the Mahmoudieh Canal, flooded all the surrounding land and thus prevented the French troops from coming to the assistance of their ships. This turned out to be an important factor in the ensuing battle and Nelson's victory. However I do believe that family legend is at least partially incorrect. In fact, the whole Maryut area was flooded three times, once from 1801 to 1804 and the second time from 1807 to 1808 (Anthony de Cosson).[2] Prior to the Mahmoudieh Canal (1818-21), the fresh water needed by Alexandria was carried by a dyke from Abukir. On 12 April 1801, the 1500 strong British forces under Hely-Hutchison assisted by the Turks, breached the dyke and flooded Lake Maryut, thus cutting off the freshwater from the French garrison in Alexandria and preventing reinforcements arriving from Cairo. The breach in the dyke was only repaired in 1804. Alexandria was at that time the capital of Egypt, which was still part of the Ottoman Empire and was therefore a most important point from which to control the whole area. The aim was to dislodge the army left in the country by Napoleon who was fascinated by the Middle East, had brought with him a multidisciplinary team. This team included the scientists and egyptologists who founded the Institut d'Égypte, later renowned for its economic and sociological studies. The second flooding in May 1807 (again by the British) as a defence, was against Mohamed Ali Pasha and was repaired in February 1808. I believe, but have no confirmation, that Lake Hadra came into being between this time and 1821 when the creation of the Mahmoudieh Canal replaced the old dyke. A height of three metres above sea level was mentioned at that time. It seems logical to have kept the land, which became Lake Hadra, at a higher level than the waters of Maryut, which had become salty from the sea flooding. Be that as it may, this created a kind of static enclosure, which on the arrival of Joseph Smouha was still two metres above the lake but had become the equivalent of a rubbish dump for the city, an infectious, smelly, mosquito-ridden and generally unhealthy area, most of which had become marshland. In fact in the two last letters that John Ninet sent to the journal *Siècle* he gave the following very specific description:

"The city of Alexandria and the surrounding areas form a peninsular encircled on the one hand by salt water marshes and muddy lakes and on the other by the sea."

2.2 Alexandria 1919

"The decade or so before 1914, that was the Golden Age, the best years." So said the old hands – French, Italian or British for the most part – in 1927, regretting that in their view, the times were not what they used to be. Some would also warn newcomers that they "had arrived too late," and must now at all costs guard against succumbing to the lure of the Orient. This for many long-term residents benefiting from the Capitulations[3] had hitherto included total dispensation from paying the Egyptian Treasury a single piaster in income tax. With the gradual withdrawal of the occupying British troops to the Suez Canal zone already in prospect, such veterans saw themselves as being reduced to the same status as Greeks or Levantines, as well as progressively subject to the extortions of Egyptian bureaucrats wearing red tarbooshes, symbol of all who aspired to the *effendi* class. Egypt's total population then was no more than 15 million, and Alexandria only some 300 to 400 thousand, in general a "mild and cheerful people." Invariably friendly too, though the WWI conscription of the able-bodied, so reminiscent of the hated corvée when the Suez Canal was being excavated, had left a generation of ordinary Egyptians resentful. While this rarely, if ever showed in day-to-day contacts with foreigners, it remained an element in nationalist agitation.

In the teeming narrow streets and lanes back from the Eastern Harbour, among them Sister Street, notorious for the nightly fracas at its wartime bars and brothels, many customs were little changed, if at all, from what Edward Lane described in his classic *Manners and Customs of the Modem Egyptians*[4]. With piercing screams of simulated grief, professional women mourners,

ALEXANDRIA. - Sidi Gaber Mosque.

their faces and black *mylahas* (head to foot shawls) smeared with mud, accompanied funerals; a few musicians would precede a procession bearing wedding gifts, perhaps an ice-box or kitchen utensils, to the bride's home; invisible behind their *musharabieh* windows, housewives, after a shouted exchange with a street vendor to fix the price, would let down by rope a basket with the money and pull it up with the item desired. Fridays saw worshippers overflowing from mosques and kneeling, arms uplifted, on newspapers spread over the roadway. The daily commotion at the Alexandria cotton exchange, its customary ambiance, determined by the imperatives of global supply and demand, appeared, at least to the uninitiated, as frantic pandemonium, much as E.M. Foster had earlier humorously depicted writing in the *Egyptian Mail* newspaper. A Greek businessman, Pericles Anastassiades, had taken him to visit the exchange:

"Oh, Heaven help us," Foster shouted.

"What is that dreadful noise? Run, run! Has somebody been killed!"

"Do not distress yourself," Anastassiades said: "It is only the merchants of Alexandria buying cotton."

"But they are murdering one another, surely?"

"Not so. They merely gesticulate."

"Does any place exist where one could view their gestures in safety?"

"There is such a place."

"I shall come to no bodily harm there?"

"None, none."

"Then conduct me, pray."

The port of Alexandria was raised to prominence by Napoleon and the transformation of the city proceeded apace throughout the 19th century by way of a series of projects, mainly the work of European architects and engineers. This period saw the arrival in Egypt of a significant number of political exiles, businessmen and entrepreneurs from Europe and the Eastern Mediterranean, but also of adventurers, aggressive professionals and emigrants

The Mosque of Sidi Gaber, early 20th century. (Collection Jean-Yves Empereur, archive CEAlex).

27

in search of fortune. Reading E.M. Forster's book,[5] or glancing at old picture postcards shows how closely Alexandria of the early 20th century resembled the larger European cities: the west port crowded with ships, the Mohamed Ali Square and Stock Exchange in the financial district, the Corniche along the stretch of water to the east where the ships rode at anchor, all sum up its typical features; the Rosetta road following the ancient Via Canopica, its route uniting ancient and modern Greek quarters, the Zizinia Theatre, the Town Hall and Græco-Roman Museum, the luxuriant public gardens. This route continues eastward along the narrow piece of land that separates the sea from Lake Maryut, and on to the Abukir promontory. Here and there along the coastal strip lie native villages, alternating with holiday resorts. Ramleh was the collective name for what was a sort of Riviera that dated back to 1863 when the railway, which to this day encircles Smouha City, was built. Its healthy climate, stable temperatures, both in summer and winter, allied to a landscape of great beauty, with the sea on one side, dunes and desert on the other, and in the distance Lake Maryut and the extraordinary scenery of the Nile Delta.

One of the first to express interest in developing the coastal strip east of Alexandria was Baron Baillot, who published an article on it in 1877. Only fourteen years after the Ramleh railway was opened and five years after the opening of the Suez Canal, he made a proposal to Khedive Ismail for founding Ismailville, a new winter resort. Inspired by European models of elite tourism, the new town was to combine the attractions of Nice and Monaco featuring large hotels, a casino, exclusive clubs and sports and leisure activities. The proximity to Alexandria was expected to ensure a quality of economic and cultural activity comparable to London, Paris, St. Petersburg and other European capitals.

Establishment of the Alexandria Sporting Club, in 1890 confirmed Ramleh's place as a centre of recreation for Alexandria's high society. The club occupied a large ellipsoidal enclosure, lying at a tangent to the Ramleh railway and the Abukir road, and was used for horse racing and other sports events.

Bedouin tents along the Alexandria & Ramleh Railway, 1920 (C. Pallini's collection).

opposite
View of the Mahmoudieh Canal near Ramleh, 1920 (C. Pallini's collection).

In 1918, the Municipal Council commissioned McLean's proposal of a new town plan with the object of correcting its somewhat random urban development which lacked any overall control. In his new plan McLean took account of a series of important projects, either already implemented or still on paper, of which the most important was the electrification of the Ramleh railway, eastward extension of the Corniche, construction of the new road to Abukir, and the drainage and reclamation of Lake Hadra. These would ready the coastal strip for the new requirements of transport, as well as assist the development of Ramleh as a suburb of a Greater Alexandria. Extending along the coast from Agami to Abukir, a distance of about twenty-two miles, with a width of between half a mile to a little over three, the modern face of the city would then be seen on the new road to Abukir in the area formerly covered by Lake Hadra: the new racetrack, the airport, all open country joined to the Municipal gardens of Nouzha and Antoniadis, with the new military airport on the Abukir promontory. (this airport actually already existed and was taken over by the Royal Air Force. Teddy Smouha spent the first six months of his war service there in the late thirties as acting Pilot Officer on probation, finishing up as Wing Commander at the end of the war).

1. Neal and Paul Linford, *Smouha District, Alexandria, Egypt. Report on Geophysical Survey*, November 2004.
1. Anthony De Cosson, *Mareotis*, Country Life, London 1935.
2. The Capitulations were bilateral contracts between the Sultan of the Ottoman Empire and European powers, conferring rights and privileges in favour of their subjects resident or trading in the Ottoman dominions. According to these Capitulations, traders entering the Ottoman Empire were exempt from local prosecution, local taxation, local conscription, and the searching of their domicile.
3. Edward Lane, *Manners and Customs of the Modern Egyptians* (1836), East-West Publications / Livres de France, The Hague / London / Cairo, 1978.
4. Edward Morgan Forster, *Alexandria: a History and a Guide*, W. Morris limited, Alexandria 1922.

3 Richard Smouha
Joseph Smouha

3.1 The man

Joseph Smouha was born in 1878 in Baghdad into a distinguished Sephardi family boasting two chief Rabbis, Haham Bashi, Bashi being the title given by the Sultan of the Ottoman Empire in Baghdad. The way he told his grandchildren about his early years gives meaning to the personality that he developed into. He would tell me how, while he was still very young, he found a window seat in his house from which he could hear the Rabbi's *daroush* (sermon) and took every opportunity to do so.

Small, tubby and uninspiring in his physical appearance, and modest in the extreme, he attracted attention by his character, intelligence and the brilliance of his entrepreneurial mind as well as the forcefulness of his speech. Clean-shaven except for a full moustache, he was easily approachable and when he spoke there was absolute silence, and everyone would listen intently. Most unfortunately this is at least one quality which I have not inherited.

Going to Manchester in his early teens in 1892, where there were mainly Baghdadi or Arab-speaking cotton traders and through some distant family contacts he found a job in, I believe, Barclays Bank. At 18 years of age he was taken on by a cotton trader, who could not speak or understand Arabic and needed someone he could trust to relay information to him on what was going on, on the floor where so much business was transacted in Arabic. George Howarth had noticed his talents in the bank, and took him on as junior partner. By the age of 21 he had already made a small fortune. Married at 26 and raising a large family, he formed his own company.

In 1914, at the outbreak of the First World War, Joseph Smouha failed his military medical due to his two bouts of rheumatic fever. In 1915, he closed down his office as a highly successful cotton broker, sent his employees off to military service and offered himself for government service, promising to look after their families and keep their jobs open.

In 1917, the value of a country's currency was of even more strategically and politically important than today. The pound had fallen to a low level in the Middle East. Joseph Smouha had been making suggestions to rectify this situation and partly because Arabic was his mother tongue. He was sent to Egypt to solve the problem and re-establish its value. He went out on a Royal Navy battleship and made his headquarters in Cairo. He already had contacts with the Arabs from his Manchester Cotton Exchange days and he was introduced to T.E. Lawrence with whom he remained friendly for years after. I remember that he would come to lunch privately with, I believe, no family in attendance. Unfortunately I have no detail of the subjects discussed between the two men but when one pictures these two personalities together it is hard to believe that their lunches and other meetings were not of great importance. At the time, there were few people whose origins were in the Middle East and this combined with a highly successful UK career would have made him much in demand.

Joseph Smouha would send goods from Manchester to the Middle East then sell the goods in exchange for gold and bought pounds with the gold. Then, in what would be considered today as a hugely successful Public Relations strategy, he opened some 32 offices around the Middle East, all carrying the slogan "we buy sterling at par."

Remember that this was at the time before Bretton Woods and not only were all major currencies linked to the gold standard but also, communications were not what they are today and even telephone calls had to pass through oft-delayed and overworked telephone operators. By this simple but effective strategy, within three or four months he had achieved his object and no one sold pounds below par anymore. Thus, and in particular, because of his strong personality and charisma, honesty and directness as well as the status provided by his Embassy support, he became well known throughout the Middle East.

Around this time, but for his own account, he was sending cotton to England. It had to go via Archangel, Russia and this carried heavy risks. He called in an insurance broker to cover the risk but the man asked for 100% of the bid price as the premium.

Joseph Smouha told him, "if I insure with you there is no point in the deal."

So he sent the goods himself.

One day he came across the broker again who asked, "So did you find anyone to insure the goods?"

He answered "Yes, I insured them with God and they arrived!"

By letter to the Secretary, Foreign Office, dated 9 August 1918, Joseph Smouha informed him "that robberies are constantly taking place from the caravans taking goods from Ahwaz to Ispahan and from thence to various places in the interior of Persia, which caused loss to traders and placed grave difficulties in the way of transit of goods ... the manager at Ispahan is a Parsee, Mr. Furrieddoon ... the firm is one of the largest importers of Manchester Cotton Piece Goods to Mesopotamia and Persia and deals exclusively in British manufacturers.

The further assistance of the British Consul-General at Ispahan is desired."

In 1918 the whole area was under British military control, and it was considered most dangerous for civilians to visit the area and they could only do so with military approval and authorisation.

I have been able to discover neither the exact problem nor any details other than the fact that my grandfather's Baghdad office had been accused of issuing false invoices. Joseph Smouha chose a well-known and highly respected solicitor from Cairo, a Mr. Devonshire, to resolve the situation.

To get an idea of the problem, the confusion and misunderstandings of the British authorities in the area, one only has to wade through the heavy correspondence between 10 September and 26 November 1918 involving, from Mr. Secretary James Balfour of the Foreign Office, down through Sir M. Sykes of the Turkish desk, Secretary of State, to Civil Commissioner of Baghdad with

Wedding photo of Joseph and Rosa Smouha: roof of the Midland Hotel, Manchester, 1904 (R. Smouha's archive).

the support of the High Commissioner Egypt, the Secretary of the India Office, Sir R. Wingate and Lord Hardinge, down to Major Ormsby Gore and the Political Agent in Baghdad.

The final result was that the Residency at Ramleh confirmed that Joseph Smouha was "well looked on by the Military Authorities" and he was allowed to go to Basra where the problem seemed to be. Mr. Devonshire, "a solicitor of high standing and repute," on the other hand, was not permitted.

Meanwhile, in England, Rosa, his wife, wanted to join him in Egypt, but she was told that they would not take her on any navy ship unless she could swim.

So she went off to the baths and learned to swim. Then she told her mother she would be leaving the five children that she now had with her to supervise; although there were two nurses, a cook and several maids, her mother said she was prepared to be responsible for the older children but not for the baby, so Rosa could not go.

Joseph Smouha was into his forties when he started the great adventure of his life, leading to the creation of Smouha City.

For the early part of my life, he remained a shadowy patriarchal figure, although as the oldest grandson of his 23 grandchildren, I was the lucky beneficiary of a lot of special attention from him, his wife, his three youngest daughters and youngest son.

I remember him as a man of tremendous intellect, an unbelievably strict self-disciplinarian, with a wonderful sense of humour

that allowed him easy contact with all those around him – unless or until he was crossed, when he would become a majestic and terrifying power – but for me, in his later years this was a very rare occurrence. From our stand point in today's world, it is very difficult to acknowledge and understand his daily life as I experienced it in the large house in Egypt. Half a century has changed the world to such an extent that it requires a book in itself to understand much of what was normal at that time. Just one small example, that for a well-off Victorian family, eight children was not considered exceptional.

His bedroom, facing the garden, on the other side of the house from the sea, was a large room with the wedding photos of his eight surviving children on the pieces of furniture around the room. On one side of the room was what was then a super-luxurious bathroom and on the other a small lengthy dressing room. A third door opened onto an enormous terrace, the width of the house; on one side the garden and on the other a glorious view of the sea and coastline from the top of the cliff on which the house was built. The fourth door led to a sizeable landing at the top of the stairs, on the other side of which was my parents' bedroom, dressing room and bathroom, with their wonderful sea view and looking down and to the right, the Corniche and coastline for several miles.

Each morning he would get up between 5:00 and 5:30, go into the dressing room, put on his *tefillin* (a set of small black leather boxes containing scrolls of verses from the Torah, worn during weekday prayers) and spend anything from 30 minutes to an hour reading the morning prayers. This did not prevent him from breaking off at any point if anything important required his attention.

Before getting dressed, washed and so on he would go to the landing at the top of the stairs where a barber was waiting to shave him, give him a haircut, etc. However just before this, probably about 6:00-6:30, he would cross the open space and knock on my parents' door to make sure my father would be on time to leave for the office at around 7:00-7:30, driven by one of the three chauffeurs used by the family (I think my father often used to take his own car!).

They would all return home for lunch, with anything from 10 to 25 family members around the table and when the morning's business was being discussed we adolescents were to be "seen and not heard." Dinner was early and also a family meal.

His habits reflected his strict personal discipline. He gave up smoking overnight after his doctor told him it was dangerous, did not drink or gamble and was manic about "cleanliness being next to godliness." In the office, he had a special washbasin which he would use whenever he could not avoid shaking hands with anyone: many in the family remember the washing of his hands.

Another personal memory was his attitude to the use of telephones. For someone of his generation, let us remember, telephones were a luxury and I remember so well the breakdowns and problems in particular especially when booking an intercity call between Alexandria and Cairo, there would be a waiting pe-

Joseph and Rosa Smouha at Richard and Sylvia's wedding, Alexandria, 1955 (R. Smouha's archive).

riod of some two or three hours. For all his life he would become impatient when someone spent an unnecessarily long time on the phone and would call at regular intervals "cut it short."

In his later years (1956-61), after what he had built was taken from him, he maintained – outwardly at least – the force of personality and his high moral tone, helped by increasing amnesic memory loss. He passed away peacefully without pain and in his sleep.

The Good Father
"From beyond the grave, cotton merchant Joseph Smouha continues to be a good father. In his will he gave this advice to his children: love and help one another, respect your mother, help people in need, be true to the religion of your fathers." Joseph Smouha was a rich man, but he left his children something more precious than riches, the path to character."
(*Daily Express*, 27.10.1961)

"In his will he said "I desire to thank my dear wife for all her kindness and help and I confidently commit to her care, our dear children. I beseech my children to be upright and of pure character in all their undertakings, to nurture no ill will towards anyone and to remain true to the religion of their fathers."
(*Daily Telegraph*, 26.10.1961)

King's Praise: "Good to Country"
"King Fuad described him as 'the only foreigner who had come to the country, brought his own money and did good to the country.' He kept a special staff to deal with charities and gave thousands of pounds (a fortune in those days!) to hospitals, schools, churches and mosques. He refused to send any of his fortune to other countries to safeguard against emergencies. When President Nasser seized his property and expelled him from Egypt the family's income dropped to about £6 per week.

The fifty-five members of the family shared £80,000 under a Government loan scheme. The value of the land should have been £15-20 million but the claim was for £12,500,000 compensation. The award of £3,106,516 came after five years of negotiation. The Estate Duty Office has judged that no duty charge arises on this interim allowance. Mr. Smouha was domiciled abroad and the Commission is merely acting as a post office in the transmission of funds to Switzerland."
(*Daily Telegraph and Morning Post*, 26.10.1961)

Notes from my Mother
"I do not recall when the following event took place, but probably in the late 1940s or early 1950s before we left Egypt in 1956. Our head Sudanese servant came back from the mosque one Friday evening (Friday being the Muslim Sabbath) and spoke to Joseph Smouha, telling him that he and the people from the Arab village near our home had to go a long way to be able to pray at

Joseph Smouha and Edwin Goar, Alexandria, 1955 (R. Smouha's archive).

a mosque. He said that they had all subscribed to buy a piece of wasteland in the village but they had no money to build a mosque on it. Joseph Smouha asked him to find out how much it would cost to build a mosque large enough for the amount of people who would pray there and for it to be a good-looking building.

A few days later he came back with the answer, but I do not know the figure. I was present at the time and heard Joseph tell him to come to his office the next day with the chief Imam and he would give him the money required.

It was all settled as simply as that, and work on the mosque was started a few days later. It was finished in what must have been record time, and was a lovely looking building. It was nice to hear the man up in the minaret calling the faithful to prayers every Friday and on special holy days. The servant came to Joseph after the first service, and told us that the Imam spoke of the man who had given the mosque to the community, and blessed him for doing so then and thereafter at most services."

3.2 Sent to Egypt

Joseph Smouha, then 45 years old and with a family (his wife Rosa 32 and children Marjorie 18, Ellis 17, Hilda 16, Edward 15, Joyce 10, Peggy 8 and Edna a baby of two) moved from Manchester to Alexandria in 1923. The "pearl of the Eastern Mediterranean" was entering its two decades of resplendence. With an economy boosted by the First World War, Egypt, though experiencing eruptions of nationalistic fervour, was a pleasant country to live in. By comparison with Manchester's winter fog and rain, the warm sunshine and cooling sea breezes of Alexandria were a near-miraculous change for the better.

Nor could the beach at Lytham-St-Annes compete with the majestic sweep of the Corniche from Fort Qaitbay, site of the Pharos lighthouse, around the Eastern harbour or with the sandy beaches of Stanley Bey, Sidi Bishr (where the family had their luxury beach cabin on Beach No. 3), Zizinia (where the Sinigalias had a family house in which Sylvia and I got married), and San Stefano. Along the coast, towards the palace of Montazah and the fishing village of Abukir with its Greek restaurants.

Bulkeley, where the family house stands, was in the very heart of Ramleh, once known as the "Ostend of Egypt."

Their first home was a rented villa at Sidi Bishr while the Bulkeley house was being built, its construction meticulously inspected by Joseph Smouha in person. But of course the *fellaheen* (peasants), toiling from dawn to dusk on the rich soil of the Nile Delta, inhabiting miserable insect-infected mud-brick hovels and infected with debilitating bilharzia from the irrigation canals "seemed both resentful of, and, with Islamic fatalism, resigned to their lot." Also, for the Mancunian family, who at that time had not travelled outside the UK, all the poverty, dirt, ignorance and misery they saw must have come as a huge culture shock to the family and been most difficult to handle.

I remember distinctly the times I would be driving through the centre of Alexandria with my father and how every time the car stopped, being surrounded by beggars, many with amputated limbs, bilharzia or other untreated incurable diseases, especially in the eyes, knocking on the windows, hands outstretched and my father or grandfather giving change to the chauffeur to give out, my father, muttering under his breath, time and time again, "poor devils, poor devils!" Take one step up from this picture, and one realises that this was but a microcosm of the whole picture of the country. I also remember most clearly my father parking his car in an unauthorised spot, calling over the nearby traffic policeman, giving him a tip of a few piasters and telling him to look after the car while we were away and not let anyone touch it. I remember stories such as the lady out shopping and telling her chauffeur to go and collect some purchases. When he returned to the car she was still reading her book, but the car was held up by four piles of bricks and had no wheels. It was most pleasantly surprising to discover that middle-class people such as small shopkeepers, office clerks, factory employees and so on, at which level one began to find a smattering of very integrated employees, led a lowly life style but had a high level of honesty and a reasonable level of that sense of humour which, I believe, still find in all corners of Egyptian society to this day. It was from this level of society and especially as of 1947 onwards that the increase of Egyptian-ization started taking over from the top, down through the professional and managerial classes until the years 1952-56, when the massive flight of

Edward Smouha, Flight Lieutenant (later Wing Commander) in the Royal Air Force, 1942. Edward Smouha was in charge of the New Sports Club (R. Smouha's archive).

non-Egyptians both Moslems and others really took off. The Suez "war" which hit not only English and French nationals and Jews, but also the Egyptian aristocracy and the Copts, initiated a reversal of status, which in the first instance immeasurably increased the influence of the military, with the officer class basically taking over the country. The experience of my father-in-law, Maître Carlo Sinigalia, is a telling example of this situation. He was an active lawyer practising in the Mixed Courts for over 30 years and with a sizeable and successful practice. One day, arriving at his office, he found a senior military officer sitting behind his desk. He said, "What are you doing? This is my office." The officer replied, "from now on it is my office and yours is at the other end of the corridor. I will be calling you in from time to time to explain and give information about the files and the clients." I seem to remember that he started playing more golf in the afternoons at the Smouha course until even that privilege was taken away from him. Shortly after that he decided to leave, sold the house for a song to the only bidder, the government, and left in 1962. The family had lived in Egypt since 1795. When I went to Egypt in 1989, the Ministry of Agriculture and Fisheries occupied the house.

4 Cristina Pallini
**Future Alexandria:
the Municipal Vision**

4.1 The Town-Planning Scheme by W.H. McLean

In 1914, as a result of the declaration of war with the Ottoman Empire (of which Egypt was nominally a part), Britain declared a Protectorate over Egypt. The result was a rise in nationalist feelings that exacerbated in the Spring of 1919, with mass demonstrations and uprisings throughout the country. Interestingly, this process was paralleled by new development projects that were to demonstrate the tangible benefits of the British rule.

In October 1918, while Joseph Smouha was corresponding heavily with the British Foreign Office on the subject of the security of trade along the routes of Persia, the Alexandria Municipal Committee asked the Scottish engineer William H. McLean to draw up a plan for the city, in view of correcting its somewhat random development.[1]

William H. McLean (1877-1967), a civil engineer from Glasgow University, had worked in Sudan since 1906 gaining the confidence of Lord Kitchener who, in 1913, transferred him to Egypt with the title of Engineer-in-Chief, Section of Municipalities and Commissions.

From 1913 to 1926 McLean worked on various urban renewal projects for some fifty Egyptian towns, spending much of his time as an engineer to the Municipality of Alexandria.[2]

McLean's ideas were quite advanced, oriented towards development planning, addressing the needs of the country as a whole and of the regions into which it might be naturally subdivided. Along these lines, he had proposed a National and Regional Development Planning Scheme for Egypt for which King Fouad had taken a personal interest. Egypt's rapidly increasing population and fast-paced growth required adequate forecast and co-ordination. In the Delta this meant improving communication between large and small towns and villages.[3]

According to the British Town Planning Institute, McLean envisioned "a grandiose scheme" that was to europeanize Alexandria even further.[4]

Indeed McLean proposed an extension of the city's boundaries, as well as a network of roads to combine projects already begun and consolidate an extremely patchy suburban area. The plan had required a preliminary survey and a report, presented on 21 October 1919 and approved 22 days later, after which the work had been finalized following comments and suggestions by the Municipal Committee.

The vice-president Alex Granville stressed the experimental nature of the plan, vis-à-vis the need to rationalise a city which was the result of successive stages of haphazard development:

"This project ... marks, in my opinion, a true step forward in the municipal life of this city and of Egypt in general. All those who had dealt with cities in this country realized the problems caused by the absence of convenient communications, in rapidly growing cities where buildings become bigger and stronger year by year. What happened so far?

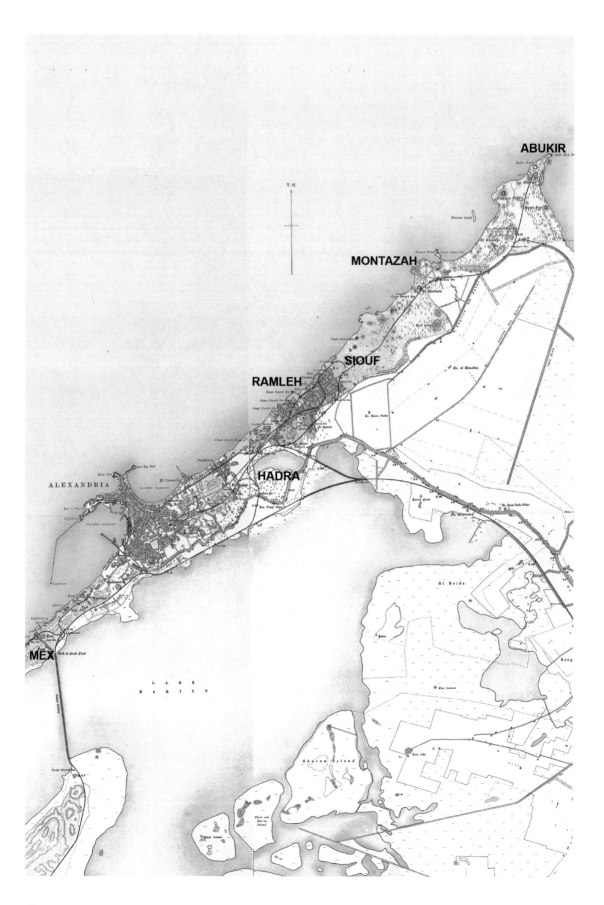

ABUKIR

MONTAZAH

SIOUF

RAMLEH

HADRA

ALEXANDRIA

MEX

LAKE
MARIUT

An area for agriculture or gardening was converted into building land. In the absence of a plan, houses sprang up in the most diverse, haphazard directions, leaving nothing else in the way of accessible roads except narrow streets with no alignment, nor leveling, nor pavement or sidewalks. Free of control, this was what previous greedy landowners left. Can we think without a feeling of regret that a city is acquiring a new neighborhood without squares or open spaces ...? If such practices are deplorable in small towns, they are disastrous in large cities such as Alexandria and Tantah."[5]

While introducing his descriptive note, McLean remarked that Alexandria was Egypt's commercial capital, with a population of 444,617 inhabitants, out of which 19% were foreigners (1917 census). Due consideration was therefore to be given to the vestiges of the Ptolemaic and Arab cities, as well as to commerce, industry, convenience and well-being of the inhabitants. In explaining the overall purpose of the town-planning scheme - untangle the built-up areas of the city, create public parks and squares, develop the main arterial roads to ensure ventilation of the city and facilitate communication between the various neighborhoods - McLean recalls the geographic setting of Alexandria at the north-west corner of the Delta, halfway along a narrow limestone ridge separating the Mediterranean from Lake Maryut.

If Alexandria was to grow as a linear city, a proper street network had to be devised. McLean proposed an extension of the Corniche into a panoramic coastal road reaching the Royal park of Montazah, as well as a 50-metres wide road to Abukir. Extension of the city along the western coast could rely only on the old Libyan route, therefore a new road along the rim of Lake Maryut was proposed. To facilitate communication between the western and eastern suburbs, new roads were to be opened through the 19th-century urban fabric. A major road connection was to replace city walls, along which a series of parks and public buildings were to be arranged. Public buildings included the new railway station and the municipal theatre, the first-aid post and the stadium, the new Græco-Roman museum, a library and an art gallery. While many of the proposed parks coincided with archaeological sites, two new squares - *Place des Obelisques* and *Place des Mosquées* – were to be arranged along the Grand Corniche, a broad boulevard forming a semi-circle of 3947,5 metres around the *Magnus Portus* of antiquity.[6]

The correlation between the proposed and ancient Alexandria were sought after also in the canal between the eastern and western harbours, as did the famous *Heptastadion*. The commercial port was to develop along the Mahmoudieh Canal as far as el-Farkha Canal. While envisaging a new suburban garden city at Agami and a smaller one between Ibrahimieh and the Latin Cemeteries, McLean also drafted a sample low-income housing project.

By reading McLean's descriptive note we find a number of references concerning the transformation of the area that was later to become Smouha City:

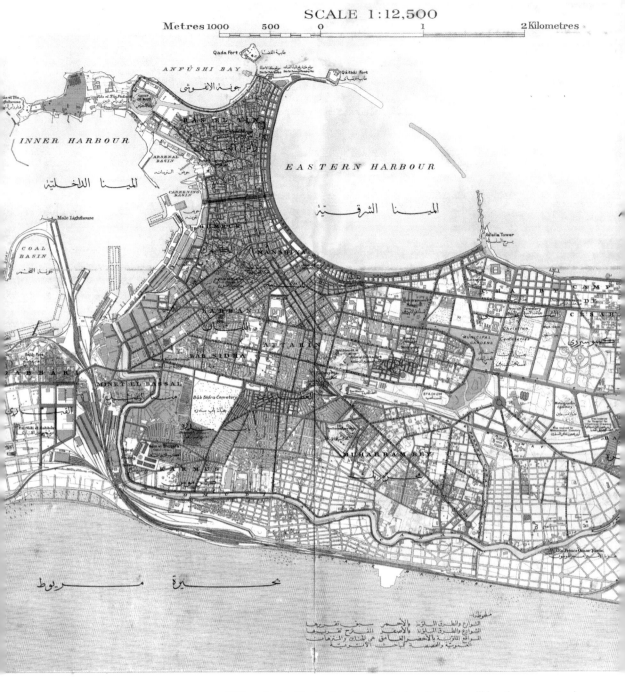

"When Lake Hadra has been drained, there will be the opportunity to develop a sporting club, a racecourse and an aerodrome surrounded by a park, across which it is proposed to open a 50-meteres wide avenue linking the city to Abukir."[7]

"When extension of the city towards Abukir reaches significant proportions, the current road to Ramleh (whose widening would be very expensive) will be too narrow for future traffic requirements, and when the need arises to extend the road southward, it will be necessary to open a major road south of the road to Ramleh and parallel to it.

It is therefore proposed a new 50-meteres wide avenue branching off the road to Ramleh somewhere behind Ibrahimieh; it would pass under the railway in two places and across Lake Hadra

(which will be eventually drained) running parallel to the coast. Near the proposed cemeteries at Sidi Bishr, the avenue is reduced to a width of 40 metres, ending in at Mandara. From this place two diagonal avenues 20-metres wide on both side of the railway will lead to Abukir."[8]

"Mention should particularly be made to the parceling out of the northern part of Lake Hadra, and to the access road to this area passing under the railway to reach the existing road to Ramleh, and to its extension to the north across the land of the Sporting Club."[9]

"The problem of traffic in a city extending over a long and narrow strip of land like Alexandria has a certain importance. It is assumed that rapid communications between Alexandria and Abukir

William H. McLean, *City of Alexandria Town Planning Scheme*, pl. 2. (Archive CEAlex).

45

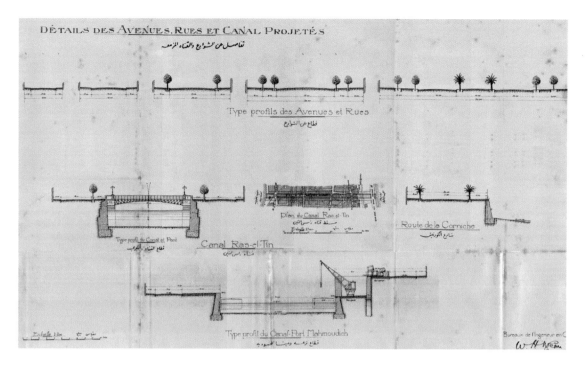

DÉTAILS DES AVENUES, RUES ET CANAL PROJETÉS
تفاصيل عن الشوارع والقناة اللازمه

Type profils des Avenues et Rues
قطاع عن الشوارع

Plan du Canal Ras-el-Tin
مسقط قناة راس التين

Canal Ras-el-Tin
قناة راس التين

Route de la Corniche
شارع الكورنيش

Type profil du Canal et Pont
قطاع القناة والكوبري

Type profil du Canal-Port Mahmoudieh
قطاع ترعة وميناء المحمودية

Bureaux de l'Ingénieur en C

and surrounding area will be granted by the State Railway, which will be doubled and electrified."[10]

"The outskirts of the city have been laid out following a garden-city scheme, so that the presence of many small parks and gardens is not so essential as in town … Plan n.4 shows a large public park formed by the Nouzha and Antoniadis gardens extended northwards up to the proposed Abukir road. It suggested placing the Sporting Club on the western part of the area, as its current location will likely be required for future construction. An aerodrome is indicated on the eastern part of the area, which in the future could be used as a civil airport for passengers, mail and similar services."[11]

It seems that Sidi Gaber and Lake Hadra were to play a crucial role in the future of Alexandria. Even though Sibi Gaber was encased by the Mahmoudieh Canal and the railway embankment, it was served by both the tramline and the railway. Other favourable features were the historical gardens of Nouzha and Antoniadis.

In agreement with the Municipal Committee, McLean envisaged the reclamation of Lake Hadra and the development of the whole area. It was divided by the new Abukir road to the north-west, a radial scheme of building lots to spring from a large wooded square along the new Abukir road, to the south-east, the new race course, the airfield and the Nouzha and Antoniadis gardens.

The new race course was to replace the Sporting Club, while the airfield - a square of 800x800 metres was to provide civil and airmail service. McLean believed that air transport was a factor to be reckoned with in considering the transport problem,[12] because at the time, the launch of airlines followed the development of the British Empire routes to South Africa, India and the Far East. Alexandria was undoubtedly a strategic location.[13]

View of the *Route rouge* to Ramleh and Abukir (Courtesy of the Alexandria Preservation Trust).

opposite
William H. McLean, *City of Alexandria Town Planning Scheme*. Sections of the propose roads (Archive CEAlex).

4.2 Between Alexandria and Ramleh

Extending 36 kilometres along the coast, with a depth ranging from one to five kilometres, future Alexandria was to absorb a number of pre-existing settlements, Dikheila and Mex to the west, Sidi Gaber and Ramleh to the east.

While Sidi Gaber was a little more than a village, Ramleh – the Arabic for *sand* – was a sort of Riviera where native settlements alternated with European-style villas and luxuriant gardens, which had developed following the opening of the Alexandria & Ramleh railway in 1863. Establishment of the Sporting Club in 1890 confirmed Ramleh's role as a place of recreation for Alexandria's high society. Later, in 1901, environmental data proved that Ramleh was superior to all other famous health resorts then patronised by Europeans.[14] E.M. Forster's well-known guide, written during the First World War, helps to visualize Sidi Gaber and Lake Hadra in the second decade of the 20th century. At Ibrahimieh station the flat fertile land of the Delta made its appearance beyond the waters of Hadra; at Sidi Gaber the best fig-trees and broad-leaved bananas were to be seen; from Abou el Nawatir, the highest hill near Alexandria, a fine view of the lakes of Hadra and Maryut.[15]

The director of the Græco-Roman Museum Evaristo Breccia extolled Ramleh as the ideal garden-city suburb:

"The origin of Ramleh is recent. Less than half a century ago, it was Ramleh, *sand* in the proper sense, except for a few groups of poor Arab houses and Bedouin tents there was not a single European house … the stay Ramleh is not only very healthy, but also very pleasant, thanks to the proximity of the beach, to the gardens surrounding most of the houses, and to the many date-palm groves. One could say that this is the ideal garden-city suburb.

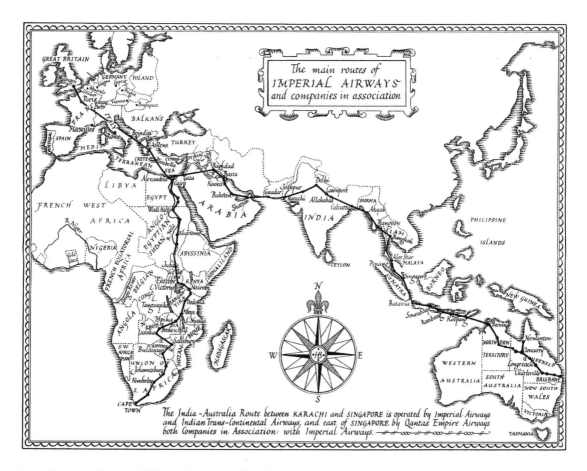

The main routes of the Imperial Airlines and associated companies.

opposite
Date-palms groves and banana plantations, the typical landscape surrounding the eastern suburbs of Alexandria.

Today Ramleh has approximately 30,000 inhabitants. … Throughout the year, in the afternoons, this promenade [along the old road to Ramleh] is a coming and going of coaches, cars, horses, bicycles. Opposite Ibrahimieh to the right of the road is the village of Hadra..."[16]

The Italian writer Fausta Cialente described this same area as a world in itself on the edge of the Delta: with its indigenous settlements crowded with chickens, goats, sheeps, colourful tents, and carts filled with agricultural produce. Around the edge of Lake Hadra, pelicans dozed and roads led out towards a flat countryside, where the eye encountered nothing but distant date palms.[17]

1. William H. McLean, *City of Alexandria Town Planning Scheme*, Cairo, Imprimerie Nationale, 1921. See also "Alexandria, Old and New," *Garden Cities & Town Planning*, January 1923, pp.8-10, and Mahmoud Riad, "Alexandria: its Town Planning Development," *The Town Planning Review*, vol. 15, n. 4, December 1933, pp.233-249.

2. McLean was member of the British Town Planning Institute established in 1914. See McLean's biography in Robert Home, *Of Planting and Planning. The making of British colonial cities*, London, Taylor & Francis, 1997, p.168. See also Robert Home, "British Colonial Town Planning in the Middle East: The Work of W.H. McLean," *Planning History*, vol. 12, n. 1, 1990, pp.4-9.

3. See, by William H. McLean, "Local Government and Town Planning Development in Egypt," *The Town Planning Review*, vol. 7, n. 2, April 1917; "Notes on a Proposed General Scheme of National and Regional Development planning in Egypt", *Journal of the Royal Town Planning Institute*, n. 21, 1924-25, pp.149-152; *Regional and Town Planning*, Glasgow, Crosby Lockwood, 1930; *The Political, Economic and Social Development of the British Colonies*, 1946.

4. "Alexandria, Old and New," cit. p. 10.

5. Alex Granville, "Préface," in William H. Mc Lean, *City of Alexandria*, cit., pp.V-VI.

6. The *grands travaux* of the Corniche were carried out by the Alexandria Municipality between 1899 and 1907 and entrusted to the municipal engineers L. Dietrich, P. Arcoudaris and E. Quellenec, chief engineer of the Suez Canal Company. Since 1901, works had been undertaken by the Italian Almagià contractors for completion in 1907. The foot of the new quay accommodated a main sewer conduit.

7. William H. McLean, *City of Alexandria*, cit., p.4.

8. *Ibidem*, p.5.

9. *Ibidem*, p.5.

10. *Ibidem*, p.5.

11. *Ibidem*, p.8.

12. William H. Mc Lean, "Notes on a proposed general scheme," cit., p.151.

13. See Robert Bluffield, *Imperial Airways. The Birth of British Airline Industry 1914-1940*, Hersham, Ian Allam, 2009.

14. Cf. Charles Pecnik, *Ramleh, La Riviera Eleusinienne et Alexandrie (Egypt), Manuals de voyage Woerl*, Liepzig, Léon Woerl, 1901.

15. Edward Morgan Forster, *Alexandria. A History and a Guide* (1922), New York, Overlook Press, 1974, pp.215-216.

16. Evaristo Breccia, *Alexandrea ad Aegyptum*, Bergamo, Istituto Italiano di Arti Grafiche, 1914, pp.11-12.

17. See Fausta Cialente, *Cortile a Cleopatra* (1935), Milan, Feltrinelli, 1962, p.88.

5 Richard Smouha
The Adventure Begins

5.1 Seen from the train

If a man makes a pilgrimage around Alexandria in the morning, God will make for him a golden crown ...

Ibn Duqmàq

The most fateful train journey Joseph Smouha ever made was from Cairo to Alexandria in 1919, a comfortable three hours and 209 kilometres in a pullman-type carriage of Egyptian State Railways, with individual armchairs and fleet-footed suffragis in white *gallabias* purveying tea or Turkish coffee.

Long before the turn of the century, the express service linking the two cities and larger towns of the Delta had attained a route punctuality akin to that later associated with Switzerland. This noteworthy accomplishment can be attributed to the assiduous endeavours over half a century of British, French and Belgian managers and engineers. Among them was Robert Stephenson (1803-1859) son of the famous "Rocket" and railways builder, who was the first Egyptian State Railways Engineer-in-Chief.

As the train slowed down to stop at Sidi Gaber, suburban station in the residential outskirts of Alexandria, it passed along a causeway crossing the eastern end of a lake (Hadra).

Joseph Smouha, newly returned to Egypt, had become aware of this site and land reclamation potential during his WWI assignment for the British Government even if he was actually seeing it for the first time. Joseph Smouha`s awareness of Lake Maryut`s history and site was acquired during that initial stay in Egypt when he was approached confidentially one day on behalf of members of the ruling family wishing to ascertain if he could arrange for them a large loan.

In pointing out to them that he was neither a banker nor a moneylender, he also said that people of their station in life should not borrow money.

On his interlocutor remarking that the persons concerned had extensive landholdings they could use as collateral, he said that in that case they should simply sell some of the land.

The reply was to the effect that the land in question was of inferior quality, much of it lake and marsh - including Lake Maryut. Before buying it, he had satisfied himself that draining the eastern sector of the lake was feasible.

Expert advice was readily come by in an Egypt whose development course had been firmly set in the 40 years of Mohamed Ali`s rule as a benevolent despot.

Since long before WWI, steam pumps had been maintaining the Maryut water level at more than two metres below that of the Mediterranean to prevent the inundation of a still larger area. Increased pump-age capacity could, in fact, have emptied the lake completely. But at that time, with the whole country`s population still under five million (today 85) and Alexandria at about 300,000, land reclamation was hardly a top priority.

Without the events of March 1801 however, there might have been no Lake Maryut to drain, no Mohamed Ali dynasty, and no Smouha City.

When Joseph Smouha came back from the Middle East he was offered a knighthood but he did not accept because he did not want the publicity, disappointing the family!

5.2 Purchase of land

Knowing my grandfather as I did, I am prepared to give free imagination to what would be going on in his head before, during and after the so-often cited train journey, with the map of Alexandria in front of him.

"Why, any idiot can see that this is a fantastic opportunity. It is not the first time that people cannot see beyond the end of their noses. All I have to do is check that there is no hidden problem." He could be scathing in his opinion about people and often was, but this did in no way interfere with his generosity to them.

What he may not have seen, but we can with the advantage of hindsight, is that being about one-sixth of the whole of Alexandria at the time and only four kilometres from the city centre, this project would revolutionise and upgrade every aspect of the city – whether property, economy, social, or sport – opening up a city that was about to be squeezed by its limited land mass extension. There had already been discussions with the Municipality without any conclusion as to price or details of the project.

The asking price by the Municipality for what he wanted to do was a sizeable sum for those days but it was agreed that if the drainage cost more than that they would cover the difference.

I feel compelled at this point to repeat what has been written on a number of occasions, but I have been unable to find any firm evidence, so I will quote almost verbatim from the texts but am reluctant to give the sources and intend to stick to this principle for the very large number of mistaken statements about Smouha City and my family.

"Smouha wants to buy the land."

"Take it."

Joseph Smouha: "No you don't understand. I am going to do something very nice with this property."

"Good idea, nobody wants it. You can have it for free."

Joseph Smouha: "No, I must pay for it because it is going to be a very exclusive neighbourhood."

"Pay us a symbolic fee."

Joseph Smouha: "Don't talk nonsense."

Finally, according to these sources, a price was reached after what could aptly be named a reverse negotiation. A French engineer, Simon Behar, confirmed that with the land anyway sloping southwards towards Lake Maryut, Lake Hadra was about two metres higher. So it was decided to tunnel under the Mahmoud-ieh Canal which was a freshwater canal which had existed since 1821, and which ran on slightly higher land between Lake Hadra and Lake Maryut.

Finally in 1923, Joseph Smouha bought 750 feddans[1] in the area. He knew that the government was prepared to subsidise only the excess over LE8,000 for the draining and that the previous owner, Prince Omar Toussoun,[2] who represented Royal family owners, had refused.

Joseph Smouha accepted the offer but the government raised it to LE10,000 and added the requirement of constructing a public drain and thereafter two more, all to be handed over to the Municipality. He accepted the revised costs of LE4,000 and LE2,000. They also required him to build three tunnels under the railway at Mustapha Pasha, Cleopatra and Ibrahimieh for a total amount of LE3,670. All these sums were paid to the Municipality by 1934.

He was also required to cede land for a main highway, which incidentally shortened the Cairo-Alexandria road through the Delta by six kilometres. In the same year (1923) he bought the shallow Lake Hadra itself, then various strips of marshland from a number of owners.

He assigned the work of reclaiming the land to the Italian firm Dentamaro and Cartareggia.[3]

By 1925 he was ready to unveil plans for a new residential suburb, and the same year he organised a public competition for a garden city – based on the new concept of Welwyn Garden City, we were always told. The jury did not select any project, but the French architect Maurice Clauzier won the second prize.

The plans included a golf course surrounded by a racecourse, a full-sized clubhouse and restaurant, six or more tennis courts and four squash courts, a residential area of villas, a few apartment blocks, an area for light industry (later a five acre Pepsi Cola plant and a Ford Motor assembly plant) a Greek Orthodox church, a Catholic church, a Protestant temple, a mosque and synagogue, horse-riding school, post office, two schools, two police stations, a fire-brigade station, first-aid post, a theatre, two cinemas, and one or two permanent markets to ensure self-sufficiency.

Further included were districts for upper-class and middle-class homes in the latter case, detached or semi-detached villas with or without gardens, and a village with working-class homes.

5.3 The Land

My mother always remarked that when she was first in Egypt in 1931 everyone spoke of it as The Land. Before that time it was The Lake. The plans for the new city had already been refined and completed from 1925 onwards. This included contractual arrangements with the Municipality regarding gifts, costs and payments for the utilities, i.e. roads, electricity, water pipes, telephone lines, etc., and in particular wide tree-lined two-way avenues with grass

midsections, squares and roundabouts worthy of any garden city.

Whenever King Fouad visited Alexandria, as he did from time to time, he always sent a message to Joseph Smouha asking him to go for a chat on Sunday morning.

He always went and enjoyed being with the King, spending a pleasant hour or so. On one occasion the King asked him how his project was going and what progress had been made, and then asked if he had thought of a name for it. "Yes" Joseph Smouha answered, "If your Majesty has no objection I would like to call it Fouad City."

"Oh no" the King replied, "You and your sons have done this great work all by yourselves, so it has to be called Smouha City."

And so it was, and still is, despite confiscation and all the other changes, especially since all other foreign names have been changed to Egyptian ones!

There are many anecdotes concerning the relationship between the two men. One, which speaks for itself, concerned the strict court ritual whereby one should never turn one's back on the King, but when it was time to leave, one had to walk backwards towards the door. Whenever the discussion with Joseph Smouha ended, the King would get up from his desk and walk in front of him to the door so that he did not have to walk backwards.

I remember that it was common knowledge in the family that things started going badly with King Farouk's (son of King Fouad) behaviour and that it was unfortunate that he had to return from boarding school in England on his father's death.

He had been sent there on Joseph Smouha's advice but the fact that he did not complete his time – he was only sixteen – contributed to his later bad behaviour.

On one occasion, Joseph Smouha was specifically invited to the palace for dinner with King Farouk. It would have been an outright

Inauguration of the drainage of Lake Hadra, 21 October 1925.
In the crowd of guests we note: HE. Amine Bey Fikri, representing the Under Secretary of State for Public Works; Mr. Enrico Pegna, General Manager of "Bonded Stores and Warehouses Co."; HE. Ramadan Bey Youssef, Municipal Councilles; HE. Joseph De Picciotto Bey, Senator; HE. Mohamed S. Khouloussy Bey, sub-governor of Alexandria; Dr. Jatis Bey; Mr. Gargour, sub-manager of the Company of the Tramways. (*Le Magazine Egyptien*, 1.11.1925).

opposite
Inauguration ceremony: H. E. Sabri Pacha, Governor of Alexandria, Engineer McLean with Mr. Daniel Delbourgo, representing Mr. Joseph Smouha (*Le Magazine Egyptien*, 1.11.1925).

problem for direct refusal, so a solution was found as Teddy and Yvonne Smouha took his place at dinner. They returned with an amazing story, that they were shown into a dining room with a small number of other guests, sometime after, King Farouk, came in, sat down, had his dinner, spoke a few words and then got up and left. It was only after that, that dinner was served to the guests.

1. A feddan (a yoke of oxen) is a unit of area used in Egypt and Sudan. A feddan is divided into 24 kirats; 1 feddan equals to 4,200 square metres, or 0.42 hectares (1.038 acres)

2. Sahar Hamouda, *Omar Toussoun: Prince of Alexandria*, AlexMed, Alexandria 2005.
3. G. Spitaleri, *Costruttori Italiani in Egitto. Filippo Cartareggia*, Alexandria, 1933, pp.25-34.

Cristina Pallini

6 The Draining and the Competition

6.1 The draining

The connections between McLean's plan and Joseph Smouha's actual decision to purchase the land and reclaim Lake Hadra undoubtedly need further clarification.

Lake Hadra was only a few feet deep, separated from Lake Maryut by the Mahmoudieh Canal and by a small strip of wasteland. When explaining the origin of the place-name "Smouha," the Egyptian scholar Radames Lackany wrote that Smouha City was originally a vast swamp known as *Mellahat Hadra* (Hadra Saltworks) belonging to Prince Wahid el Din.

When Wahid el Din untimely died in 1906, Prince Omar Toussoun acted as the guardian of his two young sons, Mohamed Ali and Amr Ibrahim, heirs of Prince Mohamed Ali and nephews of King Fouad. Omar Toussoun tried to reclaim the area with the help of Swiss engineers but, discouraged by the slow progress of works, sold the entire property to Joseph Smouha, who managed to drain the swamp with the help of British experts.[1]

According to family records and to the letter to the Sequestrator General (see chapter 10), Joseph Smouha conceived the drainage scheme after discovering that Lake Hadra was higher than Lake Maryut. He then acquired land in the area, most of which was under the control of Prince Omar Toussoun, whom he approached by an intermediary.

There had already been discussions with the Municipality as to price and details of the drainage project. A French engineer, Simon Bonan (or Behar) confirmed that Lake Hadra was about two metres higher than Lake Maryut. So it was decided to tunnel under the Mahmoudieh Canal.

Finally in 1923, Joseph Smouha bought 750 feddans of land including Lake Hadra, knowing that the government was prepared to subsidise only the excess over LE8,000 for the draining. He accepted the offer but the government raised it to LE10,000 and added the requirement of constructing a public drain and two more for the water on the lands next to the lake, all to be handed over to the Municipality. Joseph Smouha also accepted to build three tunnels under the railway at Mustapha Pasha, Cleopatra and Ibrahimieh, for a total amount of about LE43,670. All these sums were paid to the Municipality by 1934.

Joseph Smouha was also required to cede land for a main highway which was to shortened by six kilometres the Cairo-Alexandria road through the Delta.

The drainage was inaugurated on 21 October 1925 by His Excellency Sabri Pasha Governor of Alexandria and in the presence of engineer McLean, His Excellency Zaki Bey Habib and Mr. Daniel Delbourgo representing Joseph Smouha.

The draining of Lake Hadra was one of the greatest enterprise undertaken by the Italian contractors Dentamaro and Cartareggia.[2] Stretching over two million square metres Lake Hadra con-

Map of the competition area provided by Joseph Smouha to the participants (Secchi-Tarugi family archive).

opposite
View of the Lake Hadra (R. Smouha's archive).

Temporary works for the drainage of Lake Hadra, 1925 (R. Smouha's archive).

A close view of the syphon by which the waters flowed into Lake Maryut (R. Smouha's archive).

Installation of large metal pipes on the viaduct that crossed the bed of the Mahmoudieh Canal, November 1925 (R. Smouha's archive).

The surface of the Lake Hadra after the draining (R. Smouha's archive).

tained about 4,000,000 cubic metres of stagnant water, whose marshy margins made it unhealthy, particularly in the hot season. The bottom of Lake Hadra was higher than Lake Maryut, thus the draining operations required a syphon beneath the Mahmoudieh Canal, a stretch of which was to be deviated and drained. Excavation had to be made below the canal bed to build a concrete foundation with a double row of steel pipes.

The sandy soil and quicksand was dangerous for workers. Lake Maryut would ultimately receive the water of Lake Hadra, converted into 540 feddans of valuable building land.

On 6 August 1925, a selected gathering took place on the site, providing the guests with an opportunity to see the magnitude of work being carried out.[3]

Finally, on 21 October 1925, the pipes were opened. Early that afternoon groups of natives and cars flocked to the opening ceremony.

Shortly before 4:00 pm public authorities arrived - as well as a camera operator of the Prosperi Oriental Film. Among the lucky few who could enjoy the scene from a barge along the Mahmoudieh canal were some engineers who expressed their satisfaction with the work.[4]

Daniel Delbourgo declared to the journalists that, from that moment on, everything depended on the Alexandria Municipality: "We have received several proposals for the creation of a modern city. They will be examined by a very competent jury after the return from Europe of Mr. Joseph Smouha."[5]

6.2 The Competition Programme

Proposals for the creation of a modern city on the land reclaimed by Joseph Smouha at Sidi Gaber were gathered through an international town-planning competition which had a deadline of 1 October 1925. *La Construction Moderne* published the announcement on 14 June 1925,[6] while *Ingegneria* did it only in September, less than a month before the deadline.[7] Those willing to participate were invited to request any additional graphic material to Joseph Smouha, rue Port-Est, Immeuble Heikal, Alexandria.[8] The awards were LE500, 200 and 100, with honourable mentions receiving LE50.

The competition aimed at collecting ideas for the planning of a new town for 50.000 inhabitants[9] in the suburbs of Alexandria. Participants were invited to consider requirements imposed by aesthetics, health and technique, while respecting social and economic aspects.

They were encouraged to avoid monotonous layouts by devising a series of viewpoints from where peculiarities of the site and future architectural features would produce a picturesque townscape. Mr. Smouha wanted a composition of buildings and parks, squares and plantations, as well as roads, railways, tramways, and alleys for horseback riding integrating cohesively.

As explicitly stated in the competition brief, these requirements were very much attuned with the theories by Camillo Sitte and Charles Buls, who strongly believed in the aesthetical dimension of town planning.[10] For Sitte town-planning and architecture were deeply intertwined, the ultimate aim of both being the aesthetic quality of urban space. Fearing that town-planning would become a mere technical task without any artistic involvement, Sitte opposed regular layouts and symmetry, believing that due consideration was to be given to the actual perception of the proportions between the monuments and their surroundings. A supporter of Sitte 's ideas, Charles Buls clarified a number of aesthetic principles to adopt when facing problems of town-planning. Such principles concerned the direction of streets and public places and the decoration they may receive, the arrangement of monuments and public buildings, the use of vegetation, the proportions between the horizontal and vertical dimension of streets and urban areas.[11] Participants were recommended to avoid any chessboard-type layout and box-shaped houses so common in America, considering instead "all the best work of recent years in England, France, Germany, Austria, Belgium, and more recently in Italy."[12] It may be added that Joseph Smouha knew and appreciated the case of Welwyn garden city, founded in 1920 by the theorist of the garden city movement Ebenezer Howard.[13]

Welwyn (see Annexes) was the second garden city in England, whose location 34 km north of London was to be the key to success, that is the right way to provide for the expansion of the industries and population of a modern metropolis. The site consisted of nearly 2,400 acres of high ground, laid our along tree-

lined avenues, with special attention to the relationship between circulation and residential areas. The spine of the town was a scenic parkway, almost a mile long.[14]

The competition brief placed a great emphasis on the rational circulation scheme, which meant an effective layout of traffic routes enhancing the qualities of the site.

Distinctions were also made between quarters for different social classes: luxury homes, individual citizens' housing (isolated and in series, with or without front lawns), working-class district.

The plan also emphasized schools, a first-aid post, police and fire brigade stations, post-offices, one or two markets were to ensure self-sufficiency of the new town.

At the same time, a synagogue, a Greek orthodox church, a Catholic church, a Protestant temple and a mosque were to recreate the ethno-religious districts so typical of Alexandria.

A theatre and two cinemas, areas for sports and recreation, along with the nearby Sporting Club, were to attract leisure and social life.

As already mentioned, the program attributed great importance to gardens and open spaces to embellish upper and middle-class residential districts and the village of working-class homes.

McLean's idea for a new racecourse was not abandoned. Indeed, among the material to be submitted, there was a variant covering the arrangement of a sports club with a racecourse, whose total surface should not exceed 500,000 square metres. The idea of a "three-dimensional plan" and "aesthetic impression" recurred again and again.

6.3 Who was who

The competition was open only to architects and engineers invited by letter from Joseph Smouha. The jury was to be composed of Joseph Smouha, as owner, Antonio Lasciac Bey, former Chief-Architect of the Khedivial Palaces, and Paul Conin Pastour, General Manager at the Ministry of Public Works.

Research undertaken up to now has enabled us to compile a list of the competitors (See Report of the Jury in the Annexes).[15] Six teams were French: "*Urbs*" (Maurice Clauzier, Reims), *Three stars*" (Léon Azéma, Max Edrei, Jaques Hardy, Alexandria), "*Vox populi*" (Raoul, Daniel and Lionel Brandon, Paris), "*Utile Dulci*" (J. Bossard, Aisne), "*Roma*" (Marcel Portevin, Paris), "*Lys*" (René Proud'homme, Paris). Four teams were Italian: "*Ars*" (Enrico Casiraghi and Luigi Lorenzo Secchi, Milan), "*Lotus*" (S.T. de Sain ed. E. Marchettini, Cairo), "*Urbe*" (Alessandro Limongelli, Cairo), "Z" (Giacomo Alessandro Loria, Alexandria). The project entitled "Spes" was presented by Georges Niedermann from Zurich.

Two out of the six French teams included professionals with a career in Egypt, namely the Brandon Brothers and the team Azéma, Edrei and Hardy. Graduated from the Paris École des Beaux Arts in 1904, Raoul Brandon (1878-1941) worked in Cairo from

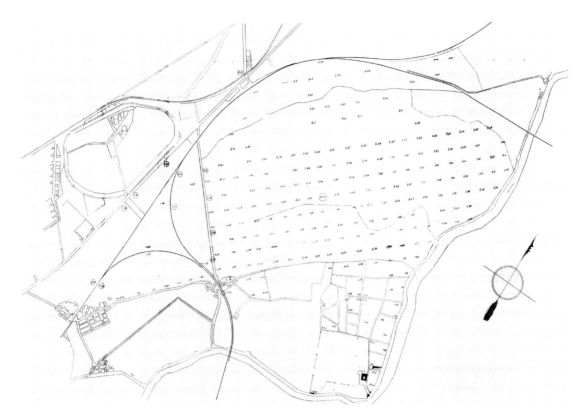

1907 to 1911, having been awarded the first prize at the competition for the new stock exchange (1907) and for the Orosdi-Back department store (1908).[16] He was well-qualified for the Sidi Gaber competition having taken part in the project of the garden city *des Grands-Champs* at Bagnolet, a semi-temporary workers' village in the eastern suburbs of Paris (1919-1923).

Léon Azéma (1888–1978), Max Edrei (1889–1972) and Jacques Hardy (1889-1974) were school fellows at the Paris École des Beaux-Arts. Max Edrei was born at el-Simbillawein in the Delta, from a family of Syrian origin who had settled in Egypt after living in Algeria. After being awarded the first prize at the competition for the new Cairo law courts (1924), Azéma, Edrei and Hardy opened an office in Egypt.[17] In 1925 the team was based in Alexandria, engaged in building the St Mark's College.

Jean-Isidore Bossard and Renè-J. Prud'homme also attended the École des Beaux-Arts.

Bossard (b. 1875) graduated in 1903 and in 1905 was awarded the fourth prize at the Concourse Chenavard with a project for a *centre d'assistance mutuelle*; he participated several times at the Salon des Artistes Français.[18] Bossard worked extensively in French Indochina, but by 1925 he was based in Jaulgonne (Aisne). Renè-J. Prud'homme (b. 1892) was a pupil of Léon Jaussely, a key figure on the international town-planning scene.[19] After having qualified in a series of architectural design competitions[20] Prud'homme worked with Jaussely in the preparation on a plan for Grenoble (1922). Grenoble was among the cities with more than 10,000 inhabitants which, according to the

Map of the competition area with indication of the ground height above the sea level (Secchi-Tarugi family archive).

pag. 60-61
Overview of the four projects (redrawn by C. Pallini)
All four project place the luxury villas near the Nouzha-Antoniadis gardens, isolating the working class district between the railway lines and the villages of Hadra and Ez-Soad.
According to Clauzier, Casiraghi-Secchi and Lasciac, the large straight boulevard from the railway station to the Mahmoudieh Canal was to become the spine of the new town, attracting most public buildings, which Loria placed instead along the new Abukir road.
Both Casiraghi & Secchi and Loria considered the Sporting Club as integral part of the new town; (Casiraghi and Secchi even sketched its possible rearrangement). Loria was the only one to exploit the triangular area enclosed by the railway lines as place for leisure activities.
Clauzier's proposal was certainly the most visionary, including areas beyond the limits set by the competition brief: the airport, the lake port and park along the Mahmoudieh Canal, extension of the boulevard towards the beach.

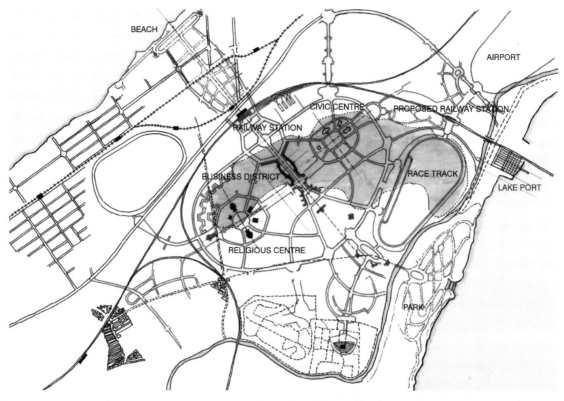

"Urbs" by Maurice Clauzier

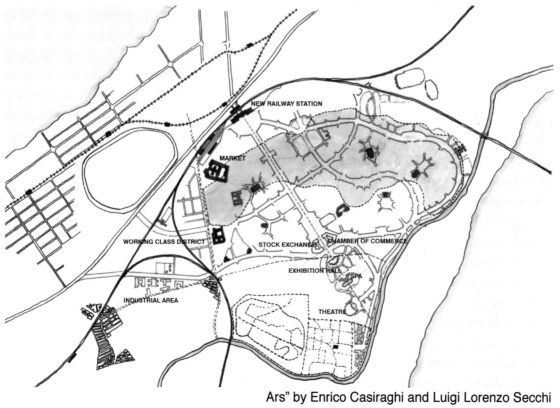

Ars" by Enrico Casiraghi and Luigi Lorenzo Secchi

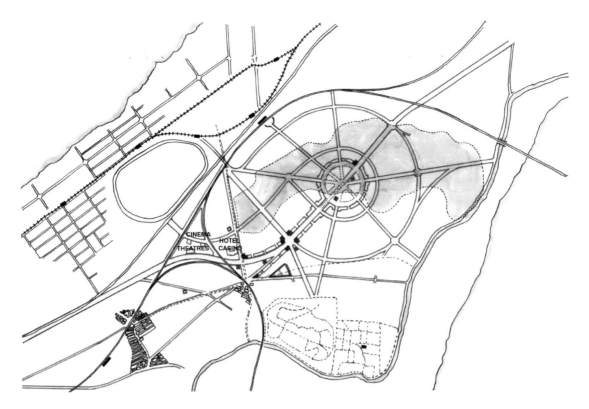

"Z" by Giacomo Alessandro Loria

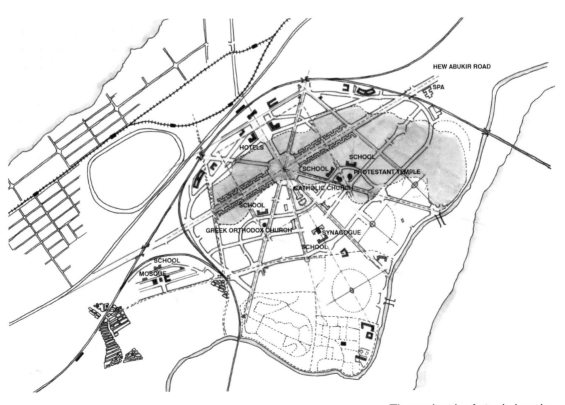

The project by Antonio Lasciac

Law Cornudet (1919), had to prepare a Projet s'Aménagement, d'Embellisement et d'Extension.

Both Maurice Clauzier and Marcel Portevin had a different background. Maurice Clauzier (1897-1984) graduated from the École des Hautes Études Urbaines under the supervision of Marcel Poëte (1922).[21] Clauzier's degree project, entitled *La Cité-jardin (Gizzy-jardin) d'un port d'aérobus de la Métropole "Urbs"*, was awarded an honorary mention at the Salon des Artistes Français, and was included in an exhibition organized by the Union Rémoise des Arts décoratifs. In 1921 Clauzier designed an industrial nursery in the suburbs of Paris.[22] In 1923, on the occasion of the Strasbourg Town-Planning Conference[23] that was to close with a visit to Reims (heavily damaged during World War I) Clauzier presented a reconstruction plan for that city partially financed by American funds (Rockefeller, Ford), inspired by garden-city principles and envisaging a widespread use of cars.[24]

Marcel Portevin (b. 1896) was trained as a civil engineer. In 1921 his name appeared in a list of registered architects in *La Construction Moderne*;[25] in 1923 he was awarded the second prize at the competition for rebuilding Reims covered market. While taking part in Sidi Gaber competition, Portevin also developed a hospital project, an architectural theme that he was to encounter again and again in his career.[26]

Georges Niedermann (b. 1878), attended the Ecole des Beaux Arts in the early years of the twentieth century, where he probably met Jean-Emil Staehli (b. 1881), with whom he designed the villa Mooser-Nef in Zurich (1912-1913). In 1922 Niedermann participated with Konrand Hippenmeier at the international competition for the Chicago Tribune skyscraper. In 1925 Niedermann was based in Zurich.

Among the Italians, Casiraghi and Secchi were the only ones who did not have a strong connection with Egypt. Casiraghi worked at the Technical Office of the Milan Municipality during the years of rapid urban change and population growth. He undertook social housing projects and plans for new schools and sport structures. Secchi (1899-1992) graduated in industrial engineering from Milan Politecnico in 1925.[27] He was then hired by the same Technical Office. While working together at the project for Sidi Gaber, Secchi and Casiraghi also worked on the "Maddalena di Canossa" elementary school.

Giacomo Alessandro Loria (1879–1937) came from a Jewish family who were long-time established in Egypt. At the turn of the twentieth century he attended the Turin Politecnico, where a lively debate was taking place between advocates of the technical or artistic approach to urban project. Loria however left Turin before obtaining a degree and went back to Egypt where he began practicing as an architect.

When he took part at the Sidi Gaber competition he was at the zenith of his career. Many of his projects had been implemented and he had qualified in many competitions for construction of important public buildings, such as Italian Hospital of Alexandria, built between 1921 and 1923.[28]

In the handwritten report of the jury the initial letter of Limongelli's name is not clear, resembling a D rather than an A. However, both Domenico and Alessandro Limongelli started their career working for the family construction firm in Alexandria. Domenico made a name for himself managing local projects for architects back in Italy and becoming well-versed in a variety of historical styles. In Alexandria (Ibrahimieh) he designed the Church of the Sacred Heart (1924). In Cairo he designed a number of private and public buildings, including the Church of the Sacred Heart near Ramses Station, the Don Bosco Institute, and the Music School at Helwan University, as well as the Armenian Nubarian school at Heliopolis (1926).[29] Domenico also worked as an expert for the Cairo Mixed Tribunals. His elder brother Alessandro (1890-1932) graduated in 1912 from the Rome Academy of Fine Arts, where he met Marcello Piacentini and Gustavo Giovannoni, two key figures of the Roman/Italian milieu.[30] In 1920 Alessandro collaborated with Piacentini and Giovannoni in the project for a number of garden suburbs in Rome. In 1926 he travelled within Egypt in search of a "Mediterranean-style" architecture, and produced a series of fine visionary drawings that were exhibited in Rome and published in *Architettura e Arti Decorative*.[31]

The hand-written report of the jury included one last group: ST de Sain and E. Marchettini from Cairo.

What was strange however, is that *Architecture e Arti Decorative* published "The plan for the new garden city of Smouha" by Antonio Lasciac, who was also a member of the jury.[32] Can we suppose that ST de Sain and E. de Sain Marchettini acted as middlemen?

It may be added then, before presenting his own project at the Museé Social (Paris) Maurice Clauzier mentioned the existence of 12 projects. Perhaps, Antonio Lasciac developed his project *hors concours*.

On 21 December 1925, at 9:00 am, the jury composed of Joseph Smouha, Antonio Lasciac Bey, and Paul Conin Pastour met to examine and evaluate eleven projects.

Lasciac Bey (1856-1946) was then a sixty-nine-year-old man with a very successful career in Egypt, where he had moved in 1882 after the British bombardment of Alexandria.[33]

Initially, Lasciac worked for prominent Levantine families. Later on, after a few years in Rome, he moved back to Cairo and made a name for himself among the Egyptian aristocracy. He became the Chief-Architect of the Khedivial Palaces (1907-1914) and a member of the Committee for the Preservation of Arab Monuments. He moved back to Italy at the beginning of the First World War and in 1919 proposed a plan for his hometown Gorizia. Back to Egypt in 1920, he was awarded the first prize at the competition for the Bank Misr headquarters in Cairo (1924-1927) and designed the façade of the new Alexandria railway station.[34]

The civil engineer Paul Conin-Pastour[35] (1855?-1933) had been

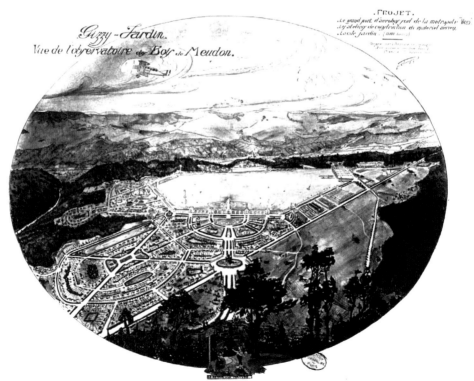

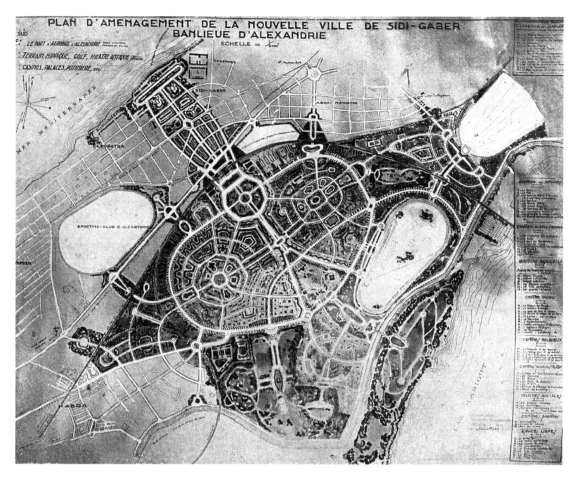

Director General of the Ministry of Public Works since 1924. He joined the service of the Egyptian Government in 1881 and was involved in the reconstruction of Alexandria's European Town. Conin-Pastour also worked on the reconstruction of Abdin Palace in Cairo, probably in collaboration with Lasciac. In 1924 he promoted the competition for the new Cairo law courts, and supervised the implementation of the project by Azéma, Edrei and Hardy. In 1925 he was engaged in the site of the Maison de France in Cairo.

Maurice Clauzier, *Plan d'amenagment de la nouvelle ville de Sidi-Gaber banlieue d'Alexandrie*, pl. II bis (from *L'Architecture*).

opposite
Maurice Clauzier, *La Cité-jardin (Gizzy-jardin) d'un port d'aérobus de la Métropole "Urbs"*, 1922 (archive of the Institute d'Urbanisme, Paris).

6.4 *"Urbs"* by Maurice Clauzier

The title of Clauzier's project evoked at one and the same time the origin and the rationale of town planning (*urbanisme*).[36] He had actually included the same Latin word in the title of his degree project at École des Hautes Etudes Urbaines: *La Cité-jardin d'un port d'aérobus de la Métropole "Urbs."* In this case, "Urbs" stood for the city of Paris, as clarified by the report, by which Clauzier tried to demonstrate how a modern garden-city could include the airport of the Greater Paris Region and some industrial units in the countryside. The headlines of his report reflected his approach to town planning: exploiting the relationship between the city and its region; rationalizing roads and other means of transport; lay-

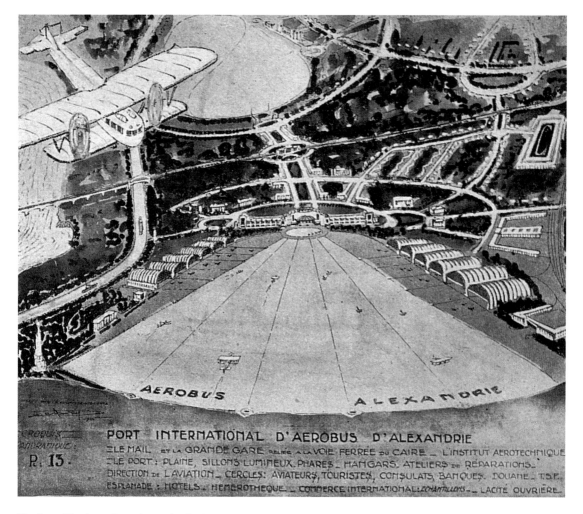

PORT INTERNATIONAL D'AEROBUS D'ALEXANDRIE
LE MAIL ET LA GRANDE GARE RELIÉE A LA VOIE FERRÉE DU CAIRE _ L'INSTITUT AEROTECHNIQUE LE PORT : PLAINE, SILLONS LUMINEUX, PHARES _ HANGARS, ATELIERS DE RÉPARATIONS. DIRECTION DE L'AVIATION _ CERCLES: AVIATEURS, TOURISTES, CONSULATS, BANQUES. DOUANE _ T.S.F. ESPLANADE : HOTELS _ HEMEROTHEQUE _ COMMERCE INTERNATIONAL:*ECHANTILLONS* _ _ LACITÉ OUVRIÈRE

Maurice Clauzier, *Port international d'aerobus d'Alexandrie*, pl. IV (from *L'Architecture*).

opposite
Maurice Clauzier, *Le quartier des affaires*, pl. 13 (from *L'Architecture*).
Legend: 1. Hotels et restaurantes; 2. Les expositions permanentes; 3. Agences des professions libérales; 4. Le commerce de luxe; 5. Le commerce d'alimentation; 6. Les banques et les bureaux privées; 7. Les grands magasins; 8. Les Garages et dépôts des commerçants.

ing out neighborhoods and public buildings; arranging parks and open spaces. In addition, Clauzier expressed his firm belief in the key role that civil aviation was going to acquire, so much so that it could help redefine the geographical distribution of the population, opening the way to new industrial sectors.[37]

Three years after graduation Clauzier applied his ideas to Alexandria, proposing something similar to what he had originally conceived for the Greater Paris Region.

"Extension of Alexandria. Creation of 'Sidi Gaber,' a luxury town:" this eloquent title introduced Clauzier's project published in *L'Architecture*.[38] His vision of Sidi Gaber was a modern city of 50,000 inhabitants, at the same time a centre for business and high finance, an "eastern caravanserai" and a place for recreation and élite tourism.[39]

L'Architecture only published three of his drawings: pl. II bis, *Plan d'amenagement de la nouvelle ville de Sidi-Gaber banlieue d'Alexandrie*; pl. IV, *Le quartier des affairs*; pl. 13, *Port international d'aerobus d'Alexandrie*. Cross-checking the information provided by these drawings and their legends, some main ideas put forth by the plan can be seen.

In line with his conviction that the future of cities depended on

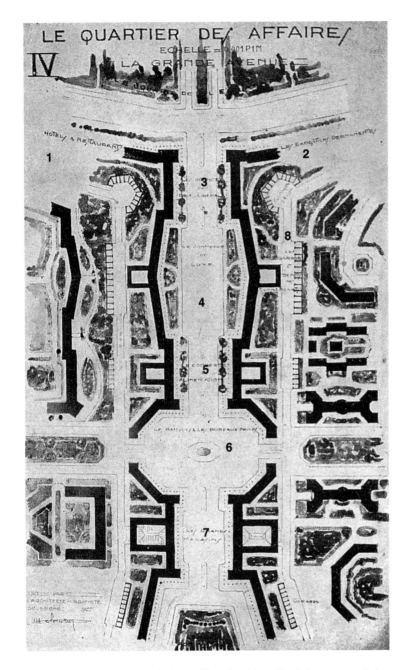

the progress of civil aviation, Clauzier identified the area of the new airport, fairly close to the one included in the McLean plan and connected to the railway. The explanatory legend of Clauzier's perspective of the airport sounded like a futurist slogan: *Le Mail et la Grande Gare reliée à la voie ferrée du Caire – L'Institut Aérotechnique / Le port : plaine, sillons lumineux. Phares, hangars, ateliers de réparation – Direction de l'Aviation – Cercles : Aviateurs, Touristes, Consulats, Banques, Douane – T.S.F. etc. Esplanade – Hotels - Hémérothèque – Commerce international : Echantillons – La Cité Ouvrière*

Clauzier developed the central business district as a scenic boulevard lined with compact buildings with arcaded basements and

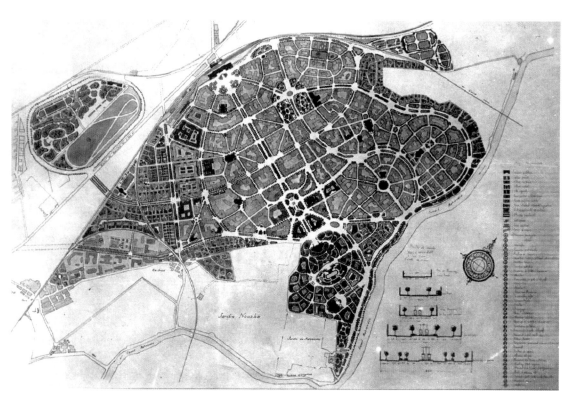

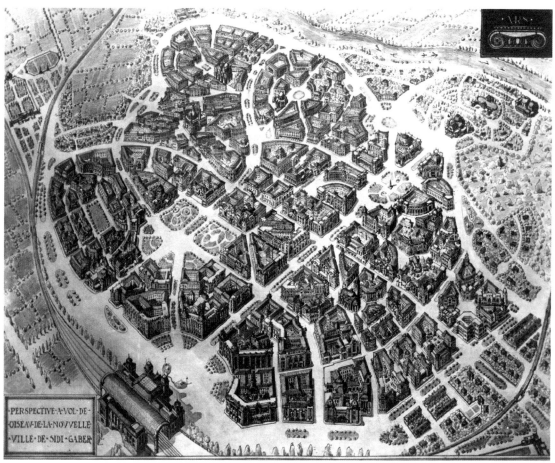

·PERSPECTIVE·A·VOL·DE·
·OISEAV·DE·LA·NOVVELLE·
·VILLE·DE·SIDI·GABER·

rear alleys leading to the garages and warehouses. His *Grand Avenue* linked the lido on the seashore (*Esplanade*), the railway station, continuing as far as the race-course and the park along Lake Maryut. After the *Agences des professions liberales*, came the square for luxury commerce and another one for food-stores; a polygonal square was to accommodate banks and private offices, followed by a smaller square giving access to the *Grand Magasins*.

The general plan shows an ellipsoidal boulevard derived from the Abukir road and crossing the *Grand Avenue*. This boulevard connected religious centres with other public buildings. Outside the boulevard were parks, urban facilities, while on the inside were residential neighbourhoods centred around religious and civic buildings (*Maison du Peuple*, Municipal Theatre, Music Hall, an open-air theatre and a spa, as well as public laundries and medical clinics).

Lafollye emphasized the isolated character of the new town, encompassed as it was by the canal and by the railway embankment, praising Clauzier's ideas to establish so many parks and gardens. He also added that Clauzier was asked to prepare a plan for land subdivision, considering that the plan would have required at least thirty years to reach completion; a lot of money for the workforce and building materials; and with bricks imported from France.

On 26 February 1926 Maurice Clauzier presented his plan for Sidi Gaber to an audience that included Alfred Agache and Paul Lafollye at the Musée Social in Paris. Clauzier explained that the financial situation of Alexandria was enviable, because people were unaware of taxes, and all expenses were being covered by the revenues of the port.[40]

6.5 *"Ars"* by Enrico Casiraghi and Luigi Lorenzo Secchi

The Italian journal *Ingegneria* published a bird's eye view and a general plan prepared by Casiraghi and Secchi for the Sidi Gaber competition.

They were rather heterogeneous drawings. While the bird's eye view showed a compact city of large blocks of four to five story buildings, the plan layout showed an harmonious network of streets.

For this project, there is also a typewritten draft of the report by the authors.[41]

"While working on the project, we have always considered both the competition requirements, and technical rules concerning public health and aesthetics that should apply to the design and development of a modern city.

Our project presented many distinctive traits, such as the necessity of ethnographic neighbourhoods to be arranged around religious buildings. As focal points of neighbourhood development, churches were situated and oriented with a kind of symmetry, near

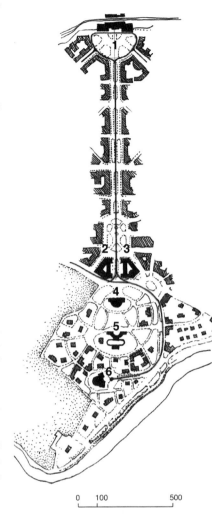

0   100   500

The main boulevard according to Secchi-Casiraghi's project, legend: 1. New railway station; 2. Stock Exchange; 3. Chamber of Commerce; 4. Exhibition Hall; 5. Spa; 6. Lyric Theatre (author's elaboration).

opposite
Enrico Casiraghi and Luigi Lorenzo Secchi, *Competition project for the new town of Sidi Gaber*, general plan and bird's eye view (Secchi-Tarugi family archive).

Enrico Casiraghi and Luigi Lorenzo Secchi, *Competition project for the new town of Sidi Gaber*, proposed sewage network (Secchi-Tarugi family archive).

opposite
Enrico Casiraghi and Luigi Lorenzo Secchi, *Competition project for the new town of Sidi Gaber*, detail of the bird's eye view showing: three religious bulidings and their squares; the park along the Mahmoudieh Canal: 1. Exhibition Hall, 2. Spa, 3. Lyric Theatre (author's elaboration).

Enrico Casiraghi and Luigi Lorenzo Secchi, *Competition project for the new town of Sidi Gaber*, detail of the rearranged Sporting Club (Secchi-Tarugi family archive).

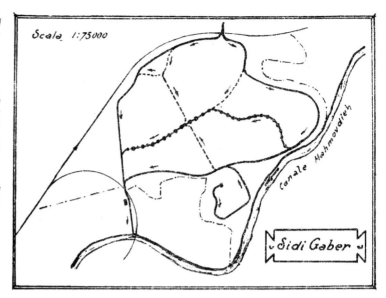

the edges of the competition area, so that agglomeration and congestion would not harm the centre of the new city.

By looking at the plan, we can observe that building and aesthetic traditions of each race have been respected, at the same time complying with every rule of hygiene, art and technology, so that each district has its own arrangement and special character ...

From the aesthetic point of view, all natural features of the land have been enhanced with the creation of picturesque areas; the elegant arrangements of roads and gardens; a road network developed following the contour lines of the arterial roads thus cutting distances and gracefully connecting them with a succession of peaceful corners, small gardens and squares.

In the most popular and picturesque part of the city, the railway station was extended and equipped with a railway siding to serve 40,000 inhabitants.

As well, the poorly-placed triangular area between the railway embankments was optimized as it was converted into a village for employees and labourers.

The village consisted of small semi-detached houses surrounded with gardens, and even equipped with a football field and tennis courts. Industrial development of the new city was envisaged between the indigenous villages of Hadra and Ez-Soad.

This because the area is encompassed by a secondary junction of the railway coming from the port of Alexandria, providing easy connections to each industrial plant, and also because it was close to the indigenous villages which could possibly provide manpower."[42]

Clearly, the project strived to settle the dichotomy between technicalities and the quality of urban space.

Casiraghi and Secchi followed the contour lines not only to rationalise the system of water supply and disposal, but also to preserve the profile of Lake Hadra in the layout of the new city.

A wide ring road departed from the Abukir road.

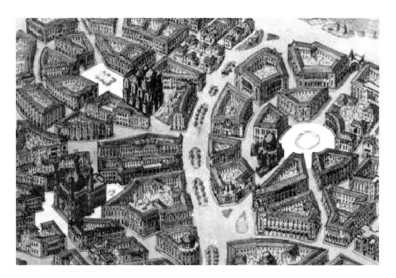

It aligned with the former shore of Lake Hadra to link the main functional areas, including the station and the theatre squares.

West of the station, along the railway embankment, space was assigned for technical needs of the city (goods yard, market, workers' district, industrial area, fire station).

An area for sports and leisure was located near the Sporting Club, perhaps considered as a potential complement of the new city. The townscape envisaged by Casiraghi and Secchi was dominated by the new railway station. Its large vaulted structure and the size of the façade (approximately 200 m) combined elements from Milan's old and new central stations.[43]

A large straight boulevard of one kilometre was to connect the station square with the central business district, a harmonious architectural grouping around the Municipality, the stock exchange, the Chamber of Commerce and an Exhibition Hall.

"The existing elevated plain was converted into an elegant public garden, with plans to build the most luxurious villas and buildings in town, such as the Lyric Theatre and the Spa.

Standing in the midst of the garden area, both the Exhibition Hall and the Chamber of Commerce serve as monumental landmarks along the boulevard coming from the station.

From this elevated spot, the large monumental axis running straight for over one kilometre can be seen dividing onto two gentle slopes, its monotony being interrupted both by the height difference between the Chamber of Commerce and the Station, and by the large parterres and vegetation obstructing the view from the bottom, leaving uncovered the routes in the background."[44]

Proposing again a solution tested in Milan a few years earlier,[45] the road-bed of the boulevard was divided into multiple tree-lined tracks, for trams, cars, horses and pedestrians.

"To avoid the unpleasant sight of the ridge of a such a wide carriageway, our main roads include two or more lanes separated by tree-lined promenades for strolling and riding … By placing the tramway track at the centre, where other vehicles are not allowed, we can push the tramway at maximum speed on long stretches of the ring-road with no danger for other vehicles."[46]

While Casiraghi and Secchi claimed that their school building proposals were inspired by the latest studies (in accordance with the competition brief), it can be noted that, at the time of the competition, they were both engaged in designing new schools in Milan. This plan differs from the others in that it paid greater attention to environmental features: the most picturesque site of the new city was to be the waterfront along the garden-lined Mahmoudieh Canal.

Here the cosmopolitan environment would be enhanced by the presence of cafes, bar, and meeting places, the site extending to the open countryside; a shady walk, with amenities for recreation, reached the Nouzha and Antoniadis Gardens; the new hospital was to exploit the salubrious air in that part of the town.

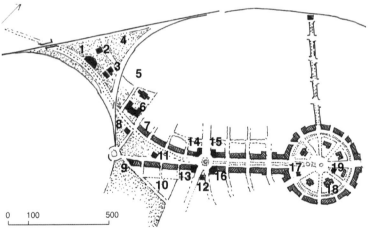

0   100   500

6.6 "Z" by Giacomo Alessandro Loria

A general plan of the project by Giacomo Alessandro Loria for the new town of Sidi Gaber was reproduced in *Studi e Concorsi*, one of the four albums collecting photographic prints of his work.[47]

Loria had grown up in Alexandria, where he started a professional career working as a draftsman for the Municipality, through where he gained a thorough understanding of the local society and urban development. As with Lasciac, Loria took careful notice of McLean's plan, he adopted the new road to Abukir as a basic feature of his plan, while changing the course of the road to divide the land into two areas of similar extensions.

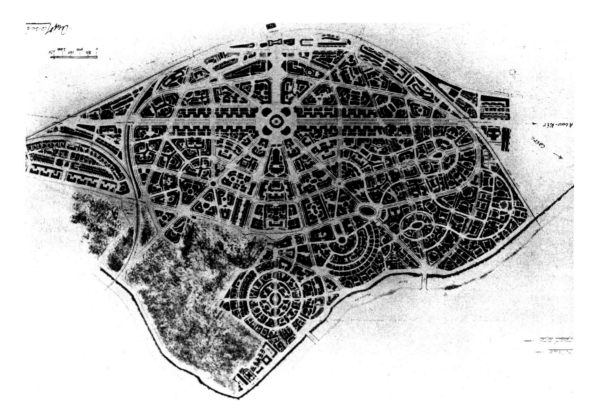

Antonio Lasciac, *Plan of the new Smouha garden city* (from *Architettura e Arti Decorative*).

opposite
The main boulevard according to Lasciac's project, legend: 1. New railway station, 2. First Aid Post; 3. Garage; 4. Hotel; 5. Hotel; 6. Public building (?); 7. Exhibition Hall; 8. Public building (?); 9. Public building (school?); 10. Public building (?); 11. PTT; 12. Synagogue and Rabbinate; 13. School; 14. Market; 15. Nursery school; 16. School; 17. Garage; 18. Café and Brasserie (author's elaboration).

Most of the public buildings were compactly aligned along this 50-meters-wide boulevard from downtown Alexandria, which at a certain point, formed the 380-m diameter of a round wooded square. All leisure facilities - cinema, theatres, hotel and casino - were set in a green area across the railway junction, followed by two parallel rows of rectangular blocks including services of public utility (first-aid post, post and telegraph office, fire station, the drinking water and electricity companies) as well as buildings of worship (mosque, Orthodox church and Catholic church).

Equally distant from the railway station and from the Mahmoudieh Canal, the round square was defined by a perimeter of regular blocks and by a central green area that included the synagogue and the Protestant church. This square was the symbolic and geometric centre of the new city, the origin of a system of concentric plots alternated with streets, some served by the tramway line, the outermost formed a ring to route traffic to and from Cairo. Radial streets linked the square to major landmarks: the railway station and the Nouzha-Antoniadis Gardens, the bridge across the Mahmoudieh Canal, underpasses and flyovers.

One of the radial streets crossed both the railway and the old Abukir road to reach the Ramleh tramway, thus encompassed the ellipsoidal Sporting Club (denominated "Hippodrome" by Loria) as a functional part of the new city. The area between the Lake Hadra and Ez-Soad was occupied by terraced houses arranged along semi-circular roads, all other quarters were characterized by a homogeneous low-density residential fabric, very similar to the surrounding eastern suburbs of Alexandria. Loria's plan may be considered as an attempt to explore the natural and infrastructural conditions that could help shape a comprehensive order in the built environment, a composition at the urban scale potentially embellished by the architecture of public buildings.

6.7 The project by Antonio Lasciac, *hors concours*

The Italian journal *Architettura e Arti Decorative* published the *Plan of the new Smouha garden city* by Antonio Lasciac,[48] which was identical to the drawing reproduced in Lasciac's photo albums held at Alinari archives.[49]

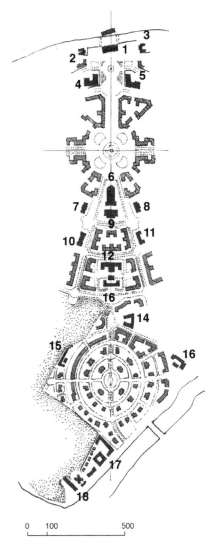

This project showed a deep understanding of both the local context and McLean's plan. The new road to Abukir, Alexandria's future backbone, was taken as a basic element of the new city, defining its layout and the densely built area. The wide roadway was lined by compact rows of residential blocks, most probably the "blocks for rent well ventilated by the courts" required by the competition brief. Lasciac also set aside a strip for public utility services between Abukir road and the railway embankment, including a mechanical bread oven, milk collection and distribution, public baths, two markets, two public laundries, and two nurseries.

Traveller facilities, parking and garage, two hotels and an apartment hotel, the public baths were grouped near the railway station. An arcaded street connected the railway station to the great tree-lined square along the new Abukir road, the geometric centre of the new city. In compliance with McLean's plan, this square was a traffic roundabout and the main access point of the road from Cairo, continuing under the railway to reach the Corniche. Other streets radiated from this square towards the Nouzha Antoniadis Gardens and towards the residential neighbourhoods, arranged in curvilinear layout along the Mahmoudieh Canal.

Lasciac also incorporated previously existing routes linking the villages of Lake Hadra and Ez Soad, which established the new Moslem quarter. A sort of ring road followed the old track between Hadra and Ez-Soad, and continued along the northern profile of Lake Hadra. Lasciac's project was criticised for its rigid geometry but recognised for the overall harmony: "the basic objectives of the road network are achieved: easy communication between neighbourhoods, clarity of layout in the main arteries and connection, a logic distribution of public buildings and facilities (station, markets, schools, hotels , etc.)."[50]

Lasciac's experience in the field of town planning included a number of proposals for connecting his home town Gorizia to the Transalpine railway (1906), and a plan for the reconstruction of Gorizia after World War I (1917).[51] Just where Secchi and Casiraghi had laid their one-kilometre straight boulevard, Lasciac proposed a monumental enfilade, aligning along the same axis the railway station, the main squares, the Catholic church and the synagogue with their respective schools.

Most probably prepared after the competition (if we are to believe Clauzier, who mentioned the existence of 12 projects), Lasciac's town-planning certainly showed a thorough knowledge of the Egyptian society, and how it had changed in the course of more than forty years.

This was reflected in his proposal to avoid a strict division of ethnographic neighbourhoods, and associating instead a school to each of the five buildings of worship required by the competition brief, so that social life was to develop in the a buffer zone between the gardens and the city centre.

Interpreting Sitte's concern for the inherent qualities of urban space - where the whole is much more than the sum of its parts - Lasciac's proposed an architectural composition at the urban scale, culminating in an oval-shaped residential district.

A garden-city pattern was to accommodate the most luxurious villas along the Mahmoudieh Canal, thus reviving its 19th role as the green belt of Alexandria (way ahead of Ebenezer Howard's time).

6.8 From 1925 to 1930

We have very little information covering the years from 1926 to 1930. Joseph Smouha was still involved in a number of other situations and we can assume that, as most of the work was done manually by many hundreds of fellaheen carrying the nine million cubic metres of earth in very primitive conditions, the workload was massive and could have easily taken the whole of this period.

The first task was to level the land. The drainage had left a large area below the level of the surrounding land and marsh.

The hilly land on the other side of the tunnel which he had bought in the meantime, was, at that time, the only way to carry this out. Over nearly the next two years the nine million cubic metres were transported through the tunnel and levelled out by nearly a thousand fellahin carrying sacks of earth and sand.

The actual transportation through the tunnel was carried out via a small old railway where the tracks were re-laid and consisted of a narrow gauge track called Decauville and a number of open trucks.

This had been constructed during World War I and had been used in Palestine to carry military supplies. Meanwhile at the prestigious Mohammed Ali Club, where the cream of business and professional men congregated, commented abounded "a mad Englishman has arrived in Egypt and bought Lake Hadra."

One can imagine that after all this major activity the years of 1928 to 1930 were taken up with preparing the land for the building of a city with many major works still to accomplish and contracts to negotiate. We do know that there was an ongoing discussion on costs with the Municipality.

One agreement carried out by the Municipality was the construction of three other tunnels which amounted to LE 43,670.

In addition, when the map of the city was finally completed, Joseph Smouha donated 721,269 sq.m. covering the streets and squares including the paving, lighting, water and electricity sup-

View of the new Abukir road (ELIA-MIET Photographic Archive).

plies, telephone and sewers all of which were included in an official contract dated 30 May 1933.

The total amount of land bought by Joseph Smouha (which included some land near the *Mellahat* and some from the railways) came to 769/20/13 feddans.

According to family records, in these early days a small oil spill or trickle was discovered, with the excitement and hopes of the millions it would bring over a short time and all sorts of plans were made. Some was sent for analysis and found to be used motor oil.

1. Radames Lackany, *Quelques notes de toponymie Alexandrine*, Alexandria, 1976, pp.28-29.
2. G. Spitaleri, *Costruttori Italiani in Egitto. Filippo Cartareggia*, Alexandria,1933, pp.25-34.
3. "Draining Hadra Lake," *The Egyptian Gazette*, 10.8.1925.
4. "Il prosciugamento del Lago di Hadra," *Messaggero Egiziano*, 22.10.1925.
5. "Le dessèchement du Lac Hadra", *Le Magazine Egyptien*, 1.11.1925
6. "Aménagement d'un plan d'une ville dans la banlieue d'Alexandrie (Égypte)," *La Construction Moderne*, vol. 40, 37, 14 June 1925, pp.144.
7. "Sistemazione di una località nei pressi di Alessandria d'Egitto," *Ingegneria*, IV, n.9, September 1925, p.346.
8. Based on what we found at the Secchi-Tarugi family archive, the material enclosed to the competition brief was a general map of the area in scale 1:18,000 and a more detailed map indicating with a great precision the level of the ground in the area formerly occupied by the lake.
9. The total population of Alexandria in 1925 was 570,000, see Isam Al-Khafaji, *Tormented Births: Passages to Modernity in Europe and the Middle East*, London, I.B. Tauris, 2004, p.91.
10. Sitte's book *Der Städtebau nach seinen Künstlerischen Grundsätzen*, Wien, C. Graeser, 1889, was edited five times between 1889 and 1922, and in 1902 it was translated into French.
11. Charles Buls, *Esthétique des Villes*, Buxelles, Bruylant-Christophe & Cie, 1893.
12. See *The Competition Programme* in the Annexes.
13. Ebenezer Howard, G*arden Cities of To-morrow (being the second edition of "Tomorrow: a peaceful path to real reform")*, London, S. Sonnenschein & co., 1902. Translated into many languages, this book had a profound impact on town-planning throughout the world.
14. Maurice de Soissons, *Welwyn Garden City*, Publications for Companies, Cambridge 1988.
15. A letter by Joseph Smouha to Enrico Casiraghi and Luigi Lorenzo Secchi, dated Alexandria, 29 December 1925, includes a copy of the hand-written report of the jury. See Annexes.
16. On Raoul Brandon's work in Egypt see Raoul Brandon, *Travaux d'Architecture Hors de France: (Etranger, Colonies, Pays sous mandat français): Travaux exécutés, projets et concours, croquis de voyage. Première partie*, Librairie de *La Construction Moderne*, 1925, pl. 1-39; see also *Brandon, Raoul et Frédéric, un architect, un peintre à travers le siècle*, catalogue of the exhibition, Chartres, 1998; Marie-Laure Crosnier Leconte, "Raoul Brandon," *La revue du Musée d'Orsay*, 8/14, n. 16, 2003, pp.46-49 ; Mercedes Volait, *Architectes & Architectures de l'Égypte moderne 1830-1950*, Paris, Maisonneuve et Larose, 2005, p.425.
17. See Mercedes Volait, Marie-Laure Crosnier Leconte, "Les architectes français ou la tentation de l'Égypte," in *France-Égypte. Dialogues de deux cultures*, ed. Jean-Marcel Humbert, Paris, Afaa-Paris-Musées-Gallimard-L'œil, 1998, pp.112-113. On Léon Azéma see Philippe Chaplain, *Léon Azéma architecte, 1888-1978*, Bibliothèque de l'Association Historique Bourg-la-Reine de jadis à demain, 2004. On Max Edrei and Jacques Hardy see Mercedes Volait, *Architectes & Architectures*, cit., pp. 428, 432.
18. *La Construction Moderne*, 10, n. 30, 22 April 1905, p.360. A. Gelbert, "L'architecture au Salon des Artistes Français," *La Construction Moderne*, 10, n. 35, 27 May 1905, pp.411-413; A. Gelbert, "L'architecture au Salon des Artistes Français," *La Construction Moderne*, 24, n. 32, 8 May 1909, p.375; *La Construction Moderne*, 24, n. 35, 29 Mai 1909, p. 420.
19. L. Jaussely was co-founder and teacher at the École des Hautes Etudes Urbaines (EHEU), member of the Musée Social and co-founder of the Société Française d'Urbanisme (SFU).
20. See *La Construction Moderne*, 36, n. 12, 19 December 1920, p.95; 37, n. 24, 12 March 1921, pp.185-186, pl. 95; 37, n. 36, 4 June 1922, p.288 ; 38, n. 20, 11 February 1923, p.239.
21. See *La Construction Moderne*, 38, 18 March 1923, p.292.
22. See *La Construction Moderne*, 4 September 1921, p. 387, pl. 193-196.
23. See *Où en est l'urbanisme: en France et à l'étranger*, Congrès International d'Urbanisme et d'Hygiène Municipale, Société Française des Urbanistes, Strasbourg 1923, Paris, Eyrolles, 1923.
24. See Pierre Bourdeix, "L'Urbanisme en pratique," *La Construction Moderne*, y. 38, n. 21, 18 February 1923, pp. 241-243.
25. See *La Construction Moderne*, 36, n. 41, 10 July 1921; 36, n. 50, 11 September 1921, pp.396-397.
26. *La Construction Moderne*, 41, n. 40, 4 July 1926, pp.493-496. M. Portevin, "Étude sur l'evolution du plan des édifices hopitaliers à travers les âges," *La Construction Moderne*, v. 61, November 1945, ed. by Paul Amédée Planat, pp.206-212; M. Portevin, "Hopitaux Suisse," *La Construction moderne*, v. 62, April 1946, pp.365-369; M. Portevin, "Hospitais Suissos," *Arquitectura Portguesa*, v. 39, September 1946, pp.6-10; M. Portevin, "Hopitaux Suisses," *La Construction Moderne*, v. 63, May 1947, pp.789-793 ; M. Portevin, C. Monteil, *Les Sujétions imposées pour l'isolement et le groupement des malades dans la conception d'un projet d'hôpital*, 1947.
27. *Milano dietro le quinte, Luigi Lorenzo Secchi*, ed. by Elisabetta Susani, Milan, Electa, 1999, pp.30-35.
28. Mohamed F. Awad and Cristina Pallini, "The Italianisation of Alexandria: an Analogy of Practice," in *Le Caire–Alexandrie architectures européennes*, ed. by Mercedes Volait, Cairo, IFAO-CEDEJ, 2001, pp. 89-98; Cristina Pallini, "Giacomo Alessandro Loria, un architetto italiano in Egitto," *Il disegno di architettura*, n. 31, 2005, pp. 44 - 49.
29. Maria Concetta Migliaccio, "Limongelli Domenico," in *Architetti e ingegneri italiani dal Levante al Maghreb 1848-1945*, eds Ezio Godoli and Milva Giacomelli, Florence, Maschietto, 2005, p.215; Mercedes Volait, "The Italian Contribution to the Construction of the New City of Heliopolis," in *Italian*

Architects and Engineers in Egypt from the Nineteenth to the Twentyfirst Century, eds Ezio Godoli and Milva Giacomelli, Florence, Maschietto, pp.72-89.

30. While Piacentini had gained a reputation with his competition project for rebuilding the centre of Bergamo (1907), Giovannoni was developing ideas on the role of urban planning in the rapid transformation of the centuries-old cities, following the theories put forth by Sitte, Buls, and Stübben. See Gustavo Giovannoni, "Vecchie città ed edilizia nuova," *Nuova Antologia*, June 1913. In 1921 Piacentini and Giovannoni founded the architectural journal *Architettura e Arti Decorative*.

31. C. Cecchelli, "Profili di giovani architetti. A. Limongelli," *Architettura e Arti Decorative*, vol. III, 1927, p.113-131. See Milva Giacomelli, "Limongelli Alessandro," in *Architetti e ingegneri italiani*, cit., pp.210-215; Francesca Marsico, L'architettura di Alessandro Limongelli, PhD dissertation, University of Roma Tre, 1999-2000.

32. L.P., "Il piano regolatore per la nuova città-giardino di Smouha," *Architettura e Arti Decorative*, vol. VI 1926-27, p.132.

33. See Mercedes Volait, "Un architecte face a l'Orient: Antoine Lasciac (1856-1946)," in *La fuite en Égypte: supplement aux voyages européens an Orient*, Cairo, CEDEJ, 1989, pp.268-281; *Da Gorizia all'impero ottomano Antonio Lasciac architetto*, Catalogue of the exhibition edited by Ezio Godoli, Florence, Alinari, 2006; Ezio Godoli, "Lasciac Antonio", in *Architetti e Ingegneri Italiani*, cit., pp.199-205.

34. See *La Liberté*, special issue published on the visit in Egypt by the King and the Queen of Italy, 1933.

35. See Mercedes Volait, *Architectes & Architectures*, cit., p.426.

36. See Pierre Bourdeix, "L'Urbanisme en pratique," cit., pp.241-243.

37. Maurice Clauzier, *La Cité-jardin (Gizzy-jardin) d'un port d'aérobus de la Métropole "Urbs"*, 1922.

38. Paul Lafollye, "Extension d'Alexandrie. Création de 'Sidi Gaber' cité de luxe," *L'Architecture*, vol. 39, n. 12 1926, pp.155-157.

39. *Ibidem*, p.155

40. For a short report of Clauzier's conference see "Section d'Hygiène urbaine & rural & de Prévoyance sociale, Séance du 26 Février 1926," *Le Musée Social*, March 1927, pp.71-73.

41. *Progetto per la costruzione della citta di Sidi-Gaber (Egitto). Descrizione generale (Appunti)*, Secchi-Tarugi family archive.

42. *Ibidem*, pp.1-2.

43. The first Central Station designed by L.-J. Bouchot was built between 1857 and 1864 and demolished in 1922; the new Central Station, still operational, was designed by U. Stacchini in 1911 and built between 1926 and 1931.

44. *Progetto per la costruzione della citta di Sidi-Gaber*, cit., p.2.

45. The reference may well be viale Zara-Fulvio Testi.

46. *Progetto per la costruzione della citta di Sidi-Gaber*, cit., p.16.

47. In 1926 Loria submitted four albums of his projects to the Alexandria branch of the Italian Board of Architects and Engineers, (Associazione Nazionale degli Ingegneri e Architetti Italiani) in order to have his authorship certified.

48. L.P., "Il Piano Regolatore della nuova Città-Giardino di Smouha," in *Architettura e Arti Decorative*, vol. VI , 1926-27, p.132.

49. Alinari photo archives, Florence.

50. L.P., "Il Piano Regolatore ...," p.132.

51. Diego Kuzmin, "Sulle orme di Antonio Lasciac," *Isonzo Soča*, n. 38, 2000, pp.2-5.

7 Richard Smouha
The Start of the Project

7.1 Municipal Commission

Most of the information in this chapter is taken directly from the many newspapers in my collection and references are given in each case. On occasion I have given more than one report of the same incident for the greater edification and atmosphere of the period. Several very important points are brought out in this chapter. Firstly, and most important, is the background of the whole way of life with the free and uncompromising relationships between races, religions and classes. Secondly, and as a consequence of this, the freedom of speech and action (which was so completely suppressed under the Nasser and Moubarak regimes) leading to a level of transparency which created – at certain levels and in certain circles – as much a western democracy as was to be found anywhere in any of the Middle East.

The following affair of the exchange of land was one of a number of teething problems brought on by the sudden appearance not far from the city centre of some 500 acres of land. This one probably caused as much problem as any. While I do not have the original minutes of the two main Municipal Commission meetings, the newspaper reports show the spirit and humour of the day.

Municipal Commission meeting of 18.3.1931

The meeting opens at 4:40 pm under the presidency of His Excellency Hussein Sabri Pasha, the Governor of Alexandria. After one hour's discussion on procedures and priorities (during which the above affair was mentioned), no decision had been taken, and the agenda had not even started. It took until 7:30, three hours of general discussion – a record.

Once it got going, the hottest point of the meeting was unquestionably the exchange of land with Joseph Smouha.

The origin of this requirement was complex. It was given by Felix Green, Municipal Councillor in charge of what would be known today as the Ministry for the Environment, but was then described as for beautifying the city and ensuring a normal traffic situation in an area destined to take on a considerable development.

Felix Green's explanation and proposal concerned improvements to be brought to the area north of the Nouzha and Antoniadis Gardens. An exchange of the two areas gives an advantage to each one, both Mr. Smouha and the City:

- The acquisition of Mr. Smouha's lot would allow a direct link between the Nouzha and Antoniadis Gardens.

- The domain of the municipality would be more complete to the south and to the east of the Mahmoudieh Canal Avenue – thus a considerable increase in the value of municipal land.

- We also thus avoid the risk of Joseph Smouha one day as owner, selling this land to build "modest and un-aesthetical constructions" for his workers.

- This exchange would also save the Municipality the expense of making a road separating the two areas as both would be joined as municipal land.

Approval has been given by the specific committees of the Municipality, the Tanzim Council, the Municipal Commission and the Ministry of the Interior.

Immediately, Councillor Mahmoud Orabi Bey (is he related to the famous Orabi Pasha of 1882?), springs to his feet:

> "I have to criticise a decision of the Tanzim Council to sell to Mr. Smouha a lot at the price of LE8,000 per sq. metre, as this lot is worth considerably more and furthermore provides a high income of many hundreds of pounds a year to the Municipality."

Our orator then proceeded to attack the Administration for allowing the sub-committees to resolve such questions instead of submitting them formally for decision by the Municipal Commission.

> "This important decision has not been submitted to any of the competent sub-committees and I am amazed that they were prepared to accept an exchange of land between Joseph Smouha and the Municipality to the detriment of the interests of the City."

The head of the Administration quite correctly acknowledged that he had not studied the question and that the proposal for the land exchange had been made afterwards.

Our orator then attacked Felix Green and got himself into a state of extreme over-excitement.

Orabi Bey exploded with anger and repeated his objections to the procedure that had been adopted:

> "I insist that the Municipal Commission throw out the exchange of land project until the question is investigated in depth."

Seddik Bey replied:

> "May I remind you that you were the first person to know of the minutes of the meeting of the delegation where the exchange was approved in principle and then sent to the Tanzim for an estimate."

Furthermore the Commission had passed this decision by approving the minutes of the delegation dated 9 December and the Tanzim Council of 8 December.

Seddik Bey continued:

> "I am astonished that Orabi Bey who visited the land in person, who was present at all the meetings of the Delegation and of the Tanzim should come today and criticise the General Management.
>
> It was Orabi Bey himself who fixed the level of the deal at one feddan for one-and-a-half feddans re-value of the lands to be exchanged. So it is really extraordinary that he should now come and protest against a level that he had previously promoted."

Felix Green then gave a resume of the whole affair, insisting on his neutrality in the matter (quite useless as his integrity and honour are known to all) but that he considers that it was necessary to speak to the landowner who was going to build workers' homes in the site.

View of the Antoniadis Gardens (ELIA-MI-ET Photographic Archive).

Green continued:

"The Committee went to the site with Orabi Bey and he, himself, carried out his own investigation. It is he, personally who suggested the 1-1.5 feddan arrangement and I believe I have a duty to ask what he meant when he said, 'Why did Mr. Green make this proposal, with what object in mind etc'."

Arcache Bey said:

"I agree with this but forcefully object to the level. This concerns 120,000 pics of very valuable municipal land. Even if Mr. Smouha has offered land for building a road, the Municipality will have to underwrite enormous expenses and the road itself will greatly increase the value of the surrounding land. We need to review everything and decide, firstly the need for this exchange, and secondly under what conditions in order to safeguard the interest of the Municipality. Mr. Smouha looks after his interest and we can help him only if it is in the interest of the public."

Orabi Bey, with a self-satisfied smile:

"I am happy that I have provoked a discussion which shows the seriousness of the case, and this was not shown up by either the Council or the Tanzim."

He did however acknowledge that it was he who had set the level at 1-1.5 feddans but he mentioned that this was just in principle and not a final figure.

Zaki Bey Raghab intervened to say:

"I regret the attitude of Orabi Bey and I also regret the uselessness of his irritability which led him to express absolutely unnecessary insinuations and criticisms. May I remind him that the Tanzim Council is instituted by decree and the whole question is therefore subject to review. I deplore the fact that the Honourable Councillor does not use a more parliamentary language vis-à-vis the General Management."

This led to an incident between our Orabi Bey and the head of the Parquet. Zaki Bey Raghab:

"We are Councillors elected by the will of the people."

Aly Bey Hassan:

"We all are and do our duty."

Zaki Bey Raghab:

"Please do not interrupt I have the right to object to the attitude of Orabi to a colleague elected like myself."

Telemat Bey:

"I can explain this incident. Zaki Bey made a distinction between the elected Councillors and those named *ex-officio*. What he meant is that the elected Councillors have a mission to represent their elector's wishes."

Orabi Bey provokes another incident:

"Our rebel, Telemat has not represented Zaki Bey's statement correctly, all he wanted to do was pacify the incident and Zaki Bey never agreed to what Telemat Bey said."

Aly Bey Hassan:

"Zaki Bey has just observed just after Telemat Bey's declaration that it is better to defend the interest of the city than to quibble over such statement. I am delighted to thank Telemat Bey for the spirit of conciliation he has demonstrated and also for his perfect courtesy."

Telemat Bey:

"Thank you for clearing this up."

Monsieur Caravia:

"I should like to emphasize the perfect harmony which reigns among the Councillors all acting in the interest of the city."

Orabi Bey:

"I consider the incident closed."

The Council voted 12-10 with 1 abstention to postpone the subject for further study. It is 8 o'clock!

"Trois heures de discussions sans aborder les questions figurant à l'ordre du jour!," *La Cloche,*10.3.1931

Do you realise what we owe to our eminent General Manager of the Municipality who has saved us some LE21,000.

Here is how he did it:

The Smouha family who acquired the Domain of Hadra reminded the Municipality that they were obliged to build access tunnels under the Cairo-Alexandria railway line. The Municipality proposed the first one near the Ibrahimieh Police Station on condition that Smouha participated to the tune of LE3,000. Joseph Smouha agreed.

Later the Municipality again backed off the proposal and informed Joseph Smouha that the expenses were much higher and he would have to pay LE6,000. Joseph Smouha, who had a horror of delays and hesitation, again accepted.

This was finally decided upon by the Municipal Delegation, approved by the Municipal Commission and sanctioned by the Minister for the Interior. Thus the Municipality was finally bound by these conditions.

Everything seemed to be in place, but our general manager looked at the file for a final time. He realized that the cost of the expropriations could be considerable. He tried out an idea on Mr. Smouha: Why commit to paying LE6,000? Let's improve this. We, the Municipality, are prepared to pay this amount and you pay the rest. Then, Seddik Bey, a consummate diplomat, pleaded his cause so well that he finally convinced him.

So, do you know how much Smouha had to pay: LE26,691, and our smart General Manager obtained a present for the city of nearly LE21,000.

I, personally, knowing my grandfather, cannot believe this to be the whole story and am convinced there must have been some trade off which while entirely legitimate would have taken some of the above glory away from the Municipality.

"Des discussions de principe qui durent des heures," *La Bourse Egyptienne,* 19.3.1931

Orabi Bey asks that the exchange of land not take place so that later no one can say that the Councillors sitting in 1931 gave the land ceded to Mr. Smouha and of great value. Mr. Green explained first of all that he had no personal interest in the affairs of Mr. Smouha and the sole reason for the decision was the beautification of the city and exactly what did Orabi Bey mean by these insinuations? Zaki Bey Raghab then calmed things down and read a note relating the history of the negotiations with Mr. Smouha:

"We are here to work."

Orabi Bey tries to interrupt him:

"You are not to interrupt me, Orabi Bey."

Things heat up again. Zaki Bey, Orabi Bey and Ahmad Hassan Bey are all shouting at the same time. Telemat Bey joins the fray to calm things down and Zaki Bey says:

"We are here to work in the interest of the city rather than these stupid arguments."

Orabi Bey jumps up at these words shouting violently at Zaki Bey. Finally calm is restored and by 12 votes to 11 with 1 abstention the meeting is adjourned.

"Affaires Municipales", *L'Informateur,* 20.3.1931

This report mentions and comments various incompetence and time wasting of this 1931 Municipal Commission. It emphasizes the fact that the 'Smouha family' being the main interested party, had not asked for any particular favour but that Arcache Bey (who seems to be the only Councillor who consistently sided with our Orabi Bey on virtually all subjects) actually acknowledged that

Mr. Smouha knows what he is doing as each square metre that he gives to the Municipality at a value of 40-50 piastres actually costs the Municipality LE1.5 for macadamising and maintenance.

"Alexandria Municipal Commission. An Exchange of Land", *The Egyptian Gazette,* 20.3.1931

Mr. Green explained the reasons for the exchange of land and made clear that the proposal for the exchange had originated with the Municipality not from Mr. Smouha.

Indeed Mr. Smouha had been reluctant to agree to an exchange on any terms and it was only when repeated proposals were made to him that he gave his consent to the transaction.

"Du bromure pour Orabi bey", *Le Phare Egyptien,* 22.3.1931

Bromide needed for Orabi Bey. This journalist really had a go at the by now infamous Orabi Bey. This meeting was even more disappointing than the previous ones. It became clear that there is a small group of turbulent Councillors who care nothing about the public's interest and whose conduct is wholly devoid of dignity. Public interest? What a joke! Wasting time? Let's enjoy ourselves! Let's discuss things, let's chat! The public? We couldn't care less … it's only simpletons who bother about such things.

Last Wednesday it was the eternal Orabi Bey who led the circus. Heavens above what on earth could be the cause of such behaviour? Why of course Felix Green and Seddik Bey! If we are to believe this excitable youngster from Upper Egypt, Felix Green and Seddick Bey, surrounded by a band of mysterious burglars, are in the process of selling the city and its suburbs down the drain, plot by plot to Mr. Smouha.

There is therefore only one man who is pure, Orabi Bey; only one man who is straight; Orabi Bey; only one man-of-the-world. Ah, this time NO, we are not in agreement with Orabi Bey.

To prove this description here is Orabi Bey raising his voice to its highest pitch screaming and shouting, turning everything upside down, stamping his feet and thumping his hands on the conference table, risking overturning it, shouting as if off his head and insinuating that Messrs. Felix Green and Seddick Bey have been bought by Mr. Smouha, especially Mr. Felix Green whom Orabi Bey cannot digest.

Let's look at the participants, on the one hand Mr. Felix Green and His Excellency the Director General.

Member of a patrician family living in Egypt from the late 1800s, known for his honesty and philanthropy, Mr. Felix Green, an elected Municipal Councillor of five years' standing, has always impressed with the correctness of his statements.

As for Ahmed Bey Seddick, Director General, he certainly has faults and weaknesses, but no one can contest that he is a civil servant of unquestioned honesty.

Finally, Mr. Smouha, a participant with a silent role who must be asking himself what he is doing in all this mess.

On the other hand, whom do we see? Orabi Bey. Where does

this joker come from? This is a present sent to us by the Egyptian Government. As an engineer in charge of irrigations, Orabi Bey is a statutory member of the Municipal Commission. It's a misfortune like any other. And by a stroke of bad luck, Orabi Bey has signed a pact of alliance with Arcache Bey, defender of the public interest ... or so he claims.

Now what is Mr. Green's crime? His constant care for the beauty of Alexandria led him to a plot of seven feddans belonging to Mr. Smouha but adjacent to the Antoniadis Gardens and where Mr. Smouha plans to build a workers' suburb.

Now you can understand Mr. Green's and Seddick Bey's worry, If Mr. Smouha manages to carry out his project that is the end of the Antoniadis Gardens. Imagine the picture—on the left of the Mahmoudieh Canal, the buildings and surroundings of a workers' city.

On the contrary, if we manage to acquire these seven feddans, we could enlarge and complete the Antoniadis gardens bordered by the canal road on the one hand and rue Albert 1er on the other, to become one of the most beautiful in the world.

Steeped with this concept, the delegation asked Mr. Smouha to exchange his seven feddans against 16 feddans belonging to the Municipality in the same area but of a much lower intrinsic value. One can easily see the advantages for both the city and the councillors from a practical point of view.

Mr. Smouha, contacted by Seddick Bey, hesitated, reflected, quibbled but finally accepted. Where is the scandal? Where is the embezzlement? Where is the complicity of Felix Green and the administration?

What on earth is all this barracking about, this Sudanese shindig organised by Orabi Bey? What are his motives and what does he really want? We cannot believe that he only had in mind the advantages of future generations that gave Orabi Bey so much worry and made him so violently agitated (lit. a devil in a basin of holy water). He is aiming elsewhere and the least one can accuse him of is that he is seeking to build a reputation as an orator. Orabi Bey, your ambition will be your undoing.

"Dans une atmosphère charge…," *La Reforme,* 2.4.1931

Discussion of the Tanzim Council on the estimate of 9 March - the land exchange.

Seddick Bey outlines the broad lines.

Orabi Bey:

> "I do not approve of this exchange. I believe it to be prejudicial to the interests of the Municipality. I do not agree with the value put on the land in question, and the confusion in the measurement of the land which includes a public road. I consider the real value of the land belonging to the Municipality to be based on the price that Mr. Smouha himself paid to acquire land in that area. He bought 8 feddans from Mohamed Tork at LE1,000.-, then 24 feddans at LE29,000.- from Mme. Jamain etc.so the minimum was never less than LE500.- and the maximum around LE1,200.-. Using this as

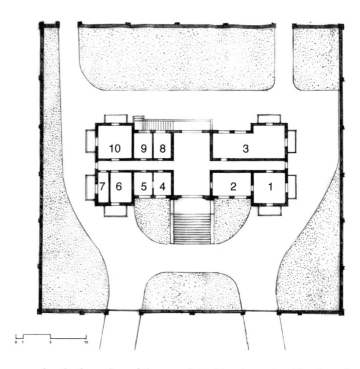

a basis the price of the municipal land must not be less than LE1,000."

Orabi Bey continued (presumably after taking breath):

"I am formally opposing this exchange. It is neither necessary nor advantageous. I do not believe this exchange will improve the Antoniadis Palace or prevent the undesirable construction of worker`s buildings and I deplore the expense of this exchange which is unnecessary for the city."

He added:

"This is a useless and costly luxury which is far and away not justified by today`s circumstances. You have the last word, you are the representatives of the City and you have to consider that the exchange is unnecessary. Mr. Smouha claims he is making a gift of one-third of the land, but that third belongs to you as it is a public utility and has been confirmed as such."

Arcache Bey praised the eloquence of his colleague:

"I am astonished that the Municipality would wish to go ahead with this exchange. The proportions are not the same and I am categoric in opposing its realisation. We could perhaps put the land up for auction or a friendly bid, but if I were not a Councillor I`d buy the lot at LE1,000 - or LE1,200 - for myself."

He developed the same point of view as Orabi Bey and proposed forming a committee to examine any offer of Mr. Smouha`s to buy the lot belonging to the Municipality. One is trying to convince us that Mr. Smouha would construct cheap buildings next to the Antoniadis Palace. One should not believe that for one instant because it would depreciate his own land and Mr. Smouha is an eminent financier who knows quite well where his interest lies.

La Bourse Egyptienne, 2.1.1931;
The Egyptian Gazette, 3.4.1931;
La Liberte, 3.4.1931

Zaki Bey Ragab:

"I really admire the eloquence of Orabi Bey. I can accept parts of his points of view but regret part of his opinions."

M. Lesinas:

"I approve the principle of the exchange but have reserves on some of the conditions."

Said Bey Telemat (to Orabi Bey):

"You know you are repeating yourself."

Mahmoud Bey Orabi (sic):

"As my speech is undesirable I will hold my tongue."

And he sat down, his voice vibrating with emotion. Telemat Bey:

"I only said Orabi Bey that you are repeating yourself. Speak if you have something new to say."

Orabi Bey stays quiet and no longer wishes to speak.

Telemat Bey, presiding, gives his resume, first thanking Orabi Bey for his zeal. He emphasizes that the question of the exchange of land has been discussed at great length and reminds everyone of all the phases that it has passed through as well as the differences of opinion between Orabi Bey and the members of the delegation and the committee of estimation.

Mr. Smouha has given the city two feddans. He offers in addition five feddans in exchange for the lot of the Municipality. That makes seven and-a-half feddans (sic). The Municipality is prepared to give in exchange 10 and a quarter feddans, that is two-thirds of 16 feddans.

As for the estimate of value, the land of Mr. Smouha is worth one-and-a-half times the land of the Municipality.

Smouha Estate Office, arch. Max Zollikofer. An additional terrace-floor was added to the building in the 1940s (R. Smouha's archive).

opposite
Smouha Estate Office (drawing by C. Pallini base on a sketch by D. Sabbah).
Legend: 1. Joseph Smouha; 2. Daniel Delbourgo; 3. Ellis and Teddy Smouha; 4. Ezra Smouha; 5. Mr. Aboaf and Mr. Seton ; 6. Mr. Russo and Mr. Matalon; 7. office; 8. Mr. Abdel Ali; 9. office; 10. Bureau d'été Direction.

Here Orabi Bey is upstanding and tells Telemat Bey that he has been mistaken in his calculations and adds that he withdraws the calculations and points of view he has developed.

Telemat Bey continued to demonstrate the advantages for the city and adds that as quickly as Orabi Bey becomes angry and argues in discussion, just as quickly he reverses his position when he sees that he is wrong. Finally the exchange of land is voted by 24 votes to two (Orabi Bey and Arcache Bey). The rest of the agenda was voted unanimously (8:45, four hours later).

7.2 The management

The nerve centre of this amazing activity was the Joseph Smouha Estate Office. It was situated at the end of a long two-way avenue with trees and flowerbeds along the middle strip and led directly from one of the main tunnels to an imposing roundabout. Joseph Smouha himself had a large office on the first floor on the right with a balcony. Slightly to the left was a smaller communicating office occupied by his right-hand man, Daniel Delbourgo. Joseph Smouha's office communicated with an office on the other side of the building occupied by my father Teddy Smouha and his brother Ellis, which had a view giving on to the Delrieux riding school, racecourse and golf course. As previously mentioned, Teddy Smouha was in charge of everything to do with the Club and its development while Ellis was more involved in the residential development; Ellis`s son, my cousin Derrick, who spent his gap year in Alexandria studying, tells how two or three times a week he would accompany his father around the land reviewing the work in progress. Teddy Smouha would often mention that, during his first year at the office, this must have been 1931, Joseph Smouha would say, "get a chair and put it just behind on my right, then sit there and don`t open your mouth under any circumstances but listen to everything."

There was no question as to who was the centrepiece of every activity in the office and I can remember Joseph Smouha shouting at the top of his voice for my father or uncle and putting questions, giving orders, in a word, until his later years in the fifties keeping a tight control of everything.

On the left hand side of the office was all the administration such as sales, correspondence, rentals and in particular an employee, one of whose daily tasks was distributing alms to "qualified" or justified beggars. While Delbourgo acted, especially in the absence of the three family members, as the general manager of the whole project, a Mr. Russo headed the back office described above with some half dozen administrative employees.

A special member of staff was Joseph Smouha`s first cousin Ezra Smouha, known in the family as Mr. Ezra, a delightful soft spoken person, who had two functions. The first, which took up his mornings, was to update the office accounts, income and expenditure, salaries etc. and in the afternoon he would go to the market and purchase the supplies for the next day mainly for the family house, but not such an easy task as he was ruled over by the tiny but commanding person of my grandmother. And at holiday time, his purchases had to provide for anything up to fifty people when you include house and garden servants, cook plus assistant, *suffragis* (waiters), nurses, maids as well as occasional such as washerwomen, dressmakers, etc.

Dr. David Sabbah from Paris, with whom I became most friendly, worked in the above office from 1946 until 1955 as translator and commercial assistant reporting directly to Mr. Delbourgo, the *wakil* of Joseph Smouha. Sadly, on my return from a week in London I found an email from his son to inform me that he had gone into hospital for a small operation and had died two days before, from complications. A most pleasant, intelligent, and modest man, he died unexpectantly at the age of 89 – and in good health! I feel lucky to have known him.

Anyway to get back to David Sabbah`s history, for the first few months of his employment he found himself in a large room with Mr. Russo, chief accountant, Matalon, an accountant, Siton, a shorthand-typist in English and Aboaf, a shorthand-typist in French and telephonist. All of a sudden, Egypt was hit with an epidemic of cholera. As he had to receive the clients, potentially carriers of the virus, he managed with the help of his fellow workers, but also by Mr. Ezra`s fear of being contaminated, to get himself transferred into an office on his own. This office gave onto a private riding school owned by M. Delrieux and frequented by the Alexandrian aristocracy, and in particular princes and princesses.

This office was formerly Joseph Smouha`s and was furnished with his old desk which took up two-thirds of the room and was totally out of proportion with his importance in the company.

They worked a 45-hour week but in reality only actually worked for 20 hours, while the rest of the time was taken up by reading. The working day started at 8:00 o`clock when Joseph Smouha reached the office thus ensuring that everyone was on time.

One Saturday, on returning from synagogue, Joseph Smouha declared that in future no work would be done on Saturdays and they would be considered as a holiday.

The reason was that the rabbi had read a verse in the Bible covering the sentence of death for anyone who worked on the Sabbath. Unfortunately, says David Sabbah, this new rule only lasted a very short time.

During this nine year period, Joseph Smouha did not come to the office in the afternoon: this was when he was aged 68 up to 77 years old and at a time when life expectancy in the UK ranged from 67 to 71. According to David Sabbah, he did however come in when necessary, for example, when tax declarations were prepared and sent, he would want to supervise.

A more recent incident that I remember, also remembered by David Sabbah - you could see in the above photo of the office two flagpoles. Everyday, one bore the Egyptian National flag and the other the Union Jack.

At one point of souring relations between Egypt on the one hand, and Israel and the UK on the other, an edict came out – this was in the early fifties after King Farouk`s departure – that the only flag that could be hoisted on private houses or offices was the Egyptian flag. A senior police officer was sent round to insist that the Union Jack must be lowered. Joseph Smouha stated that either both flags stayed up or both flags came down. Needless to say both stayed. But I remember that exceptionally it caused a stir in the family due the general unrest in the country.

Another employee remembered by David Sabbah, called Ali, was in charge of other miscellaneous sales and in particular rentals of land for agriculture pending sale for construction.

The company's outside lawyer, Moursi Badr, became very involved with everything that was going on and would come to the office every morning before going to his own. Perhaps unsurprisingly but slightly ironically there is now a road named after him, which used to be called rue Toussoun Pacha near his office not far from the Mohamed Ali Club and the tea room Baudrot, now rue Moursi Badr. David Sabbah says that he is prepared to witness that this is the only office he has known where over the period of nine years every visitor left with a present, and no request for help whether from individuals or associations, irrespective of race or religion was ever refused. This led to abuse, which was generally accepted as a normal risk of such a policy.

David Sabbah was involved in the sales and marketing of land for the construction of villas, and as such has provided us with a number of anecdotes:

"Mr. Smouha gave land to a Moslem for the construction of a mosque, as well as another lot of land to the French Red Cross to build a dispensary. I was present at both corner stone layings, one of which was attended by the famous French lawyer Maître Padoa, deputy of the French Assembly."

"The Jewish Community of Alexandria bought some land in Smouha City to build a technical college and was given a fifty per cent reduction on the quoted price."

"In the middle of an August heat wave I received a visit from an Egyptian client who wished to buy some land to build a villa. When he took his coat off he was just wearing his pyjamas and I had difficulty keeping a straight face." (This was not so unusual at the time, and unless there was a formal meeting, some people from the middle-class would wear their pyjamas all day).

"I accompanied the President of the Law Court of Tantah (the fourth biggest city in Egypt) in his limousine to show him lands for sale, when we were stopped by a police motor-cyclist who found that he had never possessed a driving licence taken to the police station of Smouha City, he actually received an apology because of his status." (He`s probably still driving without one 80 years later, wherever he is).

"I found myself in the car of a rich Egyptian property investor who wanted to build a villa in Smouha City when his chauffeur, who lived in a slummy area and slept at night to the sound of the songs of Abdel Wahab and Oum Kalthoum, replayed at their loudest from the cafes in the area, impressed by the calm and silence of Smouha, exclaimed asking the question: Is this place a *gheya*? (like a dream or wish.)"

The club had a number of secretaries, the first being Mike Marinakis who, according to David, became in fact the restaurant manager. But in later years the one we came to know best was Omar Bey Hamada, a former deputy chief of police who brooked no nonsense and from what I know ran the club like a police operation.

The office hours were 8:00 am to 1:00 pm and 4:00 pm to 7:00 pm. When Joseph Smouha left for his 3-4 months' holidays in the summer – because of the heat of 40-50 degrees this was normal for Europeans – Mr. Delbourgo cancelled the afternoon hours for the whole office but on Joseph Smouha's return Idriss the watchman/doorkeeper gave the game away and told him but it seems to have continued (see also work 8-12 on Saturday). As Club Secretary, Omar Bey Hamada had a very special relationship with my father Teddy Smouha, but also with us, the younger generation who came to play tennis, etc.

This continued after sequestration, when he kept my father up to date on what was happening at his level, either by telephone or letter. One day after our departure in 1956, he phoned in to say that under a new regulation concerning personal possessions he could arrange to send out my father's golf clubs.

He just needed a telegram (in those days!) requesting this and referring to the new regulations. You can imagine my father jumped at it. We heard nothing for quite some time. Finally my father telephoned.

"Oh no," said Omar. "It's not possible anymore."

"Why not? You said it was easy."

"Yes, but your telegram came through with a 'd' replacing the 'f', and there was an immediate un-appealable refusal to export 'gold clubs'."

Mr. Mike Marinakis, Alexandria Racing Club Secretary, 1934 (R. Smouha's archive).

Omar Bey Hamada, Alexandria Racing Club Secretary, 1948-56 (R. Smouha's archive).

7.3 The Racecourse furore

The racecourse itself had created a major furore not only in the horseracing community, but had spilled over into the Municipality's domain and various other unrelated parties.

Up till then the Alexandria Sporting Club (ASC) had been the only golf course/race course, but its development had become inadequate for the requirements of its members.

Furthermore, as was later revealed, the new addition to the ASC buildings, which had been inaugurated by Prince Omar Toussoun as Chairman of ASC, blocked out the view of one part of the races from the spectators in the stands.

The two alternatives which would, one or the other, solve the problem were Siouf or Smouha (Hadra or Alexandria Racing Club as it had become known).

A first report was carried out by a firm of surveyors and reported in the newspaper *Le Stade* of 4.4.1929, stating that, while there were indeed both grass and sand courses, they were in an atrocious state and it was easy to see how bad they could get by midsummer.

La Réforme, 1.3.1930

The discussions about how to handle the problem facing the ASC have come to the forefront.

For some time now the rapid development and increase in memberships have started to create problems for the members.

This has obviously led the committee to look for improved locations both for the racecourse and the golf course.

The erection of a wonderful new pavilion gives much more space to the members except for the race-goers, whose view of the races is partially blocked by the new building.

"As an old and fervent amateur of horse racing I was delighted to have an invitation to visit the newly projected course at Siouf, especially as I have known the best courses in the world.

Imagine my surprise to find three courses which must be among the best in the Middle East, two of grass and one of sand.

The external lane is a mile-and-a-half long, with two long straights which would allow trainers to send horses four or five abreast on training runs – a great advantage over today's situation, and more important still is that one can follow the race from beginning to end.

As far as the stables are concerned I can only confirm what I had heard, namely that they are comparable to those at Newmarket for comfort.

The stalls are spacious and have all the amenities you can find in Europe.

There is one series of 40, two of 30 and one of 20, and they are already completed – a real Horse Heaven.

Furthermore there is an unlimited supply of fresh water, not only for drinking but also for medicinal baths.

Added to this is a complete absence of flies something that you will find nowhere else. All these advantages make for much improved conditions of the horses and better racing.

Finally, in the training centre itself there is a special hygienic area for keeping the food and drink, etc.

In conclusion I am convinced that this is the finest location for a new racecourse that could be found.

I am not aware of negotiations but am sure that going ahead at Siouf would, over a short period of time, raise the level of horse racing in Alexandria from its low level of today."

La Cloche, 22.5.1930

Just before the éxtraordinary general meeting of the Alexadria

Sporting Club the Owners Association made an important delaration about the transfer of the racecourse.

On occasion in the past they had asked the Club committee to improve the conditions and in particular to improve the enclsures for the public. The Club had taken this request seriously and had studied three projects and were prepared to propose the transfer to "Sidi-Gaber-Hadra."

However the Owners Association learnt of the request of 80 club members who wanted to transfer to Siouf.

The Owners Association felt it was their duty first to declare that the transfer to Siouf would create a grave problem for the future of Alexandria racing while the transfer to the hippodrome at Sidi Gaber-Hadra under the improved conditions that the Owners Association have obtained from Mr. Smouha were without risk either for the club or for the future of Alexandria racing. A decision was taken to contact Mr. Smouha again to reopen the discussions that had been interrupted at his request.

La Cloche, 29.5.1930
"There is no question but that the Owners Association opinions carry the most weight regarding the decision on the location of any new racecourse, especially as they come from personalities who hold the respect of the public. We had the good luck last Sunday to meet up with an eminent person owning one of the best stables in Egypt and who received us most courteously and with much information.

"The transfer of the hippodrome is of capital importance for us, the owners. Apart from the real danger for the future of racing in Alexandria of having a distant racecourse without rapid access and means of communication, the nature of the ground can greatly affect the vitality of the horses. A racehorse is a delicate animal, which needs constant care. It cannot produce its best performance without continual supervision. The choice of stabling is a complex problem requiring great care. The climate, the temperature and the nature of the ground are of major importance to its condition and must be studied to the minutest detail. A hasty or careless measure can result in the worst consequences and the most elementary prudence requires us to act only with specific information. If we have shown our preference for Hadra it is because we are convinced – happily confirmed by the eulogistic report of the experts – that their land is ideal for the growth of grass, the temperature is gentle and healthy, and finally that even after rain the ground maintains a remarkable firmness. Humidity, the enemy both of humans and animals is virtually unknown and the air is dry and temperate. In a word this region is ideal for installing a modern racecourse. All this has nothing to do with personalities: it is irrelevant for us whether the land belongs to Messrs. X or Z. What is important is access and temperature without which the racing will be seriously compromised."

And he finished by confirming everything he had said. It is interesting, having read the report of the Extraordinary General Meeting of the Alexandria Sporting Club of 29 May from the newspaper report of *La Cloche* of 4 June, to compare this report with those of the *Echo Sportif* and *Le Phare* of 6th June. What was really going on, we will probably never know, but it has all the elements of a drama developing behind the scenes, a tragi-comedy which at the drop of a hat reaches its unlikely conclusion just as the curtain falls and leaves the audience dissatisfied and confused by the final decision.

The *Echo Sportif*: "Everyone was ready to vote for Siouf, "metropole of Alexandrian horse shows."

Prince Omar Pasha Toussoun opened the meeting. The object being to select either Siouf or Hadra after hearing the reports of the experts but as the racing this year has not been financially successful the committee recommends adjourning the decision sine die. A tumultuous "agreed" closed the meeting. This was bread, butter and jam for the journalist and he took up the refrain.

"The New Racecourse: Siouf or Hadra?" *Le Phare Égyptien*, 8.6.1930

The journalist said:

"In my opinion, and I can allow myself an opinion as I have shown complete independence between the protagonists - Hadraists and Sioufians, the day was useful in that it showed the need for a move from, or supplement to, ASC's being accepted by all, as at the ASC one can see nothing of what's going on at all. So whether it's one or the other it needs to be at a place where one can see the race from beginning to end. There is a 'vicious circle' (sic) – I met the ghost that from dawn to dusk haunts the most intimate corners of the ASC and opening up completely, I said, 'My dear David, what do you think of this transfer?' – 'My dear friend, I triumph! We stay and never leave: I'm telling you: this delightful Sporting, this space ideal for my poetic sauntering around and sporting activity' It's the reaction of a simple guy. I have discovered the real reason for all this lack of visibility, yet the parking lot is full, as everyone remains loyal to the ASC, but the racecourse is empty and losing money."

Our journalist gives sarcasm rein for the three main reasons put forward for going to Siouf and not Hadra:

- Siouf's distance too far from town? That's rubbish- half the racecourses in the world are in the suburbs or further afield.

- Rubbish also that 'the air of the rubbish dump' (*fosse dépotoire*) of Hadra is better than the Siouf plateau with the fresh sea breezes of Mandara.

- Preference for the earth of salty marshland recently dried out but still smelling of the leprosy of sodium chloride with large patches of a thin growth, which resembles grass as much as our friend Lebattant resembles Notre Dame.

The experts have reached the conclusion that at Siouf the earth is water resistant and the content of sand-lime is ideal for horse racing. Whether you like it or not, the earth at Hadra resembles and smells of putrid food and unhealthy organic matter to such an extent that you would have to hold your nose and cover your face!

The transfer of racing has to go through. Furthermore the Municipality is expected to expropriate a part of the ASC land. 83 members of ASC have requested confirmation of Siouf being chosen, etc. We are in the presence of two offers, one from Mr. Smouha for the dried-out Lake of Hadra, and the other, Domaine de Siouf.

Hadra is a dried-out lake, impossible to grow the right grass, the climate is damp and humid and horribly hot. However there are two advantages – closer proximity to the city and secondly also to the present stables. Siouf where the air is pure, the earth is ideal and the distance problem is solved by the city agreeing to organise a cheapened bus ride directly from the centre of town. The members of ASC have logically shown preference for Siouf rather than the Hadra marshland. It's for the members to decide but who would want a racecourse on dried-out marshland? – Unless you want to kill all horse racing in Alexandria.

"Me. Gaby Maksud Converts to Sioufism," *Le Phare Égyptien*, 22.6.1930

Thursday evening, the inauguration of the new restaurant at the Pré-Fleuri. Flowers, lights and music under a starry sky with the gorgeous dresses of chic Alexandria. But the keynote of the evening – Me. Maksud, the elegant, the irresistible Gaby Maksud decides to convert to Sioufism.

Among a group of friends led by Captain Ades he was seen to become convinced, with such grace, such charm that he disarmed anyone thinking this was not genuine. He immediately offered his resignation to Mr. Joseph Smouha and immediately became the lawyer of the Domaine de Siouf. Madame Linda Karam, presiding the party, showed her satisfaction by opening the dancing with Me. Maksud for a full five minutes alone on the dance floor, thus showing for whom and why the party had been given.

"The New Hippodrome," *La Cloche*, 12.6.1930

Prince Amr Ibrahim declares: 'If I had to choose between Hadra and Siouf, I would unhesitatingly choose Hadra.' His Excellency Ziwer Pasha, former President of the Council: 'My preference goes to Hadra which is an ideal domain for laying out a magnificent racecourse'.

"A Simple Question," *La Cloche*, 28.6.30

One wonders why Mr. Elie Shama who has never so much as owned a quarter of a horse should have been so concerned recently with the health and improvement of the equine race. 'The transfer to Siouf is of a nature to compromise most seriously the future of the equine sport in Egypt,' thus declare a number of eminent personalities. Further to the above statement, the horse owners issued the following communiqué: 'We, the undersigned owners of racehorses having learnt of the proposal to create a

new racecourse in Alexandria on the lands of Siouf, consider that the transfer of the races to Siouf would create a grave risk to the organisation of racing in Egypt and would be of the kind to very seriously compromise the future of equine sports in Egypt'.

All said and done and far be it for me, 84 years later, to comment on the suddenness of the about-turn of this decision – but something seems to be missing. As to the true reason, maybe in light of the personalities involved.

7.4 Irrigation Scandals

As all the world knows, Egypt depends on the Nile and the waters that flow from it. And unfortunately possession of the water has often been used as a means of government: it has been distributed abundantly as a reward for services rendered or for subservience shown: it has been reduced or withdrawn to punish recalcitrance and force adversaries to submission.

Thus throughout the ages the complaints of the fellahin have turned on the question of water and the most essential need is a government to listen to their grievances and do them justice. It appears quite recently that satisfaction has not been forthcoming, and that even the High Commissioner, as a result of the complaints of the fellahin, has written to the Minister of Public Works. Three cases have been brought against the Minister of Public Works by a company owning land in the Behera, who claim that because of the meagre quantity of water doled out some land has been left uncultivated and they are therefore reclaiming enormous damages for losses sustained. This situation affects four-fifths of the country. 'It is without doubt an opportunity for the new government to abolish favouritism and arbitrary action to show its spirit of justice …'.

"The irrigation scandal. Combating Favouritism and Arbitrariness. How water is distributed in the provinces," *Egyptian Mail*, 28.11.1934

M. Raphael Toriel, Chairman of Dakalilia Land Company, has brought a charge that the irrigation waters to which they are entitled have not been given them particularly since 1932, for 100 feddans and claim LE8,000 - damages + interest. He regretted that there had been publicity of his claim but added, '… near our land is a plot of barren land, about 500 feddans in extent. We refused to buy it on account of the poor quality of the soil. It was bought for a song by a neighbouring landowner. As soon as the purchase was concluded, water was so abundantly distributed that for a long while the ground was submerged. At the same time our land was rapidly losing its value on account of the deplorable conditions of our irrigation. The problem is a vital one for our country … Our company has not only considerably improved the quality of the land, but also the condition of the fellahin who

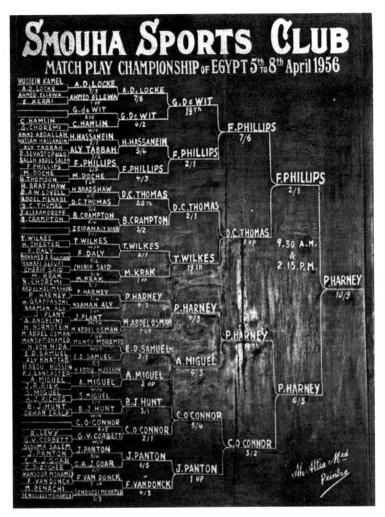

The scoreboard of the last major championship to be played on the course, 1956 (R. Smouha's archive).

E. R. Smouha presenting the prize to the winner of the Open Golf Champion of Egypt, Bernard F. Hunt (R. Smouha's archive).

opposite
Mrs Fitzpatrick (right) presenting the trophy to the winner (Captain's Prize - annual golf competition (R. Smouha's archive).

South African champion Bobby Locke (glass in hand) and M. Teddy Smouha (left of Locke), President of the Federation of Alexandria Golf Championship (R. Smouha's archive).

owe their existence to it … By depriving us of irrigation water in an unjust manner the authorities ruin the improvements we have made. We look to the new Government to remedy the equitable distribution of irrigation water'."

I have been unable to find any further references to this matter but feel entitled to conjecture what went on behind the scenes.

Firstly, M. Toriel carried out an effective and subtle diplomatic operation. Secondly, there are sufficient indications to show that the whole problem concerned the new land of Smouha City. The dates coincide with 1932, which logically is when things started to get under way, and the problems begin to show up. Also, there would not have been many size of the property, which was "about 500 feddans." Furthermore, it was "bought for a song."

Finally, it seems to me that M. Toriel was smart enough to know that Joseph Smouha would do anything to keep his name out of the media if there was going to be a problem and he would be in a far better bargaining position. Added to this is that about this time Joseph Smouha agreed to lease the unbuilt land to fellahin at very advantageous rates. Shortly after, it was decided that during the water shortage of the summer months only nine holes of the golf course would be open alternatively at a time. I am therefore convinced that smart M. Toriel played his cards extremely well and the file was closed.

7.5 The Golf course

Joseph Smouha planned to have a great open space when building Smouha City. It comprised a golf course (the longest in Egypt) and grass greens, which until then had been unknown in the Middle East, a racecourse, tennis courts, squash courts and a pony club.

My father Teddy Smouha, down from Cambridge as an Olympic bronze medallist (1928, 4x100 metres), called to the bar (Lincoln's Inn) and after an academic term at Paris University in 1929, was plunged into the start-up of this tremendous enterprise. He returned, married in 1931, to help supervise the development of this vast undertaking. Teddy Smouha was given full responsibility for the club itself, the golf course and the racecourse, which were to be built. Teddy Smouha obtained a plan for the golf course from a firm of golf course architects in England.

He went to Bingley in Yorkshire where grasses are researched. He returned with 30 different types to try out as he was determined to have grass putting greens, the first in Egypt.

All the other courses had what were known as "biscuit greens" – sand beaten down into a hard surface and sometimes flattened out with oil, which dried out in the sun. He was told it could not be done but he persisted in his idea and chose one called *Uganda Nagil* which was very successful. I personally have a distant memory – I must have been five or six years old – of accompanying him to a small tract of land – could it have been near the English Girls' College – and being shown all sorts of different grasses with their names, which I have obviously forgotten. The newspaper *Le Stade* of 4.4.29 stated, "while there are grass and sand courses in the Middle East, their conditions are atrocious even in winter and get worse by midsummer."

The *Uganda Nagil* grass that had been chosen for the fairways because of its resistance to dampness and heat was a great success. It was hand-planted by long lines of fellahin (peasant workers). With the impossible task of controlling on some days up to 1,500 undisciplined fellahin, as word got round of temporary part-time employment, Teddy Smouha resorted to creating groups of some twenty men and selected known criminals, murderers and thieves as foremen for each of these groups and who reported directly to him. These groups worked in rows planting the local type of grass, root by root all moving together in line around the three-mile racetrack. With the foremens` history and reputation known to all, the fellahin were so frightened that he never had any trouble. The design of the course itself was part of the responsibility of my father, Teddy Smouha, and the main designer was the celebrated J.H. Taylor, who learnt his golf and club making from the famous Gibson family from Westward Ho, who were professionals for over fifty years at the Royal North Devon Championship Golf Club.

The course opened in 1934, even as the last vestiges of the lake were still being drained, and already by April, the Club, by now named the New Sports Club, held the amateur Golf Championship of Egypt – won by R.L. Ravenshaw, and there was also a long driving competition won by H.H. Horwitz with a drive of 275 yards.

Play during summer weekends was on all 18 holes, but on weekdays, only nine, the other nine being flooded. This way the grass was maintained in good condition, "absolutely velvet" as one regular player put it.

Bobby Locke, a top world professional, pronounced the course, even if it was on the flat side, as one of the best in the Mediterra-

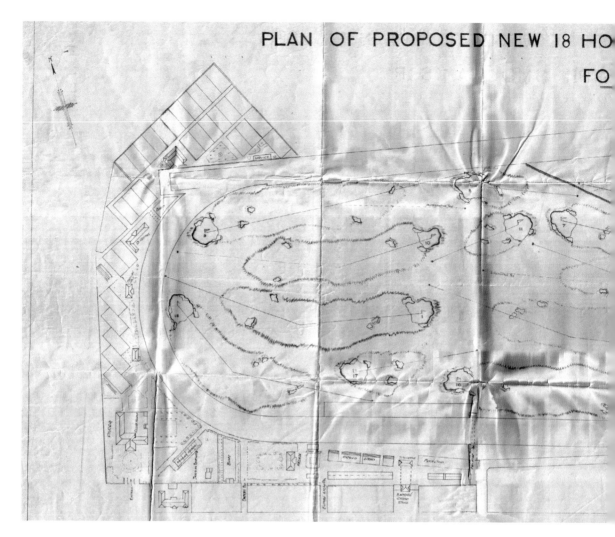

nean area, far superior to that at the nearby Sporting Club, founded by the English community, which was not so well designed.

Encouraged by the example set, the Gezira Sporting Club in Cairo converted its course to grass.

International competitions were sometimes played on this course, and Teddy Smouha received many compliments from the world's top golfers.

In the clubhouse there was the full-scale model of the course under glass, mentioned above, which I remember as being over four foot long.

After Smouha City had been sequestrated in 1956, my father requested especially, though unavailingly, that the model be given to him as a keepsake: in fact, most unfortunately, now that golf has become such a major world sport, and that the course has been completely destroyed.

There are many memories of this wonderful golf course and much that has disappeared with time and changes. Edgar Muller-Gotthard is one whose memories are not lost.

He tells how in the early 1940s he and a close friend felt that golf was exactly what they should practice. He writes:

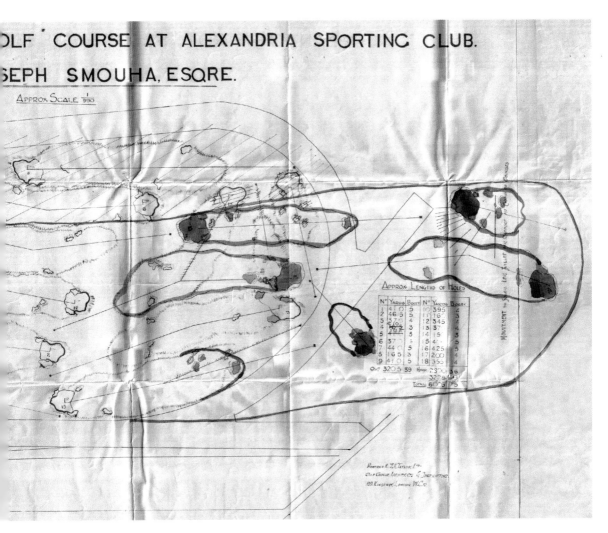

Plan of the proposed new eighteen-hole golf course for Joseph Smouha, Hawtree & J.H. Taylor Ltd (R. Smouha archive).

"but at the age of 11 or 12 with obviously no handicap, the solution was to pinch two golf clubs from my friend`s father. We rushed to the Club very early the next morning, walked to the far end of the course and entered it through a hole in the fence. So we were far from hole n. 1 and had enough time to play a few shots before club members appeared.

The add-on was that we could hide in the bunkers for a smoke! But alas we broke one of the wooden club shafts and feared returning home.

The caddy master saved us. He came up with a short copper tube which helped us re-join the two parts of the shaft and with the help of some dark shoe polish we managed to restore, well, no, to give the club a semblance of its original appearance, provided one didn`t try to use it.

This actually never happened but we were so grateful to the caddy master."

During WW II members of the armed forces were given free access to the club and its activities but it appears that tennis was much more popular with the troops than the golf.

Every year there was a caddies` golf competition and all the caddies took part, borrowing golf clubs and balls from the members who regularly employed them. They all wore "borrowed" shoes for the occasion, many limping either because they were too small for them or more likely because they were not used to wearing shoes. The winner gained a money prize.

"Communications with Smouha City," *The Egyptian Gazette*, 22.2.1935

Early on, the bus company of Alexandria started a service from town to the club and racecourse. Regular and frequent communication between the centre of Alexandria and Smouha City is now provided by an omnibus service by the Ramleh Electric Railway.—7:00 am to 9:00 pm at eight minute intervals: Place Mohamed Aly, Corniche Road, Rue Ambroise Rally, Rue Tigrane Pasha, Mustapha Pasha barracks, Sidi Gaber Station, then through the Cleopatra Subway, Avenue Albert 1er, Avenue Mohamed Aly, Avenue Victor Emmanuel, the New Sports Club, Mustapha Pasha Subway, Rue Ibrahim Sherif, Abukir Road, Sidi Gaber, and back.

Sounds great, but many of my friends to whom I told of the availability of this service, insisted that the eight-minute intervals were purely hypothetical.

The Egyptian Gazette – 17.12.1935

Alexandria now has one of the best courses in Africa and one of the best flat courses in the world. It is thus appropriate that they should have a golf professional with a worldwide reputation as a teacher of golf. Jack Gibson of Westward Ho, after war service had gone to the USA where he was full professional at various clubs in Pittsburgh, Florida and Mexico, and was invited to broadcast talks on the game. He arrived with strong recommendations from the 1934 amateur and professional champions Michael Scott and Henry Cotton.

In addition to the normal golf competitions with different formulae, singles, foursomes, fourballs, greensome, stableford etc., and as happens in a lot of clubs, there was an "exclusive" group, I think, only of men, called the 44 Club which played a money game once a week through the season. I do not know what the rules were nor any of the other arrangements. What I do know is that there was much discussion, much banter and, although it was taken most seriously, it usually ended up with laughter around drinks at the bar. Most of them were businessmen from well-known Alexandrian families, professionals, lawyers, doctors, and accountants. I remember a fair number of the regulars. There was an American, Davis (Dave), loud and boisterous but a lot of fun, Mike Choremi, Samuel (Sammy), Dr. Stergiou with his very odd style, hitting the ball so hard that he would jump 180 degrees at the end of his swing, Count Charlie de Zogheb playing I believe off a handicap of 2, hitting his ball off the first tee 30 yards along the ground to the great amusement of his regular caddy and most of the players who had participated in a very heavy liquid lunch with him. Most of them had handicaps in single figures or the low teens. My father-in-law Carlo Sinigalia (handicap 7) who was a member of the 44 Club, played there nine or 18 holes every day of the week until 1962 when he was forced by circumstances to leave Egypt, but went on playing regularly as a member of the Geneva Switzerland golf course dragging his trolley (no motor) behind him until he was 97. He finally passed away at 104, having lived through three centuries (1897-2001).

In fact the last major championship to be played on the course was the Egyptian Open Match Play competition in which many of the world's top golfers of the period took part: to name only a few A.D. (Bobby) Locke, the South African, Harry Bradshaw, Bruce Crampton, A. Angelini, Norman von Nida, Bernard Hunt, Christy O'Conner, John Panton and Flory van Donck. A photograph of the final scoreboard is shown, but, in particular for non-golfers, requires considerable explanation to appreciate what had been achieved. Even for golfers, depending on their age and knowledge of the history of the game over the last half-century, the game has developed and is still developing at an unbelievable pace from a geographically-limited and/or elite-restricted game (it is not a sport) to become a major world recognised game played by tens of millions and watched, thanks to television, by hundreds of millions. All this is to explain to all said readers:

a) the importance of what was accomplished over the first twenty years of the existence of the course which was formally acknowledged by many of the world's top golfers as being by far the best golf course in the Middle East;

b) the massive loss to the country when, in the sixties, this wonderful course was scrapped by the new Nasser regime and policy and was replaced with football fields. Today's importance of golf as a tourist attraction and the loss to the country cannot be exaggerated.

I myself remember that the day before the match play competition my father played a round with the famous Bobby Locke where I had the privilege of caddying for my father. I do remember some spectacular shots but one that I remember distinctly came at the sixth hole. This was the hole, which came after a famous short par three with a kidney shaped green with a bunker in the inner curve of the kidney. It was called the "Postage Stamp" and he had just made a mess of it. This next one was a par four and Locke was some hundred yards or so from the green for his second shot. I can remember him muttering under his breath and then ... with his back to the hole and with a fierce swing at the hole around his sizeable paunch he hit a full semi-circular ball, which finished some six inches from the hole. To this day I can remember the gasp from the onlookers who burst into applause and cheers.

I made friends with another South African pro on his first tour away from home and who was also playing in the competition, a young man of my own age called Trevor Wilkes. Some fifty years later I came across him when I was on holiday in South Africa and staying at Selborne Lodge, which has its own lovely varied golf course and where he was the resident professional.

At page 101 are the resumes of the top golfers who competed in the Egyptian Match play Championship in 1956 on the New Sports Club course in Smouha City. It is important to know that today's World Golf Rankings have only been in existence since 1986. Before that time international golf was a "fewer and far between game" - much less money, much less support, much less public interest and more primitive communications. There is much to support the view that this competition attracted as many of the top golfers in the world as any competition at that time other than the Majors. It is therefore of interest - mainly for golfers - to appreciate the following statistics.

A.D. (Bobby) Locke - could justifiably be termed the best golfer in the world at that time. In my opinion his most important achievement was not really winning any championship title (this was before the 1986 world rankings). In the Forties and Fifties the US golfer Sam Snead was generally considered the best in the world. In the short two and a half years that Locke spent in the US (where he was not treated with any favours and was never given his card which would have allowed him to play in the Majors) a series of 14 head to head exhibition matches were promoted between the two players. Locke won 12!

Of the 59 competitions he was entered for in the US he won eleven and came in the top four in 23 of the others. He won the British Open four times in 1949, 1950, 1952 and 1957. On the European tour he won 23 tournaments and on the South African 38 times. Last but not least in 1948 he won the Chicago National Open by 16 strokes, a margin which remains a record on the US tour to this day. The achievements of the players in this last competition that my father had assembled alone show the peak that had been reached: Harry Bradshaw - probably the top Irish golfer of the Forties and Fifties. Won 2 British Masters, 2 Irish Opens, 10 times Irish professional champion, 3 Ryder Cups and lost to Locke in the 1949 British Open.

Christy O`Connor Sr. - Record 10 times Ryder Cup, 15 times World Cup, won 10 Irish Opens, 6 times European Senior Champion, 2 World Senior Champion.

Bruce Crampton - 14 wins US tour, 4 times second in majors, 20 wins as a Senior.

Norman von Nida - 4 times Australian Champion, 80 professional wins.

Bernard Hunt - 1st Order of Merit 1958.60.65, 8 times Ryder Cup (Captain 1973/75).

John Panton - 3 times Ryder Cup, 12 times World Cup, World Senior Champion 1967, beat Snead in final in 1967 and 1969.

Flory van Donck - Won 50 professional tournaments, 2 times 2nd British Open.

Dave Thomas - longest drive 420 yards. Came 2nd twice in the British Open.

Hassan Hassanein - to date the only Egyptian golfer to have

reached top international level. Won 10 Desert Opens 1946-1956, four times Egyptian Open, the French Open, the Italian Open, and the Egyptian Matchplay.

The golf course was surrounded by an oblong 3-mile racecourse with a stadium - sized grandstand with private boxes as well as tiers of hundreds of seats with every seat taken at the race meetings every weekend from April to September by smartly dressed people, many of the ladies with lovely hats and the latest fashion dresses from Paris. Around the grandstand there was a paddock to show off the horses, stables and the other equine facilities.

7.6 Development and construction

The plan of the city was being refined during this period, and in particular the broad avenues, side roads, pavements, electricity, water and other utilities. Special areas were fixed for factories, shops, offices and apartment blocks. A large area was set aside for residential housing. The freeholders were subject to very strict rules in order to maintain the situation not far from the railway line at Cleopatra. Joseph Smouha also built a rest home for his Italian labourers, which were to be run by the Franciscan monks.

Derrick Smouha remembers the negotiation with the head of the congregation for a site where the monks could come after their travels. He also remembers the establishment of schools, presumably after negotiations with the Ministry of Education, for the residents present and future of the city.

It was about this time that a member of the Mohamed Ali Club was heard to say openly at the club that it was he who had advised Joseph Smouha to buy the lake and he was delighted and proud that Joseph Smouha had taken his advice! He was not the only one to make this claim.

An important rule was that they were only allowed to build on one-third of the plot and the remaining two-thirds had to be garden. Joseph Smouha gave one of the plots to the Moslem community as well as money to build a mosque, and the same for a church and a synagogue.

Derrick Smouha remembers the synagogue being the smallest of the three, as their community would have had the smallest congregation. The sale of the villas started, as far as I know, around 1933 but only really took off when King Victor Emmanuel of Italy bought one to live in. In order to attract buyers of land for the construction of the villas, they were offered tempting facilities both as to the prices and to payment conditions with the object of availability presumably to get this project started as soon as possible.

The exteriors of the villas were all built in the same style, airy and open to the sun and with a garden, the roads and sidewalks were spacious allowing easy access. Water, gas, and electricity were already completed (remember we were in a developing country eighty years ago) and the new owner only had to bring in the furniture.

Le Dimanche Illustré, 23.12.1934
About 40 villas have been built not far from the clubhouse and racecourse. One of the advantages of this new suburb, which distinguishes it from any other, is that it is only a matter of minutes from town, from the whole tramway network, from the beach and from the main train station of Sidi Gaber (to Cairo).

One must give Mr. Smouha his due as with indefatigable perseverance and after ten years of hard work, and notwithstanding numerous difficulties, he has produced such a marvellous result which will greatly benefit the city by getting rid of an unhealthy lake and in its place has brought in some two million cubic metres of good earth to a depth of 1.5 metres.

Mr. J. Smouha can now survey with pride the result of his remarkable activity and great initiative. We must congratulate him from the bottom of our hearts.

La Gazette D`Orient, 20.12.1934;
Le Dimanche Illustré, 23.12.1934;
Egyptian Mail, 23.12.1934
La Bourse Égyptienne, 24.12.1934;
Al Ahram, 25.12.1934;
La Réforme, 26.12.1934;
Il Giornale d'Oriente, 30.12.1934;
The New Sports Club is the property of Mr. Joseph Smouha. Ladies and Gentlemen who desire to make use of the premises and activities provided at the above Club, may do so after election by an Advisory Committee, which Mr. Smouha has asked to assist him for the present. Elected subscribers will become entitled to the full use of the Club up till 31 December 1935, without incurring any financial liability other than the payment of the appropriate subscription as set forth in the accompanying list and the small charges in connection with the playing of games and the like to be determined by the Advisory Committee.

The members of the Advisory committee are at present as follows: Mr. H. Bridson Chairman, Kaimakan T.W. Fitzpatrick Bey (Head of the Alexandria police), etc.

Thereafter it became a very desirable residential area. I was told that at the time of the confiscation, sequestration and nationalisation there were over 200 villas, four to five apartment blocks, a fast developing industrial area etc.

In fact documents speak of 420 villas already by 1937.

Egyptian Gazette, 22.1.1936
Sir G. Latham Corbett the Technical Expert at the Ministry of Commerce and Industry accompanied by Hussein Gayyar Effendi of the Ministry of Commerce went yesterday morning to Smouha City and inspected the site chosen for the construction of a wholesale vegetable market. They also inspected the site at

Gabbary chosen for the construction of an onion market.

7.7 The villas

The best-known villa was the Villa Jela where King Victor-Emmanuel III of Italy lived and died on 28 December 1947.

He lived there for some years with his wife Helene (Jela in the Montenegrin language).

Maurice de Piccioto's aunt (Camille Coen nee Nahon) also lived in a villa in Smouha City. Many of the smaller roads in the early days of the city were not given names: it would seem that the Municipality had a problem keeping up with the rate of development, building and occupation. Anyway, they resorted to using the mapped temporary plot numbers and road references as addresses. If I am not mistaken her address was then n. 6, Rue 47. This procedure would have been the "privilege" of the Municipality as quite early on Joseph Smouha had handed over many feddans of land to the Municipality for the construction of the roads and other public utilities, so he had no influence on this aspect of daily life.

The following story will show that situations similar to this, while not being a daily occurrence, used to happen to the great delight of those who had a good sense of humour, which is a strong attribute of the Egyptian character and personality. It also allows me to comment on an event concerning one of my aunts (my mother's sister Betty Naggar). She moved into a flat in a new building in town on a road, which had just undergone considerable construction. This led to the need to completely re-number all the buildings in the road. This was duly carried out, registered with the Municipality, creating all the documentation flowing from these changes – letterheads, post office registration, shop publicity, company paper, etc. etc. Ouf! Finally everything was completed and in order. It was only then that, probably on re-checking, it was realized that the building where my aunt lived had been overlooked in the renumbering. It was also unfortunate that not only it had no number but was at the beginning of the road. After much discussion and to avoid the enormous cost of re-numbering the whole road, it was decided to call it "n. 0, rue Mahmoud Gaber," and so it was.

To get back to Maurice de Piccioto's aunt, who wished to have a cellar added to the plans for the construction of her villa, she instructed her architect but a new problem arose. As has been mentioned in some detail, a major part of the land had been created by siphoning off the water into Lake Maryut – some two metres below. Her villa was specifically in that part of the land. So no cellar!

This problem of the relatively high underground water table combined with the lack of a city sewers system created a problem for her architect, her brother-in-law, Rinaldo Coen, who was a graduate of the *École des Travaux Publics* of Paris. So effective and clever solutions had to be found to solve these two critical construction problems. Coen's solution to overcome the high water table issue that prevented the digging of footings and standard-type foundations was to first build a fairly thick platform of armed concrete as a base or slab on which the villa could stand. I believe that the cost of building such a platform was almost as high as that of the entire villa. The lack of a city sewer system was solved by means of a very intricate underground septic tank system, which allowed the disposal of wastewaters and solid waste. Again, due to the high water table such septic tanks had to be designed in a way as to prevent overflows and this was effective, for during all the years they lived there they never had an overflow. This was very rare in Smouha.

Elio Smaga lived in a flat on the other side of the Rue Abukir and the other side of the Sporting, overlooking the ASC golf course and racetrack, with the tramline up the coast on the other side. It was only a 10-15 minute walk across the road and through the railway line tunnel at Cleopatra to get to Smouha City.

Elio describes coming through the tunnel, leaving behind the noisy hustle and bustle, the dirt and dust of the city and the main Abukir road, and coming into the haven of peace and comparative silence of tree-lined avenues and cleanliness of the villas and their gardens. At the tunnel exit, immediately on the right was the first block of flats built in Smouha City – n. 357 Binyamin Saadi. The synagogue occupied the whole of the first floor.

Apparently many of the more successful jockeys bought villas in this pleasant area – most understandably as their two places of work, Sporting on the north side and New Sports to the south were only some 10-15 minutes' walk away.

Right at the tunnel itself one could rent bicycles to be ridden in Smouha from an old Armenian who had a small bicycle shop – but it was another world.

Further on, on the left, was the largest and highest villa in the City. It belonged to Elio's aunt Nicette Abessirr, and a little further on, at a crossroads – easily spotted on the map – was the main grocery store, surrounded by villas.

While all the land was plotted to be built upon either for villas, shops, flats etc., there was a lot of wasteland ready for building where the plots were up for sale but not yet sold. During the 1939-45 war, a small part of this wasteland was used in particular by the local young Egyptian schoolboys as unofficial football pitches. This continued to be the case after the war but the space available became more and more limited as the post-war building continued. The balance of the land already plotted but which would not be required for building for some years was rented out to local farmers for agriculture. No part of the land was sold for agricultural purposes, only rented.

For most of the war Joseph Smouha gave over a very large area to the military and the Army, if I know my grandfather, the Army paying little or no rent, used it as a large tented camp. It must have been fairly discreet for I have no memory of it. (During the war, with my father posted to RAF Headquarters in Cairo, I was at school in Cairo and only spent the over-long three-month summer holidays in Alexandria).

Another nice little story which shows a number of things, first of all the varied population of Alexandria as has already been noted, and secondly how stories surface in the most unexpected way. This one came from Mrs. Chewikar Abdel-Aziz, who has a friend Mr. Fawzy Boghdadi who is the accountant at the Association of Friends of the Environment and who in turn knows Dr. Adel Abouzahra. The latter found a document at the Orthodox Coptic Patriarchate of Alexandria at their church of the Virgin and St. Joseph, a document which tells the story of a priest called Mikhail Saad who lived his whole life (19.1.1909 - 25.1.1996) in Alexandria. His father Ibrahim El Aassar Saad, born in 1861 in a small town near Dessouk, came to Alexandria and lived in the Ragheb Pacha district. Ibrahim's son Sobhi Saad became a priest and took the name Mikhail Saad.

Later he wanted to build a church. He started out looking for some land in Cleopatra but did not find what he was looking for. Then he thought of crossing the Smouha Bridge which separates the Abukir road from the district of Smouha. It was much taken by the immense area of land with banana and varied vegetable cultivation, and the exceptional calm of the natural greenery.

He caught sight of a seller of soft drinks (*gazouza*) standing by his counter and got into conversation with him about the purchase of this land. He learnt that it belonged to a Jew, Joseph Smouha, whose office was not far from there. The next day he went to the office which had been pointed out to him and had a meeting with his accountant agent "Mr. Daniel Delberg," a Jew of Yemenite origin (sic) (actually his number two, confidant and general manager, a Jew from Aden who spoke seven languages, all badly).

The priest notes as follows "we understood each other immediately. He showed me a plan with each lot of land and its exact dimensions. I chose the one I had discovered last evening just after crossing the bridge and going towards the East. Its size was 2300 *diraa* (a measurement very close to the English square yard). The price was LE2,300." This was in July 1950.

The priest then submitted his documents and was accorded a building permit, but it was only in March 1955 that the Patriarchate erected the first floor. The inauguration took place on 31 March 1956. In 1968 he wished to carry out some extensions, which is why he bought a further 6300 *diraa* at an auction of the sequestrated properties of Joseph Smouha at a price of LE3 (I imagine per *diraa*) He then arranged the construction of a dispensary, an old people's home, a shelter for young girls, a library, and more.

David Sabbah does not remember any such situation, which is surprising as he was the legal assistant in charge of producing all the documentation for each transaction.

However on a later call to me, and we can see this on the map, he remembered that there was an area, I think south-east of Cleopatra, that had been selected for the building of apartment blocks. This did not form part of his bailiwick but came under the responsibility of an Egyptian called Abd el Al who had two junior employees working for him, a Moslem and a Copt. It seems certain that this group carried out the transaction. This Abd el Al must have been quite a character: David Sabbah describes him most accurately as heavily bearded and always wearing a turban. As I understand it, one of the scandals of the office was that his daughter was married to a man who was a dealer in hashish who was caught and sent to prison and all the office knew about it before he did. He remembers that the two employees received monthly salaries of LE8 and LE10 respectively.

Mr. Niedergang from Mulhouse was sent to Alexandria as manager of the Bata shoe factory and arrived with his wife and two daughters, Rose-Marie and Simone in 1948 and stayed until 1956, returning in 1959 and staying until 1962.

When I told Rose-Marie David Sabbah's story of the man in pyjamas she remembered the hilarity of herself and her sister on their arrival for the first time in Egypt seeing men walking around in pyjamas during the daytime. I believe they stayed in an apartment for the first few days.

Then one day her parents went for a walk in Smouha City and, very impressed with the neighbourhood, made enquiries and found or saw a house for rent, took it and I think lived in Smouha City for the rest of their stay in Egypt. One of the conditions for renting the house was that they should look after the three dogs belonging to the owners.

The dogs would leave the property to go hunting and catch rabbits. Rose-Marie was eight years old when she first went to Egypt and at that age of course one remembers specific images or facts. She remembers the name of the house, Canopa, in a road called Amina Amin Fardal. And on the other side of the road was a villa owned by the Princess Fawzia called El Safa: this would have been shortly after her divorce from her short-lived marriage to the Shah Pahlavi of Persia.

She remembers that there was a Swiss nurse for the children, but what impressed her most was that the Princess would have her maid sleeping at the foot of her bed, probably on the floor. She remembers this period as a very happy one of her life, where she could walk freely at any time along lovely roads shaded with large poinsiettas.

The Smouha post office opened for the first time in 1935 and my father took the first opportunity to send out letters carrying the First day cover post office stamp.

One must remember that this was at a time when stamp collecting was a most important industry and its revenue figured respectably in all countries' budgets in the absence of fax and email, with telegrams only at an early stage. Imagine if all today's emails were in letterform and one had to buy stamps for them!

Even in my youth I was a collector – stamp collection was a major hobby for most young people – and philately shops, catalogues and auctions made an important contribution to a country's economy.

That is one of the aspects of this history that have a significant part to play in emphasizing our new world. I remember the heavy discussions round the lunch table concerning everything one can imagine, every aspect of problems with the roads, the use of water, electricity, upkeep, and much that came close to being political. The early chapter on the atmosphere in the Municipal Council will allow the reader to envision these complications. Many of the decisions and solutions were thus decided around the lunch table.

8 Cristina Pallini

A Modernist Townscape
in Construction

8.1 Town Planning

Neither a 2nd prize plan by Maurice Clauzier, nor that by Secchi & Casiraghi, awarded the 3rd *ex æquo* prize, were actually considered for implementation.

Many newspaper cuttings of 1930 bear witness to a lively debate going on in the Municipal Council about construction of a new racecourse, as the Alexandria Sporting Club was no longer considered adequate for the purpose. Siouf and Hadra were two alternative locations which would solve the problem. Siouf, in 1906 still "a distant suburb" at the terminus of the Alexandria and Ramleh railway,[1] was by 1930 the site of the new Victoria College, offering "an education on English Public Schools lines to residents in Egypt, whatever their creed of race."[2] Such prestigious British outpost could well be complemented by the new Sporting Club. However, after much discussion (see chapter 7), the decision was taken to build the new racecourse at Hadra.

By 1932, according to the Letter to the Sequestrator General (see chapter 10), the building land was plotted out and a map of the division of the city was produced in 1933, when Joseph Smouha donated the area for streets and squares to the Municipality.

The plan for the new city under construction is explained by a number of maps published between 1937 and 1958, all showing the same street layout as appeared in the plan of 1957.[3]

Among the earliest maps of Smouha City is a plan of Alexandria by A. Nicohosoff (1937).[4] It shows the whole area as a series of vacant lots with a new racecourse laid out on the site formerly occupied by Lake Hadra. The Mahmoudieh Canal and the Nouzha-Antoniadis Gardens mark the south-east limits of the new city. A network of pathways still links the villages of Hadra and Ez Soad to the Mahmoudieh Canal, while the former railway junction[5] has been replaced by new streets. The main road, shortening the Cairo-Alexandria drive by 6 Km, starts from the new 30-metre wide Rue d'Abukir,[6] named Boulevard Mohamed Ali after Khedive Mohamed Ali, the founder of Modern Egypt. The central square of 19th-century Alexandria bore that very name: more than a mere coincidence, this homonymy may indicate the intention to establish a "foundation stone" for Smouha City, "embryo" of the district to come. Entering Smouha from the Ibrahimieh tunnel below the railway lines, the Mohamed Ali road ran north-east, forming a roundabout at the centre of Victor Emanuel III Square[7] opposite the Smouha Estate Office. From there the road turned eastward, parallel to the new racecourse as far as the banks of the Mahmoudieh Canal.

Another boulevard entered Smouha from below the railway lines, following the earlier north-south Road to Ez Soad (Rue Geninet Nouzha), and a third roundabout led to the new enclosure around the Nouzha-Antoniadis Gardens. Rue Mohamed Ali and Rue Albert I[8] crossed half way through their sections from the tunnels to the roundabouts, thus setting a focal point for development of the

first residential neighbourhood, there encompassed by another road branching off the Rue d'Abukir and linking the Ibrahimieh and Moustapha Pacha tunnels. A fourth road joined Sidi Gaber station to Victor Emanuel III Square towards the entrance to the Nouzha-Antoniadis Gardens.

A 1940 map of Alexandria[9] provides another cartographic record, showing Smouha City with its network of minor streets. A much better source, however, is the series of maps published by the Survey of Egypt (1941-1943, see Annexes). When assembled they provide many important details about the city under construction, enabling us to understand how far the new plan has embodied the main requirements of the competition brief;[10] first, careful planning of the street hierarchy and related aesthetics: a subject that the competition brief stresses again and again, asking participants: to avoid the monotony of regular layouts, to shape a healthy environment with parks, open spaces and areas for sports and recreation, to study the dynamics of circulation

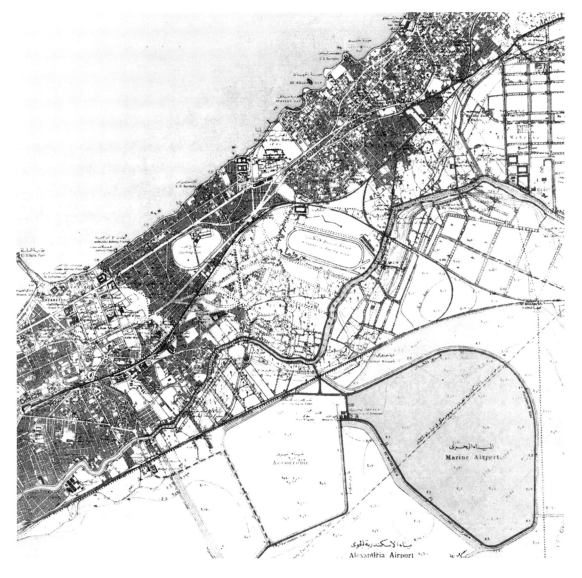

Arabic text on map: ميناء الاسكندرية البحرى
Alexandria Airport

Marine Airport / المينا البحرى

Aéroautome

Survey of Egypt, 1:25,000, 1946.

opposite
Map of Alexandria, ca. 1930 (Richard Smouha's archive).

Detail of the *Stadtplan von Alexandria*, 1940.

(level crossings, railway crossings, tram routes), to include roads and alleys for riding on horseback, to give proper dimensions to squares, crossroads and intersections, to design the roads profile to scale 1:50.

The Survey of Egypt maps show Smouha as a district planned for an early increase in motorized traffic. The street hierarchy is based on four categories, for which average speeds can easily be gauged.[11] The major road is Boulevard Mohamed Ali, 40-m wide with two or three lanes of traffic in each direction, a central path for other types of traffic, four parallel rows of trees, one at each side and two in the centre. The next size, a 30-m wide road (Albert I Boulevard linking the Ibrahimieh and Mustapha Pacha tunnels, that from Sidi Gaber station to Nouzha-Antoniadis Gardens and a road parallel to the Mahmoudieh Canal linking Boulevard Mohamed Ali to the Gardens), takes two or three lanes of traffic in each direction separated by a central island with tree-lined pavements. Local roads, some tree-lined, are 20-m wide and also take two lanes of traffic in each direction. Streets joining adjacent neighbourhoods are 11-m wide and take one lane of traffic in each direction. A small square and roundabout at each major road intersection facilitate traffic flow.

The new street layout has only partially followed the earlier one:[12] while the road to Ez Soad village had been widened to become a boulevard in the new city, the earlier road from Hadra to the Mahmoudieh Canal no longer existed.

The Survey of Egypt maps also show how land was apportioned and merit the following comments.

The new city was divided into three major areas similar in size: the residential area between the railway lines and the road linking the Ibrahimieh and Mustapha Pacha tunnels, ca. 947,100 sq. m; the quadrangular area between Nouzha-Antoniadis Gardens and the new racecourse, ca. 950,950 sq. m; the racecourse, adjoining sport facilities and the strip of land parallel to the railway (where a number of industries were to settle), ca. 1,187,370 sq. m.

The residential area along the railway line was nearer to Sidi Gaber Station and to the eastern suburbs of Alexandria, therefore easier to reach by public transport. This area was the first to be developed (94 villas had been built in 1943). It was split up into large triangular and quadrangular areas; each was further divided so that all blocks would consist of a strip of land 60 to 70 m. wide, each one parcelled into a double row of plots (an average plot measuring 550 sq. m).

The quadrangular area between the Nouzha-Antoniadis Gardens and the new racecourse was entirely vacant, so that the old paths north of the Gardens show up clearly on the map. Considering the presence of the Gardens, of the new racecourse and promenade along the Mahmoudieh Canal - lined with trees and villas since the early 19th century - this might well be the area where "luxury homes" mentioned in the competition brief were to be built.

If so, where could the areas for apartment blocks and workers housing, and the other categories mentioned in the competition brief, be situated?

Perhaps, as in Clauzier's *Grand Avenue* plan, apartment blocks were to be built along the Boulevard Mohamed Ali, still vacant in 1977?[13] The Survey of Egypt maps at any rate show that, in addition to the racecourse, related clubs and sport facilities, and to the mosque, none of the public buildings listed in the competition brief (a synagogue, an Orthodox church, a Catholic church, a Protestant temple, two schools, two police stations, post and telegraph offices, a fire station, a first-aid post, a theatre, two cinemas and one or two markets) were actually built.

The four groups totalling 94 villas were built in the area along the railway lines, each at the centre of triangular/quadrangular areas. Considering the street plan, the position of each villa at the centre of its lot, and the layout of each group around a small square, it may be presumed that the plan in course of implementation aimed at harmonizing the idea of a garden city with the concept

Detail of the first neighbourhoods units; 1. mosque (drawing by A. Scaccabarozzi based on maps by the Survey of Egypt 1:500 / 1:1000, 1941-1943).

of "neighbourhood unit." The garden city was both a movement and a planning method[14] according to which modern cities had to be self-contained communities surrounded by greenbelts (at Smouha City the railway embankment and the Mahmoudieh Canal could well serve this purpose) and include areas for residence, industry and agriculture in the right proportions. The "neighbourhood unit" was a new planning concept[15] for residential development in metropolitan areas where increasing road traffic was to create new problems. Neighbourhoods were seen as islands locked within a burgeoning sea of vehicular traffic; the concept of "neighbourhood unit" thus meaning separation of vehicular and pedestrian traffic, and arterial boundaries demarcating the inner living area. While favouring a sense of identity by grouping everyday administrative and service requirements, the cellular nature of the neighbourhood unit allowed it to be used as a building block, easy to plan and execute during periods of rapid residential growth.

More about the plan and the progress of works can be gathered by cross-checking different sources, such as the collection of newspaper cuttings held in Richard Smouha's archive.

These articles tell us that Boulevard Mohamed Ali and the road along the northern edge of the Nouzha-Antoniadis Gar-

Smouha Estate Office, Arch. Max Zol-likofer, Del Fiacco & Fils contractors (R. Smouha's archive).

Villa Harry Rofé (Abu El-Nawatir), architect John Prosper Serjeant, Mohamed Awad contractor, 1936.

opposite
Villa Jela, the residence of the former King of Italy Victor Emanuel III (from *Villa Jela*).

Princes Moritz and Heinrich of Hesse at Villa Jela (from *Villa Jela*).

Sketch of Villa for Jolanda Calvi di Bergolo, architect Paolo Caccia Dominioni, 1955 (A. Caccia Dominioni's archive, Nerviano).

Countess Jolanda Calvi di Bergolo at Villa Jela (from *Villa Jela*).

dens were built in 1931. However, in January 1934, Boulevard Mohamed Ali became popularly known as Cabbage Road; this because, despite being wide, well built, brilliantly lit by electricity and "costing the Municipality quite a lot for its upkeep each year," it crossed nothing more valuable than agricultural land.[16]

8.2 The first residential neighbourhoods

Almost a year later, on 23 December 1934, *La Dimanche Illustré* devoted an article to recent developments in Smouha City, where tree-lined roads and nearly 40 villas had been built on what was once agricultural land. Readers were informed that the Company was ready to offer ad hoc payment terms to those willing to buy a property. The villas were described as "coquettish" though of a uniform style, open on all sides to the light and fresh air, each with its small garden. Thanks to their functional layout

- including passages, balconies, and bathrooms.[17]

A publication by the Cement Marketing Co. Ltd., London (undated, most probably mid 1940s)[18] shows a number of the newly built villas in Smouha City. Each one stands in the middle of its lot, a few yards back from the boundary, and leaving two thirds of the space for the garden, so that the overall appearance would be that of a garden city. All the villas are on two floors with an articulated plan, far from the "un-aesthetic box-shaped home" stigmatized as such in the competition brief.

All these villas are of a modern style, with flat roofs, plain façades and clean lines, laying emphasis on horizontal elements (balconies, loggias, etc.). The steps leading to the entrance protected by a balcony is another common feature, as are the carefully-designed fences. Each of the 17 villas, a picture of which was published in *Les Enduits Decoratifs*, bears the names of the owner, architect, contractor and decorator.

Five of the owners were either members of the Smouha Es-

Villa Ahmed Bey Sadek, Ing. Carnevale contractor (enduits Mohamed Badr).

Villa K. Kabalan, Arch. Léon Barcilon, M. Voyazis contractor. (bigger)

Villa M. Fouad Naggar, Ing. Ferreri, Cardinael & Paumen contractors (enduits Hadjidimitriou).

opposite
Villa M. Ghorbal Bey, Arch. Max Zollikofer, G. Galiounghi contractor (enduits Alfred Barbier). (bigger)

Villa Delbourgo, Arch. Max Zollikofer, Cardinael & Paumen contractor (enduits Vafiadis & Centofanti).

Villa Max Zollikofer, Mohamed Awad contractor (enduits Vafiadis & Centofanti).

Sales contract, 9.3.1938 (R. Smouha's archive).

.

tate staff, or architect-contractors working on the site: Daniel Delbourgo was Joseph Smouha's right-hand man, and Ezra Smouha (Joseph Smouha's first cousin) was a member of the office staff. Cardinael & Paumen was running a building company, while the Swiss Max Zollikofer[19] was a well-established architect in the Alexandria of the time: besides his own villa, he also designed the Smouha Estate Office and the villas of M. Ghorbal and D. Delbourgo.

The remaining seven owners were Ahmed Bey Sadek, a member of the Egyptian Constitutional Committee in 1923; Fouad Haggar, owner of a number of cinemas in Alexandria (1942), K. Kabalan, a Coptic priest (?); Jean Placotaris; Ghorbal Bey, who represented Egypt at Unesco from 1946 to 1951; J.C. Corbi; P. Capponi. Documents from Richard Smouha's archive bear also the names of engineers John and Paul Zouro, and of architect B. Mustacchi. The names of Eva Crell, Marcel Zaghekian, Isaac Fisher and Maitre Antoine Ayoub appear on a contract as the purchaser of a plot of land dated 9.3.1938.

A more recent publication by Awad & Partners shows three villas built by Mohamed Awad Senior at Abu El-Nawatir (north part of Smouha City), namely Villa H. Good designed by S. Katarincek (1936) and Villa Harry Rofé and adjoining complex by John Prosper Serjeant (1934-1936).[20]

Though only a partial list, these names show that the first inhabitants of Smouha City represented the upper middle class in the Alexandria bourgeoisie. Conversely, the list of the Alexandria Racing Club members (see Annexes)[21] shows how the new racecourse was at one and the same time the jewel of Smouha City and a meeting place for the cosmopolitan high society in the Egypt of the time.

CITE SMOUHA

Procès-verbal de cousignation du lot No. 78 Planche 𝒟

Ce jourd'hui 9 Mars 1938 à 5 heures en présence de

1o L'Architecte D. Mustacchi de la part de l'acheteuse Eva Orell

2o De l'Ingénieur Paul Louro, de la part de Monsieur Joseph Smouha, vendeur

On a procédé au mesurage contradictoire du lot précité, préalablement borné par des cornières de fer entourées de béton. Les opérations ont donné les résultats suivants :

Nord Sur une longueur de 14m 590 (quatorze mètres & 590 mm), par la propriété de Monsieur Marcel Laghnikian

Sud Sur une longueur de 18.86 (dix huit mètres et 860 mm) par la rue décilée No 2969 bis.

Est Sur une longueur de 31m 315 par le lot No 79 (au vendeur)

Ouest Par une ligne brisée formée de 2 tronçons, l'un de 27,21 (vingt sept mètres & 210 mm) par la propriété de M Isaac Fisher, l'autre de 9m 525 (neuf mètres & 525 mm) par la propriété de Maître Antoine Ayoub

La superficie a été trouvée égale à Pics² 1100 (mille cent)

L'Acheteur   Pour le Vendeur

Villa M. Ezra Smouha, Arch. Léon Barcilon, Mohamed Awad contractor.

Villa M. P. Capponi, M.M. Veras & Arida contractor, enduits Vafiadis e Centofanti.

Villa H. Good (Abu El-Nawatir), architect S. Katarincek, Mohamed Awad contractor, 1936

opposite
General view of Smouha City (Sandro Manzoni's archive).

The Club included tycoons like the Swiss *hotellier* Charles Baehler,[22] the Belgian capitalist Baron Jean Empain,[23] the wife of the Irish-American mining magnate Alfred Chester Beatty, the banker Robert S. Rolo.[24] Others, like Jacques O. Matossian[25] and Fernand Rossano,[26] were great industrialists and import-export dealers. Parissi Belleni,[27] Théodore P. Cozzika and Théodore Th. Cozzika[28] were among the most prominent members of the Greek community in Egypt. Ambroise Sevastopoulos was manager of the National Insurance Company of Egypt,[29] and Vittorio Giannotti Managing Director of the Fiat Oriente.[30] Members of the Alexandria Racing Club included S.E. Ahmed Ábboud Pacha[31] one of Egypt's leading financiers and industrialists.

Victor Emmanuel III and Helen of Savoy arrived in Alexandria on 12 May 1946, three days after having abdicated in favour of their son, in an extreme attempt to save the Italian monarchy. At first they were hosted by King Farouk I, by October, they had found accommodation at 31 Constantin Choremi Street in Smouha City. Standing along a nice road lined with *flamboyant*, Villa Jela appeared to be a peaceful house where an old couple spent the time growing flowers, strolling around, receiving guests. Among the most assiduous were Baron Tito Torella di Romagnano, Countess Jaccarino de Rochefort, Count and Countess Calvi di Bergolo, Philipp, Moritz and Heinrich of Hesse,[32] exiled members of the Bulgarian Royal Family. They all lived in Smouha City. Other usual guests were the Romanovs. Villa Jela was very similar to other nearby villas.[33] Almost every day Vittorio Emanuele compiled his *Memoire*, aimed at drumming up all charges against him and the monarchy; he died on 28 December 1947 and was buried in the catholic Pro-Cathedral of St. Catherine in the centre of Alexandria.

8.3 Industrial settlements

The competition brief made no mention of industry but, even so, the plan defined in 1933 by Joseph Smouha and his collaborators may well have envisaged its location between the racecourse and the Cairo railway (ca. 189,630 sq. m.).

In the maps drawn up by the Survey of Egypt (1941-43) the area is still seamed by tracks and narrow canals with the racecourse stables situated in the south-east corner: "a long row of boxes built of concrete, roomy, clean and well aired,"[34] where horses were certainly well provided for.

An ice factory, already there in 1919, lay near Nouzha Railway Station, while the early buildings of a working-class district could be seen in the triangular area north of the Hadra-Ez Soad Road.

But as early as 1937 Anderson and Butterworth of Manchester had already purchased land from the Smouha Estate, possibly for a textile factory.[35]

During WW II the airport and adjoining marine airport were built directly south of Smouha City after another part of Lake Maryut had been reclaimed.[36] Alexandria's strategic position in the Middle East encouraged the arrival of engineering and construction companies, needed to meet the needs of the Allied Forces. Among these was the Ford Motor Company who shipped materials to Alexandria for use by the British in their war against the Italian armies in Libya, Eritrea and Ethiopia. Ford had established a branch in Egypt as early as 1926. For the year 1935, Ford-Egypt showed profits higher than those of any European Ford company except Dagenham.

Operating from Alexandria mainly for sail and service, with no assembly plant, it conducted Ford business in Iraq, Ethiopia, Saudia Arabia, Cyprus, Rhodes, Italian Somalia, Oman, Mus-

cat, Bahrein, Malta, Sudan, Syria, Iran, Eritrea, Yemen, Albania, Sinkiang, Mongolia, Transjordania, Hadramaut, and Kuwait.

Sales rose sharply during the war so that, by the early 1950s, Ford-Egypt had become the company's regional headquarters for the entire Middle East, the Balkans, and Northeast Africa.[37]

The 1957 plan of Smouha City shows the premises of the Ford Motor Company adjoining the racecourse and the Smouha Club;[38] they were "modern and impressive buildings and included a mosque in one corner of the property."[39] Nearby stood the Transport and Engineering Company, established a few years later to make tyres for cars, light trucks, buses, tractors, bicycles and motorcycles licenced by Mansfield Company from USA. A small area was used by artisans, while the large adjoining area is identified as "Property Heirs Reget Pacha."

These early buildings of Smouha City marked the beginning of a new phase in the industrialization of Egypt.

A 1958 map published by the U.S. Army[40] (see p. 164-165)

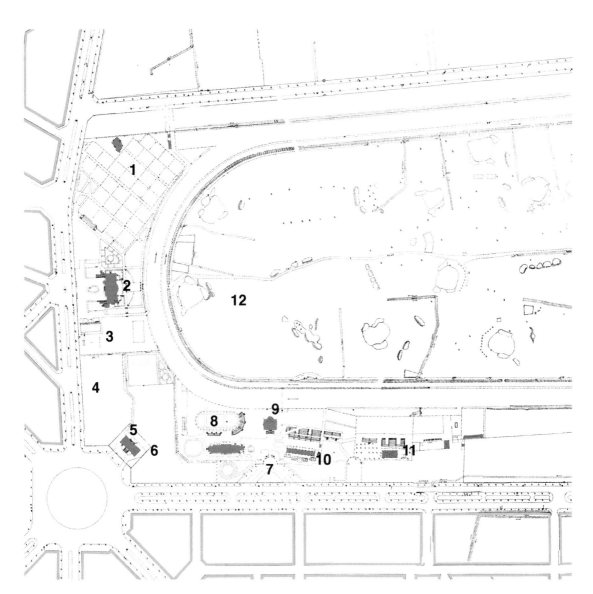

also shows the Ford-Egypt and adjoining Transport & Engineering Company, as well as a large textile complex on the Hadra-Ez Soad Road and the wholesale fruit and vegetable market along the agricultural roadfrom Cairo and the Delta on the right bank of the Mahmoudiah Canal. Crossing Smouha City from east to west, Boulevard Mohamed Ali had become the main point of access to Alexandria. The Sidi Gaber railway station had been rebuilt and construction had begun on the Nouzha station and railway siding. Most of the earlier industrial districts lay along the Mahmoudieh Canal: a match factory, Mobil Oil Egypt, the Weaving Company, rice mills, a cotton-spinning works, ice factories, a brewery, paper mills, the gas works, a Salt & Soda plant. The Minet el-Bassal canal-port comprised an large warehouse district (for cotton, cereals, timber, and tobacco) and included cotton pressing plants and several factories.[41]

Close to the Gabbari railway siding there was another huge area of workshops and warehouses. Industrial buildings stretched

Map of the sport facilities at ARC (drawing by A. Scaccabarozzi).
Legend: 1. Tennis Courts; 2. Smouha Club; 3. Squash; 4. Furusia Riding School; 5. Smouha Office; 6. Delrieux Riding School; 7. Main entrance to ARC; 8. Pesage/Paddok; 9. Royal Stand; 10. Grand Stand; 11. Tribunes of 2nd and 3nd class; 12. Golf-course.

opposite
View of tennis-court and Ford factory, 1951

Views of the Ford Factory.

The Grand Stand and the Royal Stand,
Eng. Alexandre de Naglowsky, E. di A. De
Farro & Co. contractors.

opposite
The Grand Stand (from *The Illustrated
London News*, 1959).

Royal Stand, Eng. Alexandre de Naglowsky, E. di A. De Farro & Co. contractors.

along the western harbour as far as Mex: lumber yards, cotton
warehouses, a slaughter house, tanneries, and fertilizer plants
alternated with oil and petroleum storages.

8.4 A statement of modern architecture

Much attention was given to the new racecourse in the months
of its completion, and even more in the weeks before and after
its inauguration on 14 April 1934.

A bus service to the new racecourse was instituted at the end of
January 1934.[42] At the beginning of February, while the workers
of contractors E. di A. De Farro were busy at site, many newspapers published the first photos of the racecourse showing its
fine tribunes protected by projecting roofs. In March a number
of journalists were finally admitted to the site by the Secretary of
the Alexandria Racing Club, Mr. Mike Marinakis.

The article published by *Le Favorí* emphasizes the quality of
the landscape project, suggesting the racecourse as the best
panoramic viewpoint from which to admire the new city under
construction.[43]

On 7 April, just one week before the opening ceremony, *La
Gazette d'Orient* published a complete map of Smouha City. *Il
Giornale d'Oriente* gave prominence to the modernity of the new
structures and to their efficiency on the opening day when five-
thousand people flocked there.

"The public showed its enthusiasm for the modern and elegant
features of the construction … Our city thus acquires a new
building model and, at least from the worldly aspect, reaches
the same level as Cairo which already has two racecourses."

The article lays emphasis on the Italian contribution, given that
the E. di A. De Farro building company had taken care of the
whole project and of the structures in concrete, completing the
works in only eight months.

"The architectural expression embodied in execution of the

structures has aroused unanimous admiration. It may be said that these buildings provide a seal of approval to the modern architecture becoming ever more widespread in our city …

Special praise is due to the simple and elegant style of the Royal Stand, and to the Grand Stands from where a full view of the course, of the weighing room, of the comfortable and hygienic stabling, and of the paddock may be had. An audaciously designed achievement – the only one in Alexandria – is the roof that extends ten metres outward from the Grand Stands, protecting them from the sun.

Added to its overall simplicity and to the luxurious Royal Stand is a grass-covered area, a charming relief to the eye.

All this enables the public to feel surrounded by exceptional comfort, partly because offices are available inside as well as outside the stands, for the purchase of tickets and for collecting betting wins. No distance therefore has to be covered for these purposes and crowding is avoided. By construction of the Alexandria Racing Club, the city as a whole, and especially the area where once lay an unhealthy stretch of water, acquires an outlet of first-rate importance towards the outside world and, when the town plan has been realised, will serve both tourism and summer residence."[44]

The Sprinter gave its readers a technical description of the racecourse: its track one mile round with a straight of five furlongs (ca. 1 km)[45] long was 400 yards longer than that of Heliopolis, and 30 yards wide allowing 35 horses to run abreast.

The Grand Stand lay at an angle to the track, so that the public could follow the race at any point.

"The Grand Stand, which is the same style of that of Heliopolis, has a seating accommodation for over 1000 spectators, who are well protected from the sun all times in the afternoon. To the left of the Grand Stand are reserved seats for the public …, and special stands for owners, reporters and trainers; and higher up are the stands for the stewards and distinguished guests. On the terrace from end to end there are two rows of 58 boxes

and behind them is a spacious tea-room, beautifully decorated. While having their tea, race-goers will have no difficulty in carrying on their bets seeing that the ARC, sparing no efforts to please the public, will place small booking-offices for the sale of P.T. 100 and P.T. 20 tickets. The ground floor consists of a vast hall where the most important bets will be taken. Large windows give access to plenty of light and fresh air. Booking offices for the sale of tickets, Double-Totes, boards Owner's Credit Tote, and the paying-desks are so placed as to offer the most rapid service with the least confusion."[46]

Following inauguration many more articles appeared praising the new racecourse built on such a grand scale, regardless of space and expenses: it was indeed a major feature of the town-planning scheme, the very heart of the new city and a hub of high-class social life. A golf course - the longest in Egypt - was laid out on the lawns at the centre of the racecourse to a plan by the British architectural firm run by John Henry Taylor, a member of the so-called Triumvirate of Golf in the late 19th and early 20th century who had became a famous golf-course architect.[47]

The adjoining sport facilities included 16 tennis courts, four

squash courts, hockey pitches, rugby and association football grounds, a bowling green, a cricket pitch, ping pong tables, a children's playground.

Complementary to these were fine terraced buildings with lounges, dance floors, card-playing and reading rooms, where members could enjoy all the amenities. All accessory buildings along the racecourse shared the same simple lines, features conveying the idea of a modern environment based on principles imposed by technique, aesthetics and hygiene.[48]

Les Enduits Decoratifs described the quality and an number modernist buildings which were changing Alexandria's and Cairo' townscapes. It included a photo of the Grand Stand and of the Royal Stand, indicating Alexandre de Naglowsky as the engineer and E. di A. De Farro as the building contractor. The information about Alexandre de Naglowsky is scanty. Most probably he was one of the many white Russians who left their country following the 1917 Revolution. His studio in Alexandria was full of sculptures and paintings;[49] his fame as constructor of all-welded barges[50] showed an eclectic personality, whose interests ranged from art, to archaeological survey, to the technicalities

Club Smouha Estate, Arch. Léon Barcilon & Max Zollikofer, Cardinael & Paumen contractors (enduits Hadjidimitriou).

A view from the Smouha Club (from *The Illustrated London News*, 1959).

The verandah of the Smouha Club (from *The Illustrated London News*, 1959).

opposite
Aerial view of the Alexandria Racing Course, ca. 1933 (Archive CEAlex).

of engineering problems. We may presume that de Naglowsky worked in the Project Department of the E. di A. De Farro building company, which had taken care of the whole ARC project and of the structures in concrete.

This was one of the major Italian construction firms in Egypt, operating there since the early 20th century and specialized in reinforced concrete and structural steel construction. International directories cited De Farro & Co. for its loose-soil consolidation technique. They knew how to compact unstable soils, typical in Lower Egypt and even more so in Smouha City (particularly in the area of the racecourse formerly occupied by Lake Hadra) by using compression pillars, which also functioned as foundations. Among the public buildings which made a name for E. di A. De Farro was the Alexandria's Municipal Stadium (1927), whose tribunes feature immense cantilever roofs in concrete, very similar to those of the Smouha racecourse. The company's achievements also include the Royal Littorie Schools at Alexandria (1931-33) designed by Clemente Busiri Vici along modern-

MOUSTAFA PACHA محطة مصطفى باشا

ist lines.[51] Most scholars agree that these schools were the first modernist buildings in Alexandria, a style soon to be followed by other public and community buildings in the same area.[52]

In Smouha City the architecture of private villas was perfectly attuned to the functional lines of the new buildings around the racecourse, thus shaping a homogeneous modernist townscape that marked a clear break with the eclectic townscape of central Alexandria.

1. Sahar Hamouda, Colin Clement, *Victoria College. A History Revealed*, American University of Cairo Press, Cairo-New York, 2002, p.34.

2. Edward Morgan Forster, *Alexandria: A History and a Guide (1922)*, Peter Smith, Gloucester, Mass., 1968, p.182.

3. *Smouha City* (scale 1:2500), 31 March 1955, revised on 1.1.1957, R. Smouha's Archive (see *Annexes*).

4. Alexandre Nicohosoff, *Plan général d'Alexandrie avec ses embellissements récents*, revised in 1937, 1:20.000.

5. The railway junction between the line leading to the port and that joining Alexandria's Cairo Station to the Egyptian network.

6. The new road to Abukir, also called "route de Siouf", was built by the Italian contractors Dentamaro & Cartareggia and reached Bulkeley in July 1931. See G. Spitaleri, *Costruttori Italiani in Egitto. Filippo Cartareggia*, Alexandria, 1933, pp.73-76.

7. Victor Emmanuel III (1869 –1947) belonged to the House of Savoy and was King of Italy (29 July 1900 – 9 May 1946).

8. Albert I (1875 –1934) reigned as King of the Belgians from 1909 to 1934.

9. *Stadtplan von Alexandria*, Berlin 1940, 1:15.000.

10. *The Competition Programme. Concerning the arrangement of a plan of a city - Sidi Gaber, Suburb of Alexandria*, typewritten document held at the Secchi Tarugi family archive, Milan (see *Annexes*).

11. See Ernst Neufert, *Enciclopedia pratica per progettare e costruire*, Hoepli, Milan 1988, p. 519.

12. This can be clearly seen by comparing the Survey of Egypt maps with those provided to participants in the competition.

13. See the map series Survey of Egypt 1:5000, Dressé par Consortium S.F.S/I.G.N. France en 1978, aerial photo of 1977.

14. The main theorist of the garden city movement, which gained a foothold in the UK at the turn of the 20th century, was Ebenezer Howard, who wrote *To-morrow: a Peaceful Path to Real Reform* in 1898, republished in 1902 as *Garden Cities of Tomorrow*; this book offered a vision of towns free of slums and enjoying the benefits of both town and country.

15. A concept originating in the earlier social and intellectual attitudes, see Clarence Perry, *The Neighbourhood Unit* (1929), Reprinted Routledge/Thoemmes, London, 1998.

16. See "La 'route des choux' - Des questions à la Délégation Municipale," *La Bourse Egyptienne*, 2.1.1934; "The Mohamed Aly road - Councillor's question to delegation," *Egyptian Mail*, 4.1.1934; "Another inquiry into municipal affairs? - The building of Mohamed Aly road," *Egyptian Mail*, 21.1.1934.

17. J. Assémani, "Le Développement d'Alexandrie. La Cité Smouha," *La Dimanche Illustré*, 23.12.1934.

18. *Les Enduits Decoratifs en Égypte*, published by the Cement Marketing Co. Ltd., London (no date).

19. The Swiss architect Max Zollikofer (b. 1898) had a brilliant carrier in Egypt. His works include a plan for the industrial town of Beida Dyers, a subsidiary of Bradford Textile Industries in Kafr el Dawwar near Alexandria (designed with John Prosper Serjeant); other works by Zollikofer are: Villa M. G. Tambay, Moustapha Pacha; Villa M. E. Foa, Sidi Bishr; Desert Home, King Maryut; Villa H. Landart, 1945 ; Drive-in of the Bank of Belgium, 1954. In 1956 Max and Claude Zollikofer were called upon by the British administration of the Victoria College to estimate the entire property of the school, see Sahar Hamouda and Colin Clement, *Victoria College*, cit., pp.207, 304.

20. Rosemary Kitchen, *British Influence on the Architecture and Built Environment of Alexandria*, University of Newcastle-upon-Tyne, 1995 (typewritten report), p.51.

21. See *La Gazette d'Orient*, 14.4.1934.

22. Charles Baehler had built a hotel empire in Egypt and promoted urban development at Zamalek, see Samir Raafat, "The Baehler Skyline," *Cairo Times*, 28.10.1999.

23. Son of the founder of Heliopolis, Jean Empain was said to be one of the richest men in Europe and to represent the biggest capitalist group in the Belgian Congo. See Carolyn Burke, *Lee Miller: On Both Sides of the Camera*, Alfred A. Knopf, New York 2007, p.153; and Patrick Balfour Baron Kinross, *Lords of the Equator*, Hutchinson, London 1937, p.189.

24. Robert S. Rolo was a prominent figure in Egyptian economic affairs and social circles, who held a number of directorships on the boards of the Crédit Foncier, National Bank of Egypt, S.A. du Wadi Kom Ombo.

25. Together with his brothers, O. Matosian ran the leading cigarette company in the Middle East.

26. Fernand Rossano was a partner in the F.B. Rossano & Co. established in 1886, he was also member of the Alexandria Cotton Future Exchange. See *The Egyptian Cotton Gazette: Journal of the Alexandria Cotton Exporters Association*, vol. 14-17, 1952, pp. xxiii, xxiv ; Elwyn James Blattner, James Elwyn Blattner, *Who's who in U.A.R. and the Near East*, Paul Barbey Press, 1953, p. 54; *Who's who in Egypt and the Near East*, vol. 18, Paul Barbey Press, 1952, p.79.

27. Parissi Belleni was a Greek from Leros who set himself up as an engineering contractor, taking part in important public works, becoming one of the richest men in Cairo and a member of Egyptian high society. Elwyn James Blattner, James Elwyn Blattner, *Who's who in U.A.R.*, cit., p.261.

28. The third generation of a very powerful family in Egypt closely linked to the development of Egyptian economy and society, and to the organization and progress of the Hellenic Diaspora. Theodore P. Cozzikas was for a long time president of the Greek Chamber of Commerce Cairo and president of the Greek Community in Cairo. Théodore Th. Cozzika, son of Theocharis Cozzikas, founded the Greek Community Hospital at Alexandria. See E.Th. Souloyiannis, *The Greek Community of Alexandria, 1843-1993*, Athens, 1994, [in Greek], pp.331-332.

29. See Elwyn James Blattner, James Elwyn Blattner, *Who's who in U.A.R.*, 1952 (see also 1955, 1951), p. 587; Margaret Pope, *ABC of the Arab World*, The Socialist Book Centre Ltd., 1946, p.97.

30. Ahmed Ábboud Pacha owned the Egyptian Sugar and Refining Company and held 14% of Bank Misr. After the revolution his property was expropriated. See Marcel G. Laugel, *Sur le vif. Dépêche oubliées de la Mauritani eau Yemen*, L'Harmattan, Paris, 2008; Gamal Essam El-Din, "Political economy of the revolution," *Al-Ahram Weekly on line*, 18-24 July 2002, issue n. 595 special.

31. See *The Grace Log*, vol.14-17, W.R. Grace & Company, 1931, p. 128; Elwyn James Blattner, James Elwyn Blattner, *Who's who in U.A.R.*, 1952, p. 395 (see also editions of 1955, 1953, 1951).

32. Moritz and Heinrich of Hesse were sons of Mafalda di Savoia, who had died at Buchenwald.

33. See Tito Torella di Romagnano, *Villa Jela*, Garzanti, Milano, 1948.

34. See *The Sprinter*, 6 .04.1934.

35. See Robert L. Tignor, *Egyptian textiles and British capital 1930-1956*, The American University in Cairo, 1989, pp. 38-41.

36. See Survey of Egypt, Map series 1:25.000, 1946.

37. Mira Wilkins, Frank Ernst Hill, *American Business Abroad: Ford on Six Continents*, Cambridge University Press, 2011, pp. 258-261, 320. See also Robert L. Tignor, *In the Grip of Politics: the Ford Motor Company of Egypt 1946-60*, University of Nairobi Department of History, 1989.

38. The factory and offices were built around 1946.

39. Gordon S. Riess, *Confessions of a Corporate Centurion: Tales of International Adventures*, AuthorHouse, 1998, p. 4.

40. Map published by the Army Map Service, Corp of Engineers, U.S. Army, Washington DC, compiled in 1958 from Egypt City Plans (Alexandria n. 2 and n. 3) 1:10.000, Survey of Egypt 1:25.000; Directory Military Survey Sheet 94/510 printed in 1952.

41. See Charles Goad, *Insurance Plan of Alexandria, Vol 1: Minet el Bassal*, 1898, 1:4000.

42. "Bus service to the new racecourse," *The Egyptian Gazette*, 22.1.1934.

43. See *Le Favorí*, 12.03.1934.

44. "L'inaugurazione del nuovo Ippodromo di Hadra," *Il Giornale d'Oriente*, 15 April 1934 (author's translation).

45. A furlong, a measure of distance widely used in horse racing, equals one-eighth of a mile, though its exact length varies slightly among English-speaking countries.

46. See *The Sprinter*, 6.04.1934

47. John Henry Taylor (1871-1962) had learned the game as a caddie at North Devon Golf Club and had turned professional at the age of 19. His most notable works as a golf-course architect are Royal Birkdale and Ahburnham golf courses. His books on golf include J.H. Taylor, *Taylor on Golf: Impressions, Comments and Hints*, Hutchinson, London, 1902; J.H. Taylor, *Golf My Life's Work: Taylor autobiography*, Jonathan Cape, London 1943. On J. H. Taylor see also Bill Mallon, Randon Jenis, *Historical Dictionary of Golf*, Plymouth 2011, p.289.

48. "The Smouha Affair," *The Illustrated London News*, 28.2.1959, pp.336-338.

49. A photo entitled "Studio de M. A. de Naglowsky, Alexandrie" was published in *Les Enduits Décoratifs en Egypte*. Alexandre Naglowsky in mentioned as "a giant Russian sculptor" in Gabriel Josipovici, *A life*, London Magazine Editions / The European Jewish Publication Society, London, 2001, pp.112, 114.

50. See "All-welded Barges Constructed in Egypt," *The Welder*, vol. 16-18, 1947, p. 133.

51. On E. di A. De Farro contractors see *Annuario degli Italiani d'Egitto*, Pubblicità Anglo-Egiziana, 1933, pp. 135-137 and Milva Giacomelli, "Italian construction companies in Egypt," in *Building Beyond the Mediterranean. Studying the Archives of European Businesses (1860-1970)*, ed. by Claudine Piaton, Ezio Godoli, David Peyceré, Arles, Honoré Clair, pp.50-57.

52. Such as, for example, the nearby St. Jeanne Antide Schools by Ferdinand Debbane (1934-35), the Greek Community Hospital by Jean Walter (1932-38) and the El Mouassat Hospital by E. Kopp (1936).

9 Richard Smouha

Sports and Social Life

9.1 Alexandria Racing Club (the club pre-inauguration)

"Alexandrie Nouvelle – L'hippodrome Smouha," *La Gazette D'Orient,* 3.2.34

"The final touches by specialist workers will be completed in time for the inauguration in two months, a magnificent racecourse, large, spacious, luxurious, modern. The firm De Farro have completed an admirable task. All along the green ribbon of turf there runs a brown wooden barrier of gracious design.

The entrance, sober and elegant with a turnstile system allows for crowds to pass easily.

The first building, the Royal Box, majestic with delicate decorations, is surrounded by flower-beds. Further over are the first-class stands, vast, comfortable and sheltered by a huge cover.

A hundred metres away the second class stands, also protection from sun and rain, an innovation compared to other clubs. On the left of the entrance are the weigh-ins and paddock for the horses and further over, their boxes, with running water and protected against both heat and cold.

Finally the taxi from Sidi Gaber and Cleopatra takes only four minutes and costs only four piastres – that's of course for the snobs. As for the sportsmen and journalists (!) they go by bus taking five minutes but costing only ten milliemes. The macadamised road is luxuriously comfortable."

The Club Pre-inauguration

"L'Hippodrome de l'Alexandria Racing Club," *The Egyptian Gazette,* 9.3.1934

"The Jockey Club of Egypt has approved the programme for the season of the two clubs. The Alexandria Sporting Club has increased the prizes by 20%.

The Alexandria Racing Club's programme for its opening on 14 April will run 14 races, two of which are major prizes namely the Alexandria Gold Cup (LE1,000 - offered by the owners) and the Smouha Cup (LE350 offered by Mr. J. Smouha).

The promoters have made a great effort to reduce the admission prices that will be:

Grand stand-men PT (piastres) 20; Grand stand–ladies PT 15; Small stand general PT 8; Third class PT 4

Finally it is decided that the promoters will never receive more than 4% and the balance will go to improvements and prizes.

"The Alexandria Racing Season," *The Egyptian Gazette,* 6.3.1934

"It is regrettable … a reluctance to support the club which for so many years has provided Egypt's summer racing. Unless there are entries in larger numbers, the club will suffer and so will the public. The owners and trainers have for several years considered that they have not received their due. The Alexandria Sporting Club has 1,880 members of whom the majority are not interested in racing. The club has had to cater to the general interest of its members and from time to time has had to look for a compromise between racing and other sports. The committee have tried to maintain a balance and the evidence of the large membership and candidates for election shows that they have done their task.

Recognising the needs of the local racing world, the committee of the Alexandria Sporting Club has from its inception been friendly towards the new racing club at Hadra. Alexandria Sporting Club was unable to accept a working arrangement proposal, which would have meant a certain loss for them. In spite of this they have continued to maintain a friendly attitude, helping with organisation, pari-mutuel etc.

The Alexandria Sporting Club seem to realize that in the not very distant future, all racing in Alexandria may be on the new course and the Sporting will become purely a games and social centre. But before that can happen, the new racing club must establish itself and prove its capabilities in the eyes of the Jockey Club and the public. If this does happen it is only fair to recall the many years that ASC have led the way in increasing prize money. Since 1912 they have paid out more than both Cairo clubs put together.

Such methods should have no place in sport and it is inconceivable that the Jockey Club of Egypt or the public could view them with approval."

"The Alexandria Racing Season – The Two Clubs, ARC's Position," *The Egyptian Gazette*, 17.3.1934
"It took just 10 days for Alexandria Racing Club to riposte to all the implications of this article with a communiqué in an article in *The Egyptian Gazette*, dated 17 March 1934, it refers to the owners and trainers not receiving the consideration they felt due to them. But certain parts of the article appear to suggest that the owners and particularly those associated with Alexandria Racing Club have not treated the Alexandria Sporting Club fairly and have acted in a way detrimental to the sport.

To any such suggestion they take exception and insist on taking account of: the new racecourse could have been run as a business proposition. Instead they approached Alexandria Sporting Club to negotiate an amicable arrangement but this fell through.

And also that a few owners after prolonged negotiations obtained a lease of the new racecourse in order to promote the sport by ensuring that a first-class racecourse would be available to the public, and that the profits if any would be used to improve the racing. They therefore assumed a heavy liability.

Nearly all these members were also members of Alexandria Racing Club and far from wishing to do it any "injury" had inserted a clause allowing them to transfer the lease to Alexandria Racing Club.

The only condition that they required was reasonable representation in the management to ensure adequate racing.

Unfortunately the proposal was not accepted nor did Alexandria Racing Club make any counter-proposal.

Under these circumstances the owners had to take over; they formed a company and other owners joined. The management was given to men who have served as stewards of the Jockey Club and on Alexandria Racing Club committees and they have divided the racing equally between the two clubs, fixing the amount of the prizes on the same basis as in recent years.

'This action can hardly be construed as an attempt to injure the Alexandria Racing Club, but the Alexandria Racing Club's reply was to increase considerably the amount they had offered last year. Is this attitude consistent with recognition of and sympathy with the needs of the local racing world and a friendly attitude to the new venture? It can only make it more difficult for Alexandria Racing Club and therefore not surprising that the owners give their support to Alexandria Racing Club'."

Anyway the Alexandria Racing Club members stated that they have no wish to indulge in recriminations and look forward to the day when a satisfactory solution will be arranged as it was between the Gezira Sporting Club and the Heliopolis Racing Club in Cairo. Freddy Martell writes (sic) "Un peu dédaigne par les aristocrats juifs, il (Joseph Smouha) ne fut pas admis au sein de leurs groupes notamment pas au Sporting Club!

Joseph Smouha déclara alors "s`ils ne me veulent pas chez eux … ils viendront chez moi."

(Somewhat ignored by the Jewish aristocrats he was excluded from their circles, and especially at the Alexandria Sporting Club, generally referred to as Le Sporting. Joseph Smouha then said: If they don`t want me there, they will come to me.")

9.2 A visit to ARC

"Notre visite à l'Alexandria Racing Club," *Le Favori*, 12.3.1934

"By taxi we went to visit Mr. Mike Marinakis, the alert and courteous Secretary General of Alexandria Sporting Club, a trip, which took us hardly five minutes from Sidi Gaber. Today we enter via the large door of the main entrance, which in the future will only

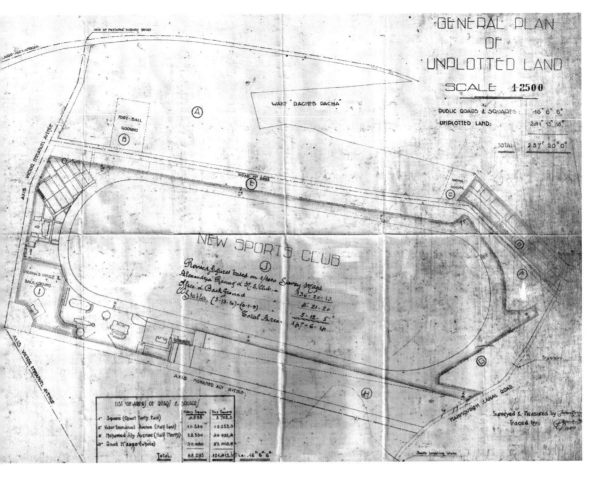

be used by His Majesty and celebrities. We observed four entries operated on rollers to allow access of crowds.

After passing by several blocks with workers applying the final touches we arrive at the course. And suddenly we give a spontaneous exclamation of wonder. We are gazing at a panorama of great beauty – on the horizon, a necklace of villas of various colours ascending the clear hills of Sidi Gaber that with a slight imagination one could be viewing a mountain range – admittedly tiny. To the north a small clump of date palms from which from time to time there surged a white train curving round the hippodrome and leaving a trail of greying smoke. Now we reach the course itself, where with the pure air brushing our cheeks, we hurry to take our places.

The course itself, 27 metres wide, is fully covered by a curtain of master gardeners bent over the grass which is 1.5 metres higher than the former Lake Hadra, and covered with sand and grass. The course itself, 2800 metres long allows for a start of 34 horses abreast, and the straight of 1000 metres is 300 metres longer than at Heliopolis in Cairo. It is at the end of this straight line that the real expertise and dexterity of the jockeys comes into play, just before the bend.

The whole area with the golf course covers an area of 120 feddans. After this we climbed into the stands, with their colour

scheme of pea-green and beige.

The style and conception have been cleverly studied so that it is protected from the sun but has total visibility via its angle to the track. The main stand seats 1000 on comfortable seats and we are informed that their dimensions were established after anatomical studies. We were shown the special places for the owners, the press, the trainers and higher up just below the stewards, the important guests

This brings us to the very top of the stand where there are two rows of 58 spacious lodges and behind them an immense tearoom with flowery pots which allowed the race goers to have meetings in private with their buddies and girl-friends and at the same time participate in the races via a desk which allowed them to bet in all privacy and security.

We retrace our steps to the great hall where the betting takes place. There are many points of access allowing a large number of participants to operate at the same time. And the spaciousness of the hall creates an area of cool air away from the heat outside. Four groups of betting desks separated by a mount allows for easy and speedy action. In the centre are the desks (guichets) of the parolis, and further over the Owners Credit Tote and in a corner away from the rest desks for paying out the winning tickets. At the other end of the hall there is a large screen where all indications concerning the mounts and the results are set out in large letters as well as any other information such as protests.

Finally to console the losers a well-equipped bar is available, also for the winners to celebrate their luck.

We find ourselves in front of the royal box decorated with taste. A little further on, the jockeys' weighing room with the jockeys' rooms each with its shower, washbasin etc.

Further on again, the secretariat linked to the infirmary equipped with everything necessary to carry out surgery.

Yet another hall for the amateur jockeys, then the boxes for the horses, some specially equipped for the nervousness of the thoroughbreds and protected from the flies and the heat.

Finally the small third class stand near the parking lot from where one can catch a speedy bus no more expensive than the tram. A last mention, the 24 founder members prepared to receive only 4% for their 10,000 pounds invested in this hippodrome and whom I list ...

Yesterday, I telephoned to Mr. Mike Marinakis to fix a rendezvous. The indefatigable Secretary replied that these days he is still in the office at midnight. Only then did I understand why he has recently lost seven kilos. This 'right man in the right place,' by his pleasantness, by his courtesy, by his politeness impresses all who visit him.

As soon as he took over his function, he put the press in the forefront of his cares, and served them with fairness above all suspicion."

The following newspapers also reported, but in slightly less detail, the visit conducted by Mike Marinakis:
Le Dimanche Illustré 04.3.1934;
The Egyptian Gazette 17.3.1934;
Le Gazette d'Orient 24.3.1934;
The Sprinter 06.4.1934;
Le Favori 10.4.1934;
Jocker 13.4.1934;
Le Turf 13.4.1934.

The Under-Secretary of State for Finances, Amine Osman Pacha discussing with Mr. Joseph Smouha and the national swimming champion Ishak Helmi bey, Alexandria, 1934.

opposite
Entrance Smouha Club (from *The Illustrated London News*, 1959).

9.3 Alexandria Racing Season

"Alexandria Racing Season - Jockey Club Notice," *The Egyptian Gazette,* 20.3.1934

"It has come to the notice of the Jockey Club that both collective and individual pressure has been brought to bear upon certain owners and trainers to boycott racing at the Alexandria Sporting Club by partisans of the Alexandria Racing Club and vice versa.

The stewards decided that this most reprehensible conduct shall cease forthwith, otherwise they will take drastic action against the guilty party or parties by the application of their powers to the utmost limit.

They are determined to protect fully the legitimate interests of all concerned in racing under their rules.

They request that the clubs concerned shall at once agree upon ways and means of restoring the friendly and sporting attitude that is essential to the best interests of racing as the Stewards of the Jockey Club view with regret the possibility of necessity of intervention on their part."

9.4 The Inauguration - 14 April 1934

"Le Nouvel Hippodrome," *Le Phare Égyptien*, 15.4.1934
"The inauguration at Smouha was truly a world event.
Feast of elegance. Feast of horse racing where people who had

Abdel Fattah Pacha Yéhia, President of the Council, Joseph Smouha and S.E. Emine at The Alexandria Racing Club.

M. Clément Ades receiving the "Smouha Cup" from Joseph Smouha for his win with "Churbara."

The winners of the meeting of the inauguration of the Alexandria Racing Club.

opposite
H.E. Ahmed Ziwer Pacha, former President of the Council of State and Mr. Joseph Smouha following the horses parading with amusement, Alexandria, 1934.

never put foot on a racecourse dared timidly and fearfully.

There was happiness and discontent, those who were lucky and those who were unlucky, lovely ladies in pursuit of a race tip and our 'turfists' in the pursuit of lovely ladies. There was the inevitable procession of officials, jetsetters, demi-monde and hangers-on, and all the rabble of adventurers and others that one meets at the races."

"A Huge Success - The First Race Meetings at the Alexandria Racing Club," *Egyptian Mail*, 17.4.1934

"The first day the crowds were already in place by 2:00 pm, way before the time fixed for the first race at 3:00 pm.

More than 5,000 people turned up for the first meetings at the new course each day. The main race on the opening day, Saturday, was the Gold Cup carrying a prize of LE1,000. This was won by Mrs. J. Matossian, the wife of one of the Stewards, himself an important member of the Owners Association. Her horse,

Panache, was trained by Mr. Simon Tasdjian Sunday's main race was the Smouha Cup + LE 350. This was won by Mr. Clement Ades who received the cup from Mr. Joseph Smouha himself, the winning horse being Churbara."

I give below a combination resume of reports on the inauguration appearing in the following newspapers between 15.4 and 22.4: *Le Phare, Egyptian Mail, La Bourse Égyptienne* (2), *The Egyptian Gazette, Il Giornale D'Òriente, Jocker* (2), *The Sphinx, Le Turf, Le Stade, Le Favori, Sporting* (2), *L`Echo Sportif, The Sprinter* and *La Réforme Illustrée*, as well as *Al Riadah* and *El Safir*.

The Egyptian Gazette, 15.4.1934

"This magnificent race-course with the majestic stands, able to hold more than a thousand sportsmen comfortably seated, the Royal Stand, royal in its splendour in the vast paddocks, the new track levelled like a billiard table or the green and soft turf inviting the steeds to perform exploits ... All this is a pleasant change from the Sporting and its wooden stand, its track hidden by an ugly clubhouse, the scanty enclosure and its course spoilt by sharp bends." Mr. E. de A. de Farro, an expert who has visited many courses in Europe and America stated, 'this course is twenty years ahead of any I have seen in Europe.' The whole organisation has been delegated to a person well-known for his courtesy and competence and particularly his knowledge 'from A to Z' of this sport, namely Mike Marinakis, the ARC club secretary. This weekend as from 2 o'clock each day, all roads led to Smuha (sic)."

"The Smouha City Racecourse," *The Egyptian Gazette*, 19.4.1934

"Considering the short time available it was gratifying and pleasantly surprising to see that assembling such a system of correlated parts was carried out without a hitch.

View of golf-course and Ford factory in the background, ca. 1940 (R. Smouha's archive).

The turf proved to be as good as it looks. One reason for its excellent quality may be that for 128 years, this land was under sweet water. When the lakebed was drained, millions of small fish died and so provided a dressing of excellent fertilizer for the soil. This venture by the group of owners who have laid themselves out to make a new ear for the Egyptian Turf, has commenced auspiciously with every sign of continued prosperously."

The photograph showing H.H. Omar Toussoun has much present relevance and significance as it was from him in his position as trustee for certain members of the royal family that Joseph Smouha bought the Lake and Land.

Also significant the two extremely pleasant meetings that I, as grandson of Joseph Smouha, had with his grandson H.H. Hussein Toussoun, first in Paris and then at our home in Geneva.

Not surprisingly and despite the large prizes, the pari mutuel (tote) profits reached record highs.

A few constructive criticisms were made in the press which would have been followed up and rectified – for example that the Stewards from their place next to the Royal Stand were unable to see the horses at all times after the race, giving rise to a lack of control, and that the Steward in the 'Crows Nest' had no means of communicating any objections he may have had.

The comment: even a red flag would have been enough. My comment: long live mobile telephones! More importantly and understandably eighty years on, that with the unexpected thousands of spectators, the parking lot was insufficient.

The Alexandria Racing Club made a much-appreciated gesture by offering gifts to the owner, trainer and jockey of the winning horse of the opening race. Nor were others forgotten such as Mr. Marinakis and the Judge of the Course Mr. R. Brassard, who were similarly spoilt.

"The magician of this fairy-like transformation of a dirty old lake showed emotion at the evidence of the fantastic success which henceforth bears his name."

"To have built in such a short time such a fine hippodrome on the land of a former lake indicates a skill and intelligence which does honour to the founder."

The thousands of spectators, arriving from all over the country, crowded everywhere even taking over the weigh-in area, the paddocks and the tote, and the amount of business transacted will never be seen again.

Notes from my Mother

"On the day of the race-course was inaugurated, a box had been assigned to our family. It was a very exciting day, with crowds of people – the ladies had new dresses made for it and lovely hats, good enough for Ascot. I was sitting in our box with my parents-in-law and one or two members of our family. Teddy, my husband, had gone off to 'talk to people and find out how things were going.'

As we sat waiting for the start of the first race, Teddy came back with a trainer who had asked him to introduce him to Mr. Smouha who had 'made this wonderful course.' The trainer responded to my father-in-law in flowery words his appreciation of the work he had done to accomplish something that would give pleasure and work to as many people. Then he said he had a horse running, an outsider, which was sure to win and the stakes were high, so would Mr. Smouha give him some money to put on it for him? My father-in-law pretended not to hear, but Teddy nudged him, and said: 'go on, give him some money to put on the horse.' Very slowly, Mr. Smouha put his hand in his pocket, brought out a 5-piastre piece (one shilling), handed it over and I clearly heard him say: 'if they had known in Manchester that I gambled on horses, no-one would have done business with me.' The trainer took the money politely, but looked as if he was just going to die of shock."

"Le Second Gala Hippique – Le Président du Conseil y Assiste," *La Bourse Égyptienne* and *Le Stade*, 30.4.1934
"The Second Gala meeting on Saturday and Sunday 28/29 April was almost equal to the first. This time the guest of honour was the President of the Council or Prime Minister S.E. Abdel Fattah Yéhia who had come on a special trip from Cairo for this reason. He and his wife stayed for tea with Joseph Smouha and Me. Gaby Maksud. Yet again, as for the inauguration most of the big Cairo racegoers came to the meeting."

9.5 Alexandria Racing Club *versus* Alexandria Sporting Club

"Un hippodrome est né sur l'emplacement d'un ancient lac", *le Turf,* 20.4.1934
"All last week various rumours indicated that the revenues of Alexandria Sporting Club were heavily insufficient. It is this situa-

At the New Sports Club, the first Annual Open Tennis tournament winners with Lady Barker who offered and presented the prizes.

The tournament of the New Smouha Club: Miss Michailidis and Mrs. Smart, women's singles finalists.

opposite
Announcement of the ARC inauguration, *The Gazette de l'Orient,* 07-04-1934.

tion, which is creating a most painful atmosphere that is harming not only the turf but also all the organisations connected to it.

It is greatly to be desired that a speedy arrangement be reached in the interests of the two clubs and the future of horse racing in Egypt. In the meantime let us thank Mr. J. Smouha who, at great risk, has succeeded in beautifying the city of Alexandria with this monumental construction. 'We are happy to announce that the news film of the inauguration of Alexandria Racing Club was carried out by Mr. Leon Suares and has been showing at the Majestic cinema.'

The Need for an Agreement
The need for an agreement between the two clubs is being felt day by day. The gap in their approach threatens to become insoluble if they remain inflexible. The interest of horse racing has greater priority and an agreement must be reached speedily. In this case the only way to reach a final conclusive agreement is via reconciliation, concessions and by abandoning other requirements. Last Tuesday the Alexandria Sporting Club committee held an important meeting to this effect. The discussions and decisions remain secret but they were not contrary to the interests of this sport."

"La Semaine," *La Réforme Illustree*, 22.3.1934
"… Naturally as with every question there are two sides – the Smouha clan and the Sporting clan. The first is reactionary. New and modernistic – grand, large and rapid. The second is conservative, has small corners, old memories, small attitudes. So there is a battle with each side presenting its advantages. Then the interests of each side are put forward leading to trifling arguments and interminable discussions. Where is the sense of reasonableness and where the sense of truth? Qui vivra, verra."

"Sporting," *Jocker,* 25.4.1934
"… The birth of a new racecourse should logically have led to an improvement to the racing world of Alexandria. Alas, it is not so. Due to misunderstandings, insufficient clarification and explanation, Alexandria Sporting Club and Alexandria Racing Club appear to be waging a desperate fight against each other.

Without going into further details, this state of affairs in itself is unacceptable: racecourse professionals – the jockeys, the trainers and all the back-up employees have the right to live and are here to work.

Last week's Alexandria Sporting Club meeting confirmed a sad reality, really badly attended with only 25 horses for the six races several Alexandria Sporting Club Steward's decisions only made the situation worse than it was.

There are personalities, members of the Jockey Club who have great influence and it is they who have an obligation to use this influence to bring the two clubs to an agreement.

It's the public that suffers."

"Une éclaircie à l'horizon," *Le Turf*, 18.5.1934

"The horizon clears – the rumour ran like a powder train that an agreement had been reached after heavy discussion. There is as yet no confirmation but both sides are anxious to reach a conclusion. The differences will disappear if the correct concessions are made."

After the war, the racecourse and facilities had been rented out on a twenty-year lease to the owners in 1934. This was up for renewal in 1954, and the family, i.e. Joseph Smouha, was not interested in taking over but still wanted a good deal. Derrick Smouha, my cousin, was in the office during his gap year and remembers heavy negotiations.

9.6 Sports and social activities

"Alexandria's New Games Centre – Smouha City Sports Club," *The Egyptian Gazette*, 19.12.34

"Many parts of Alexandria have changed greatly over the past few years but nowhere has there been more has there been more rapid or more complete transformation than on the estate at Hadra where Smouha City is quickly rising from the ground. The disappearance of the lake was the first and most conspicuous of the changes. The making of the Alexandria Racing Club's magnificent course with its attached buildings completed the conversion of that part of the estate into the best racecourse in Egypt. An eighteen-hole golf course … an area where four years ago there was little but market gardens … All the amenities including the serving of meals by a reputed firm of local caterers.

The Club has 16 tennis courts, 4 squash courts, rugby, hockey and association football grounds, a bowling green, a croquet lawn, ping pong tables, a children's playground, card room and reading room, lounge, terraces, dressing rooms and baths and two dance floors, and inevitably a large and active card-playing "fraternity."

All this required a degree of active management and a goodish number of employees /caddies/indoor servants, etc. A tea dance at the club: the Smouha table. (p.155, left to right) – Yvonne, Joyce (later Mosseri), Peggy (later Setton), Rosa (nee Ades), Joseph and Edward (Teddy) circa 1937.

A tea dance (these were held weekly).
The clubhouse itself is particularly attractive, built on the architectural conceptions of today and so designed that members have the maximum of light, air and views from every part of the building. The terrace is one of the most delightful spots, commanding a view of the golf course in front, with the Mahmoudieh Canal in the middle background, while to left and right respectively can be seen the tennis courts and the children's playground. This ter-

race is certainly as pleasant a place as any in Alexandria.

The children`s playground turned out to be in fact and un-expectantly a huge success. First of all it had as good a combination of swings, roundabouts and climbing games as anywhere and was always inhabited by English nannies that appreciated the spaciousness and enclosed space, which made supervision so much easier."

Another, and in a sense more amusing, situation concerned the one sport which was in private hands. This was the Delrieux riding school owned and run by Monsieur Henri Delrieux. I have no idea how this came about but he had got hold of a plot of land immediately behind the Joseph Smouha Estate Office and just under the windows of my father`s and uncle`s office but most importantly with the racecourse on the other side of his school. This enabled himself - presumably duly authorised - to take his pupils on rides around the racecourse. Among the many photographs from this period is one showing three prizewinners of a jumping competition at the school. One of the three prizewinners is Prince Hussein Toussoun, whose grandfather Prince Omar Toussoun was the main seller of the future Smouha City to my grandfather. Another prizewinner is my wife (on the right)! 1946.

Advantage was taken of this great open space so close to town and especially Alexandria with its polyglot multitudes, its multi-faceted groups of highly educated and cultured peoples mentally and socially jostling each other to outdo and outperform. The main evidence of this is the production by the next two generations of the disappearance of this Alexandria, of fascinating literature about the atmosphere and personalities of this period. One of the many objectives of this work of mine is that this exceptional society shall not be forgotten in our new world.

There must have been many special occasions stemming from such a life. One, which I am happy to be able to recount is the annual "Concours d`Elegance Automobile" which was held I believe in and from the Smouha Club. One of our photos shows Freddy Mizrahi at the wheel of one of the winners, a Bentley, with Joyce Magar who most certainly contributed to the prize by her presence. Both have also contributed to this history and both also joined the "lost everything" crowd of Alexandria.

Claudie Wouters-Dambach and her husband, as have many, benefited from the new or comparatively new activities stemming from the existence of a club with wide-open spaces almost within walking distance of their homes or schools or offices. Many of these former Alexandrians have emphasized the sense of freedom and safety just walking on one's own in the road. While they remember from just a mile away the deafening noise of the traffic, the dust the people and a little closer in, the mass of beggars who would surround any likely looking European.

Maryse Pastroudis, Prince Hussein Toussoun (grandson of Prince Omar Toussoun), Sylvia Smouha (grand-daughter in-law of Joseph Smouha), horse-riding prize winners (R. Smouha's archive).

Delrieux riding school (R. Smouha's archive).

These club facilities also took over the role of one of the favoured places to hold celebrations.

On 17 May 1937, *The Egyptian Gazette* published a letter from G.H. Dempsey (I think I was at school in Heliopolis with his son) "May I, as another of the great audience which had the privilege of witnessing the Coronation Display at Smouha City join 'Delighted' in appreciation of the finest show of its kind ever staged in Alexandria…"

"Une exquise oasis à Smouha City," *La Gazette d'Orient*, 20.12.1934
The organisers who had the happy inspiration of introducing the Cypriot and Maltese Episodes, performed entirely by those communities, are also to be heartily congratulated, emphasizing thus, the voluntary association of nations which is changing the imperialistic sense of Empire into a worldwide Commonwealth.
"Yesterday was a dull day with nothing to do so I found myself visiting the Alexandria Racing Club. Imagine my surprise on a dull winter's day to find a long line of cars parked at the entrance to the New Sports Club. My professional curiosity drew me to push a glass door behind which stood a Nubian dressed in an impeccable commissionaire's uniform.
From the entrance a sober décor of small tables covered with damask tablecloths, large inviting armchairs, a beautiful parquet floor and on the left a large marble fireplace.
On the other side of a large bay window you find yourself on a beautiful verandah bathed in sunlight with a view stretching to the horizon of this immense racecourse.
Colourful flowerbeds a profusion of greenery favour long drowsy moments in the sun.
But then pushing a door on the right of the entrance one finds

Participants in the Concours d'Elegance Automobile at Smouha City (Joyce Magar, Claudie-Dambach).

British journalists at a tea offered by Joseph Smouha.

A group at the New Sports Club, Smouha City after the close of the Open Tennis tournament. Front row from the right - Peggy Smouha (wife of Ellis), Yvonne (her sister and wife of Teddy), Teddy Smouha.

opposite
At the weekly tea dance, 1937; from left to right: Yvonne Smouha, Joyce Smouha, Peggy Smouha, Rosa Smouha, Joseph Smouha, Teddy Smouha (R. Smouha's archive).

oneself in an American bar with bottles in a thousand colours, gleaming crystal glasses, comfortable armchairs, high stools, in a word a sumptuous temple of liquid pleasures.

On the other side of the terrace there is a large reading and writing room, also for bridge and whist. Then a music room with a piano at the end. At the exit, toilets and bathrooms.

We go upstairs to the next floor – a royal staircase – more like an ascension, and you can imagine the beautifully impressive view all around 180 degrees. Upstairs there was additional space for a card room, billiard table and ping pong.

As already mentioned, horse racing and golf took first place, and while there was less activity in the minor sports, tennis had a largish number of supporters, but I cannot remember a time when all 16 courts were occupied, but probably this would have occurred in big match competitions. The tennis really got off to its start with the first Open Tennis Tournament in February 1936. Nearly all Alexandria's leading players participated and the presence of the Royal Navy in port added spice to the competition. The first surprise was the defeat of the Navy Champion Commander P. Glover by Contmichalos, who himself lost in the next round. Glover made up for his loss by winning the Plate – open to all first round losers.

For a first it was most successful with 36 entries in the men's singles, 25 in the women's and 53 in the three doubles categories. Michaelidis won both singles and doubles.

Dinner parties were not so commonplace in the thirties as they later became during the war. However many businessmen quickly got into the habit of having lunches there as it was only a 5-10 minute drive from their offices: and the ladies got together for tea

parties, at that time much in vogue for gossip and exchange of information over cards, cucumber sandwiches and cakes - even in those days being spurned by weight-watching younger women. Such parties were precisely timed - 3:30 to 5:15.

The Advisory Committee of the New Sports Club issued a report on the working of the club for the first 10 months – a satisfactory position. If revenue does not yet cover expenditure, the figures show a deficit of only LE103, but this has not included depreciation and write-offs.

There are 402 resident and country members and 260 family members but many more were needed to keep the Club prosperous. The Honorary Secretary by now is Group Captain Cull D.S.O. RAF retd. whom I remember well and who was well suited to the job. I also remember his wife who was also extremely active but not always in the direction he would have wished. While it was considered too early, there were already discussions about the possibility of forming a members' club, which would negotiate a lease to take over the premises and the grounds. In the meantime Joseph Smouha had generously guaranteed the members against any financial deficit.

10 Richard Smouha, Cristina Pallini
War Years and Sequestration

10.1 The war years 1939-1946

These years saw a complete change in the structure of management of Smouha City. Of the three main protagonists Joseph Smouha, Teddy and Ellis Smouha, the last, who, for health reasons always returned later than the others after the heavy heat of the Egyptian summer, was caught out by the breakout of the war on 3 September 1939 and was forced to pass the duration in England. Teddy Smouha, on his return from England, was immediately posted to RAF Abukir as an acting pilot officer on probation (the lowest of the low in terms of commissioned officers), served out the war in Cairo after the six-month probationary period in Alexandria and towards the end of the war was sent to Transport Command Headquarters in Bushey. He only became reactivated in the business after demobilisation at the end of 1947.

I have copy of a letter dated 21 February 1940 from Joseph Smouha to Mr. Riding, Headmaster of Aldenham School (who had become a close friend of Joseph Smouha, as with so many he has come to contact with).

"…Desmond (his youngest son) is working very hard and sends his love to all of you.

Teddy Smouha had joined the Royal Air Force, Headquarters, and after an absence of seven weeks we only saw him yesterday just for the day.

As you know Ellis had another operation in London, and he is still there to be treated by Mr. Harmer.

The building trade here has stopped at present, and I am working on the land, trying to put every bit of it into cultivation. Although it may not give me much return, nevertheless it is for the good of all.

It is sad to see the losses that our brave merchantmen are suffering in the Sea. (sic)

Mrs. Smouha has bought the little stock of English blue wool she was able to find here, and we are having about 50 ladies to come to our house every Wednesday afternoon from three o'clock till eight o'clock to knit stockings and shawls for our sailors …

I hope that England will soon triumph over Germany for the great cause of liberty and humanity."

The most important of the three, Joseph Smouha, rented a flat in Zamalek in Cairo at Bodmin House. In 1940, a list of the ten most wanted men to be executed by hanging in the public square in the middle of Cairo, on the arrival of the Germans in Egypt, was found on a captured German officer: n. 1 on the list was Joseph Smouha. An eavesdropping on a cocktail conversation between civil and military high-rankers was reported back to my father "… and what are we going to do about old Smouha?"

It was immediately decided to evacuate him to South Africa. However he refused to go without his family. The authorities caved in and we found ourselves on a Short Sunderland flying boat headed south. There were my grandparents, Aunts Peggy and Edna, my mother and us three children plus nurse and maid. Quite a household! And in those days quite an aircraft-full.

I do not know the reasons or technicalities but the trip from the Nile River take-off to the Durban sea landing took four days with stops every four hours or so and overnight landings at (then) primitive places such as Wadi Halfa, Khartoum, Malakal, Kissoumo on Lake Victoria, Mozambique and Mombassa, before our arrival at the final destination, landing in the sea off Durban. We spent four months in South Africa. Joseph Smouha rented a house in Johannesburg in a suburb called Parkview – not far from the zoo, and the whole family lived in it. He became active in a numbers of fields but as a small boy of only eight years old then and had only had home education. I had to walk up the hill to school and back. Here I was like a boy from outer space parachuted into a group of small boys who had never been outside of Parkview. I was a strange animal and like all little boys they made the most of it. In recreation they would form a circle around me, then one would hit me in the back and when I turned round another would take over.

One day my mother found me in tears and soon found out what was going on. She said, "no problem. You've forgotten your boxing lessons with Sergeant Bob Scalley (Scottish heavyweight champ). Just pick one boy and go and punch him."

The next day I did just that, his lip started to bleed, he burst into tears and all the others scattered.

The day after that this boy brought me a present of a model aeroplane and became my best friend. I remember the walks home with my new group of friends, buying "an ice-cream dolly" (like today's Magnum) with a ticky (three penny bit). I still have the copy of my school report showing zero out of 20 in Afrikaans!

Back from South Africa, back to the war theatre, but there must have been very little new business done in terms of building and sales on the land, with Joseph Smouha in South Africa, my father in the RAF and Uncle Ellis in the UK.

However, I remember that day-to-day life continued but at a much slower pace in Alexandria. It was about this time that Joseph Smouha paid for two Spitfire fighters for the RAF and the

The Smouha Estate in 1959 from *The Illusrated London News*, 1959 (R. Smouha's archive).

opposite
Registration certificate of "Joseph Smouha" on of the two Spitfires he paid for in WWII.

details are recorded here as being significant to show the high level of his participation in the war effort, in addition to his three sons and his youngest daughter in the RAF.

The war brought a tremendous increase in sporting activities at the Club, directly attributable to the military.

The newspapers of the period talk of "several playing fields" without specifying their exact location. My guess would be (see p.129) the far side of the tennis courts.

And of course this brought a whole new social activity (see Lawrence Durrell).

The newspapers give full rein: "now is the time for the Municipality to provide permanent grounds for sport and they might conceivably pay a useful visit to Smouha City."

Two items show the extreme importance of Alexandria for the Royal Navy's Mediterranean fleet.

A good indication is to take a selection of the several hundred guests at the Ball of the British Benevolent Fund in 1937: 2nd Lord of the Admiralty, Kenneth Lindsay MP, C-in-C Med Fleet and Lady Fisher, Admiral Sir Dudley Poumd Vice-Admiral Sir Alexander Ramsay, Vice-Admiral Sir Charles Forbes, Rear-Admiral Raikes, Captain Sir Maxwell and Lady Anderson, Sir Ralph and Lady Cator, Baron and Baroness Pfyffer, as well as all the local potentates, jet set, business moguls – far too many to name.

Added to this, the much used rugby football pitch, remembering this is 15 a side: HMS Sussex 26 beat HMS Ajax 0, HMS Renown 16 beat HMS Beswick 3, Alex Sporting 20 beat RAF Amria 8, Cairo 0, RAOC 18, Alex Sporting 10 beat Melita 8, RAF depot 0 HMS Glorious 22, HMAS Australia 16 beat HMS Exeter 0.

Cricket, hockey and football all benefited from the situation between 1938 and 1947. After that tourism started taking over and group visits such as that of the combined Oxford and Cambridge golf team which had a match against the club, which probably got hold of some of the local scratch players such as John Plant.

I don't remember the result but that at the first hole, a par four of some 300+ yards, Eustace Crawley was the only one to reach the bunker in front of the green with his drive.

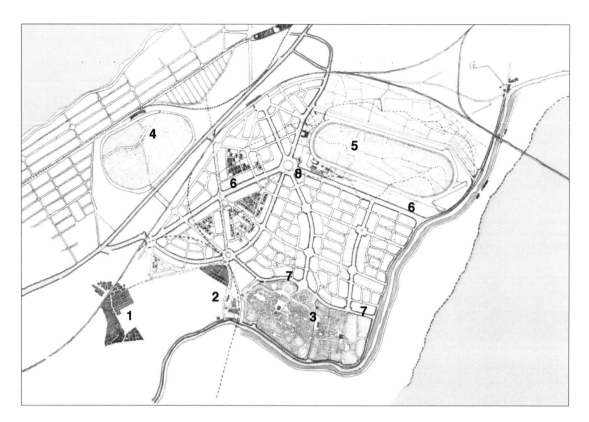

Smouha City in 1943 (C. Pallini's reconstruction).
Legend: 1. Hadra; 2. Ez Soad; 3. Nouzha-Antoniadis Gardens; 4. Alexandria Sporting Club; 5. Alexandria Racing Club; 6. Boulevard Mohamed Ali; 7. Boulevard Albert I; 8. Victor Emanuel III Square.

10.2 Post-war business

As with all, especially major, projects, every now and then they enter a new phase in their development. This is what happened with Smouha City. While the structure remained the same, the activity of the management of the city calmed down. Greater emphasis was put on the sale of villas and other constructions and with the end of hostilities and the departure of British and allied troops, mainly to the Canal Zone, and the return of top management to the Estate Office, a very different atmosphere prevailed.

Much of this new Smouha City was greatly affected by what was happening outside it.

The greatly diminished British influence found a replacement in the increasing influence of local politicians.

Add to this the striking new existence of the foundation of Israel and the early power of anti-royal (Farouk) political sentiment in Alexandria as in the rest of Egypt, which fast became a very different country in which to live and do business.

More and more often the Smouha lunchtime business discussions concerned politics and – I clearly remember – politicians. Smouha City was no longer a developing former lake but was fast becoming part of the City of Alexandria – in fact at that time approximately one-sixth of Alexandria's land-mass.

Despite all this, Joseph Smouha never wavered in his attitudes and way of life.

Nevertheless, by the Fifties and way into his Seventies he left much more daily power in the hands of his sons but still maintained complete control over policy and major decisions. At this point I feel compelled to return more specifically to a remark made in my introduction – life expectancy.

Just after the war life expectancy in the developed countries in Europe was 67 years, so that with the inevitable effect on his energy and capacity, Joseph Smouha living in Egypt could easily have been described as an "old man."

To complete my argument the equivalent life expectancy today is 82, indicating an increase of one year every four years. At the same time, both his sons, and I clearly remember this, took time to settle down after the strains and tensions of the war. Uncle Ellis had been invalided out of the RAF, and Teddy Smouha who had had an extremely active but exhausting war, were no longer in the same form as they had been eight years earlier.

My father was only "demobbed" in 1947 and even then did not rush to get back to Egypt until he had settled, among other tasks, the all-important aspects of his children's education.

10.3 Politics and Sequestration

The copy of the letter from the Sequestrator of Smouha properties to his boss translated below is indistinct and complete accuracy of the translation cannot be guaranteed at every point.

To the Sequestrator General, the property of British Subjects.
Sharia Bustan, Cairo, March 16, 1958.
After compliments.
With reference to your letter No. 3961 (*the number is indistinct*) of the 11 instant concerning the properties of Youssef Smouha, I have the honour to inform you that I have learned that the Office of the Sequestrator-General has sold to the Agricultural Reform Co-operative Societies the lands which we previously handed over to the reform to be administered on the account of that organization. This sale is not in accordance with the law nor with the true situation, since all these lands, and the remaining properties of Youssef Smouha which are now under my sequestration, are building lands divided into plots and situated within the boundaries of the city within the meaning of the decision of the Maglies Tanzim of the city of Alexandria issued in 1932 and confirmed by the decree issued on April 17, 1941 and published in the Journal Official (*Journal Officiel*) n. 58 of May 12, 1941.
I therefore consider it my duty to explain to you the history of this matter in as much detail as possible, relying on •••••• (*word illegible*) and maps and contracts and decrees: so that if you are satisfied with the points of view and the proofs which are laid before you, you may stop this sale and withhold authentication of it.

In 1923 Mr. Youssef Smouha bought 750 feddans in the neighbourhood of Al Hadra and Antoniadis and Sidi Gaber, that is Lake Hadra.

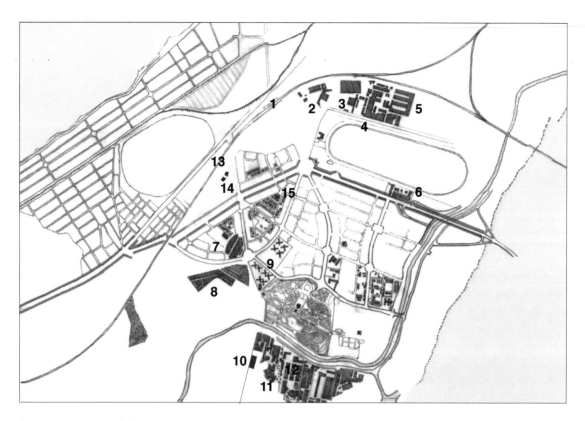

Smouha City in 1978 (C. Pallini's reconstruction).
Legend: 1. Sidi Gaber Railway Station; 2.
"El Nil" Public Transport Co.; 3. Ford Egypt;
4. Transport & Engineering Co.; 5. Tyre
Factory; 6. "El Nil" Public Transport Co.;
7. Textile Factory Stéa; 8. Textile Factory;
9. Cité des Etudiants; 10. Nouzha Railway
Station; 11. Brick Factory; 12. Société Nasr
Appareils Electriques; 13. Coptich Church;
14. Catholic Church; 15. Mosque.

opposite
Map of Google Earth, 2014.

He knew at the time that the question of draining the lake was under discussion between ex-prince Omar Toussoun as heir of the
two ex-princes Mohammed Ali and Amr Ibrahim, and the Ministry
of Works, the Government requiring in this case the payment of
£8,000 and undertaking to pay anything in excess of this, but
presumably Toussoun did not accept this.

Mr. Smouha then came forward with an acceptance of this offer; and the Government made it a condition that he should pay
£10,000 and build a public drain at his expense and thereafter
hand it over to the municipality; and moreover that he should
construct two other drains to lead off the water arising from lands
next to the lake. He accepted this. The cost of constructing these
drains amounted to £4,000. He was then obliged to pay a further
sum of £2,000 to the Municipality in 1934.

In order to facilitate communication between Ramleh, Alexandria, and the gardens of Antoniadis and Al Nouzha, constructing
three tunnels under the railway. These are the Mustapha Pasha,
Cleopatra and Ibrahimieh tunnel; and they cost about £43,670

When he produced … the map of the division of the city in 1933,
Mr. Smouha donated to the Municipality 721,269 square meters,
or the equivalent of 172 feddans, in accordance with an official
contract on May 30, 1933, that is the streets and squares in which
had been completed the paving, lightening, water and electricity
supplies, telephone and some sewers, the rest of which will be
completed soon.

Mr. Smouha then bought some land near the Mellahat land and
donated some of it to the Municipality, also for streets.

He also bought from the railway some land from which the lines had been removed elsewhere. The total amount of land bought by Mr. Smouha in this area eventually amounted to feddans 769/20/13, and the amount, which he donated to the Municipality, came to 195 feddans. All the lands owned by Mr. Yousseff Smouha and his sons, except the land of the Sports Club and the race track, are divided into plots of varying areas, as is confirmed by the maps attested by the Municipality of Alexandria which are in our possession.

These plots were offered for sale by the pic, at prices varying in accordance with the situation of each plot, and on long-term instalments. Mr. Smouha used to provide the purchasers with credits for building over a long period. Conditions in the second World War, however, caused him to stop the provision of these credits, and he confined himself to the sale of the land on instalments, placing on building •••••• (*words illegible*) certain conditions, in that he fixed certain plots for the building of villas, others for blocks of flats and others for construction of workshops, garages, schools and other things. For the comfort, security and peace of the inhabitants of the city he created on his own account a Post Office and a Police Post let at a normal rent and built a Sporting Club race track which he let to the Racing Club for twelve years, providing that they should hold races once a fortnight alternating with the sporting club – all this in the knowledge that the idea of building a race track was one of the most important points in the expansion and development of the city of Alexandria. He also built 306 stables which he let on yearly

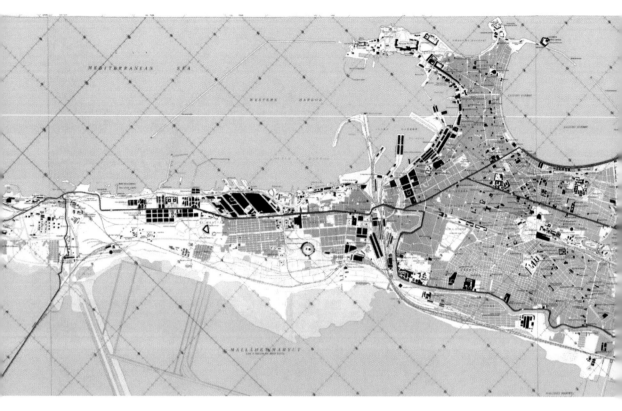

Map of Alexandria, U.S. Army Map Service,
Washington, 1958.

leases to race-horse owners and •••••• (*word illegible*) and built a
riding school. The joint Transport Administration put on two lines
of buses, which passed through this city to the middle of Alexandria. Again, the Ministry of Education built primary, preparatory
and secondary schools for boys and girls and set up lodging for
foreign students at the university.

How could all these things be put in the middle of fields if these
lands are not building lands?

But in view of the size of this city and the long time needed to sell
it all Mr. Smouha decided to use some parts of it for cultivation
by leasing it to dealers in vegetable and fruit. These leases, however, resulted in swarms of mosquitoes and flies and unpleasant
odours, which came from the manure which had to be put on
the fields. This caused the inhabitants to complain and grumble,
and some of them decided to leave the place and go elsewhere
and there were few people ready to buy the land. So the owner
evicted the farmers from some of the land near the middle of the
city (about 75 feddans) and left the remaining part away from the
city (214 feddans) around the racecourse on lease to dealers in
vegetables only, not fruit, stipulating in the contract of the lease
that they should leave any plot which was sold. He did in fact
carry out this condition with some farmers when he sold some
plots near the entrance to the city on the side of Moustapha Pacha tunnel.

Among them was a large plot of land on which the Ford Company constructed a large workshop for cars round which was a
garden which improved the looks of the entrance to the city. The

joint Transport Administration and United Spinning Company proposed to ask that we should sell them some of this land for garages and workshops, and we turned the matter over to the Agricultural Sequestration.

When the Office of the Sequestrator-General decided to hand over these agricultural lands to the Agricultural Reform to administer them on the Office's behalf and to its account, its agents took over 214 feddans of agricultural land under cultivation and 36 feddans from within the land near buildings, although there was absolutely no cultivation on it, claiming that it was land suitable for agriculture. We objected to this at the time and wrote on this question to the Agricultural Reform and to the Office of the Sequestrator-General. But receiving no reply, we said no more, taking into consideration that the Agricultural Sequestration and the office of the Sequestrator General were twin branches of the same office. But when I learned that the office of the Sequestrator-General had in fact sold these lands to the Agricultural Reform Co-operatives Societies for a sum equivalent to 70 years' tax, I hastened to write you this letter. The office of the Sequestrator-General may get in touch with the Municipality of Alexandria to discover the truth of all these facts which I have mentioned about Smouha City and about its division into plots from the year 1933 including the lands which are cultivated now; and about the Municipality's ownership of the streets which exist in the middle of the cultivated lands, which shows that the cultivation of the lands is a temporary matter.

The office may also ask the Provincial Government of Behera

about the 78 feddans which ceased to be cultivated in the year 1954, when the provincial Government lifted the tax … from this land in consideration of the fact that it had been laid out for building. The office of Taxation also has definite information about all this, for they are partners in the profits. They have details of the land, which has been divided into plots and their area and price. I wish to explain this to you so that I shall not be blamed in future for failing, as the person responsible, to draw your attention to the facts.

Please accept my highest esteem.

Signed
Ahmed Kamal Raouf
Sequestrator of the Smouha family properties etc.

Copy to:
H. E. the Minister of Agriculture and Agricultural Reform,
H.E. the Minister of Economics.
The Deputy Sequestrator-General for British properties in Alexandria, The Director-General of the Municipality of Alexandria, The Director Of Direct Taxation.

"Incredulity in Cairo over British Role - Smouha Land Claim," *The Daily Telegraph*, 1958

It is interesting to note that no mention in this letter was made of the Villa Smouha, wich was held under separate ownership.

"Cairo newspapers published in English and French today joined their Arabic contemporaries in expressing incredulity that the British should have left the Smouha claim out of account when negotiating the still-unsigned Anglo-Egyptian financial agreement.

The Smouha property is in Alexandria and it is understood that Britain expected that the greater part of it would be returned as sequestrated property. It is believed that the Smouha family are claiming 12,000 sterling pounds an acre."

The *Egyptian Gazette* wrote:

"Mr. Smouha had publicised full details of the claim he was making long before the agreement was initialled last month and had submitted the claim to the British Treasury. If the British had the slightest doubt about the figure they agreed to in respect of the claim, why in heaven's name didn't they voice their doubt before reaching the agreement with Egypt? To haggle with the United Arab Republic on the signing of an agreement to which the British are already committed is not likely to lead to any improvement of in Anglo-Arab relations."

Le Progrès Égyptien:

"After saying that Britain had retreated from her first demand for the establishment of diplomatic relations, asked whether she had

not raised the Smouha question in the hope of obtaining other advantages.

Is it conceivable that British policy has fallen into such a degree of infantilism that its negotiators should have allowed fraud on the part of the Egyptian authorities?"

Transport & Engineering Co. (photo A. Scaccabarozzi, October 2008).

opposite
Smouha mosque (photo A. Scaccabarozzi, October 2008).

These comments are typical. There is no doubt that the agreement will be signed in the end because on practical grounds the Egyptians want it as much as the British. But it looks as though the Egyptians are determined to exploit to the utmost the propaganda value of the situation. According to *Al-Shaab*, 289 feddans of the Smouha Estate have been acquired under the agrarian reform law at the generous price of 420 pounds a feddan. A feddans is just under an acre.

Another account said 30 feddans remained under sequestration and would, presumably, be returned.

10.4 Smouha City, 1956-1977

The years of the sequestration of Smouha City coincided with the adoption of the new Master Plan of Alexandria (inaccessible so far) put into effect in 1960. Those were the early years after the Free Officers' Revolution, marked by State Socialism and so-called decolonization: the building industry was nationalized, as were most buildings owned by foreigners or by members of the Egyptian elite; these were converted into state departments and public institutions (schools, hospitals, etc.).[1]

The Master Plan envisaged industrial development, and areas for social housing in the poorest districts of the city. Abdul Nasser

Sidi Gaber Station (photo A. Scaccabaro-zzi).

Smouha Club at Burg el Arab (photo A. Scaccabarozzi).

Road, the former Rue d'Abukir, was envisaged as the main representative axis of the future. But war with Israel, the subsequent War of Attrition and the run-up to the 1973 war, completely prevented any such formal development. The nation's public funds were entirely devoted to the war effort while demographic growth and migratory movements from the Suez Canal Zone led to a rapid increase in urban population. It may be asked whether or not developments in Smouha City were held back after sequestration, when the land was managed by the Agricultural Reform Cooperative Societies.

A partial answer may be found on comparing the 1958 map with another by the Survey of Egypt drawn from aerial photographs taken in 1977.[2] By that year the four neighbourhoods nearest to Sidi Gaber Station included some 130 villas, while the working-class district between Hadra and Ez Soad had been almost completed. A Coptic Church and a Catholic Church had been built along Rue Tout Ank Amoun parallel to the railway lines. The fine neo-Islamic mosque of Nabi Ali Taleb with its tall minaret marked the point where Rue el Shahid Gawal Hosni (former Boulevard Mohamed Ali) crosses Rue Albert I. Most of the plots along the boulevards were still empty, some owned by the *Garage de la Société de Transport*, the *Depot de la Société de Pétrole de Suez*, the *Société Internationale de Pétrole Egyptien*, the latter two being major oil and gas producers.[3]

The Ford complex had attracted a group of transport-related industries: *the Société de Transport Public el Nil*; *Société de Transport Public*; *Société de Transport et Etude, Usine de Pneumatiques el Nasr*. All these buildings, still standing in 2008, feature a modern style, in line with the townscape of Smouha City. An *Usines de Cuivre* stood by the railway junction of Hagar El Nawateyah. The quadrangular area between the racecourse and Nouzha-Antoniadis Gardens was still mainly devoted to agriculture; a large plot at the entrance of the gardens had been occupied by a religious institution, and a new *Société de Tissage Stéa* plant had been built along Rue Albert I near the Nouzha roundabout.

In front of it were the nine residential units of the *Cité des Etudiants*. Following the 1965-1975 five-year plans, a complex of state-owned industries was built along the left bank of the Mahmoudieh Canal near the railway siding, overlooking the Nouzha-Antoniadis Gardens.

A number of earlier villages - Ezbet Prince Omar Toussoun, Ezbet Baraweyah, Ezbet El Nouzha - had given place to the *Société Nationale el Madareb, Briqueterie, Société Nasr Appareils Electriques, Société de Tissage el Nil, Société de Tissus el Nil, Imprimerie Moharram, Service des Eaux*.

1. See M.F. Awad, R.S. Youakim, "Nouvel Ordre Urbain et Nouvelles dynamiques 1958-2005", *ROMM* 45, 1987-4, pp.187-194.
2. See Survey of Egypt 1:5000, Dressé par Consortium S.F.S/I.G.N. France en 1978, aerial photo of 1977.
3. The Gulf of Suez Oil Company (GUPCO) was established as a joint venture owned in equal shares by BP and EGPC (The Egyptian General Petroleum Company) to extract oil and gas from the Gulf of Suez basin, the Western Desert, and the Nile Delta.
Most wells became operational in the early 1960s. The International Egypt Oil Company (IEOC) was a state-owned oil company established by President Nasser.
See Soala Ariweriokuma, *The Political Economy of Oil and Gas in Africa: The Case of Nigeria*, 2011, p. 7.

11

Marie-Cécile Bruwier

Archaeological Research, 2008 to 2012

The first geophysical survey took place in November 2004 in three different sectors: a bus parking belonging to the port authorities (zone 6), the schoolyards of the Al-Ibrahimieh School (zone 4) and of the Ashraf el-Khaga School (zone 1). "In search of Cleopatra's temple" is the title of the report Dr Sally-Ann Ashton devoted to the results of this survey.

The project was funded by the British Academy and *The Seven Pillars of Wisdom Trust*. Paul and Neil Linford, geophysicists, have conducted the electromagnetic and radar analysis, registering several "positive" anomalies.

From 2008 to 2012, excavations were funded by the Musée royal de Mariemont (funds from the Ministry of the French-speaking community of Belgium with support of the association *Les Amis de Mariemont*), in close cooperation with the Supreme Council of Antiquities and with the logistic and scientific help of the CEAlex.

In November 2008, 25 core-drills were performed, followed in 2009 by archeological surveys and digs. The core-drills suggested that in antiquity, part of this ground served as an "inundation" basin for the Nile, and contributed to clarify the muddy waters coming from the yearly flood.

In Summer 2009, the archaeological survey in the schoolyard of the Al-Ibrahimieh school (zone 4) revealed a large number of granite and limestone blocks covered with hydraulic mortar, as well as limestone capitals and granite columns.

Smaller artifacts were also brought to light, such as fragments of a terracotta oil lamps representing Isis, with her specific crown and two corn ears, and a small bust of her consort Sarapis; at the same time, was discovered a granite block showing a hieroglyphic inscription as part of a royal title.

In 2010, other architectural remains were unearthed, such as the basis of a portico (?) and part of a red granite column, which almost certainly belonged to a large structure, as well as several columns fragments. So-called Gaza amphoras, containing remains of skeletons, and a Saint-Menas bottle tend to date the last use of the site in the Byzantine period.

As for limestone kilns found *in situ*, their use is clear: the dismantling of the monument's stones and their burning for re-use as lime! From January to May 2011, the Supreme Council of Antiquities conducted the excavations on one adjacent grounds, owned by the private companies Al Baroun wa Al Negm Al-Sahily (zone 2). Archeologist Dr Oussama El Nahas conducted the work under the direction of Dr. Mohamed Moustapha Abd al-Megid.

Finally, during the 2012 season, it was decided to explore the last piece of land still to be investigated, situated on the other side of the Lewaa Fawzi Moaaz street (zone 5). 19 trenches, mostly perpendicular to the Moaaz Street were dug, but no further significant parts of the architecture of the antique monument was unearthed there.

What was the Purpose of the Buildings?

Different interpretations regarding the attribution of the monument

The six investigated lands (Google Earth, 2011).

opposite
South West views of the sectors-zone 5 (photos: Vincent Euverte).

are proposed. According to Strabo, there was a place outside Alexandria, called *Eleusis*, in the eastern suburb of the city. But he places this *Eleusis* near the canal.

Other authors, such as Polybius, talk about a *Thesmophorion*: but is this building in the same area? 19th-century scholars seem to interpret the building as the *Thesmophorion* mentioned by Polybius, and created by Ptolemy II, or more simply as a temple of "Demeter and Persephone" or "Ceres and Proserpina." The fragment of lamp with Isis wearing ears of corn was discovered; in 2011, two other fragments of lamp were found, one showing a figure of Sarapis and the other the image of Isis suckling Horus: they do attest to the presence of an Isiac cult. We would remember that Isis was closely related to Demeter by the Greeks. Another interpretation of the "temple" structure could be a *Lageum*, which is a temple dedicated to the Ptolemaic deified kings. Two hieroglyphic inscriptions were unearthed in 2009 and 2011, showing the end of a king's titulary: they indicate that some royal statues or inscriptions mentioning royal persons were present in the excavated monument. The research revealed that the history of the site can be divided into periods.

A monumental structure built on the site was later seriously damaged at various times.

Traces of a group of buildings in their original location were found to be very damaged. During the following period, the monumental structure was dismantled and various parts of the building moved, reworked, or used to stroke limestone kilns. Several of these kilns were found, indicating reuse of the site. In the last period, the loca-

tion was leveled and used as a cemetery. Gradually the site was abandoned, until the draining of the Lake Hadra.

Richard Smouha considers that the Romans prized this area because of the fresh air. The draining of the lake uncovered remains of a Roman spa and many artifacts were rescued. Where have they ended up wonders Richard Smouha.

In the 1960's, several schools, a bus depot, and a police station were built there. In the layers that had not been disturbed, a great deal of archaeological material was found, mainly from the Roman and late Roman periods. The Smouha site definitely dates from the late Roman period, but stone objects have also been found that indicate the existence of a Ptolemaic monument.

The excavations have at least proven that a significant monument once stood on this spot, which was outside Alexandria in antiquity and that an important complex was built on the banks of Lake Hadra.

12 Richard Smouha
The National Archives & the Smouha Family House

12.1 The National Archives

You will have read (see *The Man* and *Sent to Egypt*) some divergence of the story covering Joseph Smouha's trips to the Middle East and many of the facts covering these journeys. The main reason was that during the period at the end of the First World War, the whole area covering Egypt, Persia, Mesopotamia, Palestine, etc. was under strict British military control, some of which was carried out on the spot (I have already discussed at enough length the state of communications nearly a century ago) and some from London, a situation that created confusion. I therefore decided that I would check whether there was anything in the UK National Archives in Kew, which could provide more information on the subject. That turned out to be an adventure on its own.

The National Archives are housed in a huge modern building some 10-15 minutes' walk from Kew underground station, fronted by an enormous pond. Once inside one discovers that one does not exist without a Readers Card. To obtain one of these, one is placed in front of a computer and must answer some 30 or so triple-choice questions. Getting there and all this had taken up nearly all the morning. I am ashamed to say that I rushed through questions such as, "If you see a book on the floor, do you pick it up, call someone or stop people touching it?" I was told that my results were among the worst anyone had seen but I would nevertheless be awarded a card: I think my age, and the fact that I was wearing a tie, helped.

By telephone I had discovered a file FOI 1004/525 under the name Joseph Smouha. I asked to see it as his grandson and was told it was closed until 2045. In shock, I said I was also looking for files between 1917 and 1921. They could not find them and let out that this one covered 1959 to 1969. I had to leave. Sometime later I received a very detailed letter from the National Archives giving information concerning eight files covering 1917 to 1919. On my next trip to London – remembering the importance of the Readers Card, I had put it in the safest place I could think of, and promptly forgot where that was – I was fortunately not required to go through all the original rigmarole as they had a copy of my card and photo on computer. A number of the eight references have been discarded as historically irrelevant but the results of the information from the others can be found in the chapter *The Man*.

So I was left with the Joseph Smouha file closed until 2045. With the assistance of specialist lawyers I applied as Joseph Smouha's grandson to open it. In vain it was refused. I appealed and received a second non-motivated refusal, other than an explanation of the reasons that the regulations gave for a refusal.

I have asked for evidence or at least confirmation of any work carried out in justification of the refusal. At a later date I discovered two further files carrying the Smouha family name and which are closed until 2055. I had always assumed that the longer legitimate closing of file was thirty years. But it is not so. There is no official limit and the criteria for the decision to close for this abnormally long period are, I am told, extremely complex. Later still I discovered the first 75-year closure via a book by Saul David called "Mutiny at Salerno 1943 – An injustice exposed". I believe that such a long period raises all kinds of doubts and questions. An article in *The Times* newspaper dated 7 April 2011. On Page 2 – concludes, "The truth is long overdue."

12.2 The Smouha Family House

In one way the situation of the family house does not fit into a history of Smouha City. In another way it does: Smouha City was held in the name of an entity called Smouha Family Estates whereas the house was in Joseph Smouha's personal name. While the one was confiscated, sequestrated, nationalizad, the other was left untouched and was never formally taken out of the family ownership but used by the State.

Alan Mcgregor, who was *The Times* correspondent in Egypt for 25 years and who has left me all his research on the Smouha family, wrote the following delightful description about the house entitled: *The Big House Near Stanley Bay*.

"The high garden wall, red bougainvillaea spilling over it, of the house into which Joseph Smouha and his family moved in 1927, abutted on the road above the Corniche at Bulkeley, a tranquil residential area cooled by fresh breezes from the sea. Near the delectable beach of white sand at Stanley Bay, it forms part of suburban Ramleh, once known as the 'Ostend of Egypt,' located seven or so kilometres east along the coast from the centre of Alexandria. This was to be their home for almost three decades, until, that is, the precipitate enforced departure from Egypt of many foreign and Jewish residents in 1956, after Britain, France and Israel had tried unsuccessfully to unseat Gamal Abdel Nasser's government and reverse the nationalization of the Suez Canal the previous year. The Italianate-style mansion built about the turn of the century and set in a vast garden with carefully tended lawns and flowerbeds, jacaranda, eucalyptus, acacia. Aleppo pine and flame trees, and also a big swimming pool, underwent several structural alterations for its new occupants, living in a rented villa nearby while the work was in hand. The most obvious change was the creation of a large lounge, some 25 metres by ten, most of one side being an extended window with a heart-stirring panorama of sea and Corniche. The dining room overlooked the garden to the rear, and the library and billiards room were similarly of generous proportions, complemented by two drawing rooms, kitchen, scullery and storerooms. The first floor contained bedrooms and bathrooms, plus boxrooms and linen cupboards."

In the 1930's another building was added, at the far end of the garden. This had a garage for seven cars on the ground floor, and, above, two stories, each with a family-size luxury flat – but no lift – that would later house Ellis and the youngest daughter, Edna,

Villa Smouha in Bulkeley (R. Smouha's archive).

each with their two children.

It was only at the turn of this century that we became aware of two pieces of supposed information concerning the family house. The first was that sequestration did not apply to houses, which had been in use as family houses. I personally believe that this simple statement was a misinterpretation of some specific rule and not a generalization. The second was that our family house had been overlooked, had never been sequestrated and was still in our name on the Land Register.

The house, inhabited by a succession of government entities and then occupied by successive Presidents, still belonged to us! Without going into more detail, my brother Brian and I decided to follow this up.

My brother Brian was friendly with the then Egyptian Ambassador Dr. Mohamed Shaker in London, and discussed our problem with him. Dr. Shaker recommended a friend of his, a former ambassador turned lawyer, called Salah Bassiouny. He sent me a resume of the series of decrees and laws that had been promulgated since 1962. In particular a number of new laws and court decisions from 1981 have specific relevance. The 1981 law states that properties not sold are to be returned to owners (natural persons) and must be compensated with the sale price plus 50% plus annual interest.

On 21 June 1986, the High Constitutional Court ruled unconstitutional Article 2 of the 1981 law and that all properties should be returned to their owners. Since the publication of that judgement in the Official Gazette, on 3 July 1986, any owner had the right to reclaim his property. Then, on 22 March 1998, the Prime Minister of Egypt issued a decree by which all insurance companies and government organs were obliged to return the properties that were sequestrated and not sold again to third parties.

Then followed a long and highly frustrating period during which we tried to obtain the required documents: proofs of inheritance and especially translations and confirmations of everything. It was however finally completed and we were then able to start with the real issue at hand.

I was lucky enough, at the time of improving relations between Israel and Egypt, to meet Salah Bassiouny, on a diplomatic mission in Geneva, one year or so before his untimely death. I remember him well, a man of my own age and of a rare kind of personality and whose chemistry and attitudes fitted so well with mine.

He advised that the only effective way to obtain satisfaction was through the courts. He brought an action in court on our behalf after the months that it had taken to obtain the necessary documentation and authorisation proving our identities and entitlement as heirs to our grandfather. To give only one example of the complications of documentation through three generations was the added fact that the address of the house had changed, as had also the name of the road.

In an email received from our lawyer on 29.12.2001:
> ... we dig in your file (sic)... was not an easy job which cost us a lot of time and money ... and the following is a resume of his advice:
> 1. The Compensation Agreement between Egypt and the UK on 28.2.1959 which dealt with UK properties under sequestration did not include the house. The only reference to Smouha in the annexe to the agreement refers to the agricultural land.
> 2. Because the house was excluded, a new order, No 140 of 1961 imposed sequestration on Joseph Smouha and family (the list includes 261 names, many are good Egyptian families).
> 3. Based on this order the Sequestration Department sold half the property to the Egyptian National Insurance on 1.1.1964.
> 4. The other half was sold to the Ministry of Finance on 22.4.1967, both were notarised in 1977 and then the whole property was delivered to the Presidency and became the Residence of Vice- President Mubarak. After he became President, it became the Presidential guesthouse and still is.
> 5. The High Constitutional Court ruled that all laws, which gave the Government the right to sell properties under sequestration, are unconstitutional.
> 6 ... The counter-argument ... is prescription of 15 years. But such argument could be forfeited so long as the possession of the property was unlawful from the start and the owners were in no position under prevailing unconstitutional laws to claim it.

We believe we are in a fairly good position to proceed before the Court of Ethics for the return of the property (not compensation).

Finally and most importantly, I received an email giving a summary of the claim submitted to the Court of Ethics, which reads as follows:

1. Legal proof of the property through four consecutive notarized sale contracts (1924, 1939, 1932, 1944) by which Mr. J. Smouha bought four plots of land which constitute the whole of the property (details).

2. The Egyptian/UK agreement of 28.2.1959 excluded the property of Mr. J. Smouha, the property of 48 Mobisson Street, Bulkeley was not mentioned and not compensated for (details and analysis).

3. In spite of the above, the property was put under sequestration without any legal grounds.

4. Then on 1.1.1964 the Sequestration Department sold part of the property to the National Insurance Company. On 22.4.1967, it sold the other part to the Ministry of Finance. In both case the Sequestration Department claimed wrongfully that these properties were part of the Egyptian/UK agreement! (details).

5. According to Article 1 of Law 141 of 1981, "sequestration to be lifted on properties of natural persons which were imposed on them by Presidential decrees based on the Emergency Law." Article 2 of this law stipulated that properties, which became property of the State, should be compensated to the owners. The High Constitutional Court rules that Article 2 is unconstitutional; accordingly, the State is obliged to return the properties to its owners (details and legal interpretation).

Based on the above facts and legal grounds, the claimants demand return of their property and all accrued benefits and interest since 1956, to rule that the two sale contracts of 1.1.1964 and 22.4.1967 are null and void.

6. We presented with the claim all the relevant documents which we were able to acquire through our means during the past months and expect the court to inform us of the date of the first hearing.

At first I could not understand the purchase of the additional plot in 1944. Then it suddenly came to me. How ironic! This has to be the plot that my grandfather bought and gifted for the construction of a mosque, paying also for the building. (see *The Man*). Was the intention really to include this in the properties supposedly to be sequestrated but in fact overlooked?

The first hearing took place on 15 June 2002 before the Second Circuit of the Court of Ethics. The legal summons, the legalized part of the will and the powers of attorney were all accepted. The State lawyer asked for a postponement and the hearing was adjourned to 5 October 2002. At this hearing the State Attorney requested another postponement to examine further the claim and the case. The court deferred to 16 November 2002 for the state to submit its memorandum and present its documents. Bassiouny then informed us that in another case where he represented the plaintiffs, the Court of Ethics had ruled against prescription and that this should have a bearing on our case.

Then – I don't have the exact date – a sad, sad event at the end of November: this man to whom I felt so close, for whom I had such great respect, died in his sleep prematurely at the age of 71.

A few days later in a long email his son Omar Salah informed me that he was taking over his father's practice and would be happy to take over the case. At the same time he gave me an update on the latest hearing, which took place on the 16 November when the State lawyer presented its documents. The hearing was postponed to 1 February 2003 to allow time to review them and prepare a reply.

The following is a resume from Omar of great significance from 23.12.2002:

23.11.1967: refusal by the Confiscation Department to hand over funds and shares belonging specifically to Yvonne Smouha (presumably in answer to a claim that she was not part of the sequestration of the Smouha Family Estates, being the entity, the subject of the sequestration); and the appearance of an undated letter from the State Properties Department that per the Egypt/UK agreement dated 24.4.1969 "family" includes wife and children but not grandchildren!

As well as a 1969 letter from Confiscation Department to Bank Misr authorising release of shares.

And lastly an undated agreement with Moursi Badr authorising release of shares but no evidence that this was carried out.

Replies:

The above documentation concerning liquid funds and shares has no relation to the subject matter of this case, being real estate. This documentation obviously weakens the State's position as no reference is made to real estate, the subject of the claim. Contradictions in the comments concerning the shares and liquid funds:

a) they say they are not available,

b) in agreement to release them and

c) there is no evidence of releasing them.

Lastly and most importantly, the 1967 Convention refers specifically to shares and liquid funds with the exception of real estate, which, in accordance with Egyptian Law, may be re-appropriated in favour of the grandchildren of the person subject of the confiscation or nationalisation. Again we ran into problems of documentation – this time the powers of attorney of my mother and brother – which took us right through the end of the year and through January and February of 2003, then a public holiday in Egypt. In the meantime the judge set the next hearing for 15 March. After all this we were sent a copy of a recent judgment where the Court of Ethics had decided that it should not deal with cases of sequestrated property! Then on 15 March the hearing was adjourned to 19 April for judgment.

A long email from Omar starting, "Dear Richard, I trust this email finds you in great spirit" 15.5.2003. He then informed us that someone from the Experts Office subordinate to the Ministry of Justice will be appointed to examine the documentation (or its absence!) on two properties (we are only concerned with one: the house), to report on the surface, specifics, legal owner and title deeds and that the Smouha family were owners at the time of confiscation.

If this is found to be the case, the next question is whether they were compensated under the 28.2.1959 Compensation Declaration or any other. The expert must then identify the share of the two properties and the possibility of returning the properties in kind. If this is impossible, the expert will identify the value in the current market price and each share, the total accumulated proceeds from the date the custody was imposed and the share to date. The hearing fixed for 7.6.2003. Expert's fees paid by Omar.

We then received the following information every few months from Omar:

28.10.2003: "We are still at the stage of waiting for the court to name the official from the Judicial Experts Office who is to do this."

6.12.2003: "… we are still attempting to expedite the first experts session. I share your frustration in relation to this unreasonable delay which is completely out of our hands in light of the bureaucracy associated with litigation in Egypt." He continued saying that he sent a senior litigator to attempt to expedite the process through his contacts in the Official Bureau of Judicial Experts.

3.3.2004: "we attended the first expert hearing session last Sunday. Our counterparts, the State lawyers did not attend the session and hence the expert postponed the next session to the 24.4.2004."

My frustration shows:

3.3.2004: "Dear Omar, the expert must be getting quite old now -yani- min zeman. (that is, it`s been a long time). Whose turn is it next "not to attend"? I presume there is nothing else we can do except wait and get older."

5.4.2004: "... the expert has issued a letter last week… requesting the court to appoint a tripartite committee of experts as he feels an "embarrassment" in light of the identity of our opponents (i.e. the President of the Republic of Egypt). In our personal assessment, we believe that the expert has feared to issue his opinion in connection with our claims. I attach a copy of the expert's letter to the court as well as the letter he received from the Cabinet of the President (which was attached to his letter to the court and which in our opinion triggered his fear) … to discuss the matter further."

Court of Ethics Judgment, 15.5.2004

Whereas … the expert returned the file without completing his mission because of "embarrassment" because of some circumstances he did not disclose but the court noticed that he attached a letter from the Presidency.

> "Whereas, according to the law of evidence, claiming any of the responsible persons personally or by his capacity don't give the reason … the Ministry of Finance (my note: the seller of the property) is the only one competent in all cases of sequestration as head of the Sequestration Department."

Nevertheless the court "approved" the expert's desire to abandon his mission and instructed the experts office to delegate a "superior committee of three experts" to carry out the mission.

The experts must deposit the report two weeks before 2.10.2004. The case was postponed till 18.12.2004.

But during this period, our lawyer reported that the expert got frightened, tore up his report and resigned (I wonder if he kept a copy or whether we can still locate him). Anyway during this period our lawyer pressed the court to go forward. The judge suggested proceeding along the same lines but this time would appoint a Commission of three experts whom he considered to be sufficiently resistant (correctly as it turned out).

30.11.2004: Brian and I agree to this idea and give "court action" one last chance, asking for details and cost. Omar Bassiouny offers to bear the costs because he is so disappointed with the situation in Egyptian courts.

8.12.2004 and 21.2.2005: In view of everything Brian and I agree to pay 10,000 dollars, treating this as the equivalent of an appeal in line with our agreement.

10.5.2005: "… At last the Tripartite Committee Experts hearing has been scheduled for 15.5.2005. The initial scheduling we received was for 14.7.2005 but we submitted a petition to the Head of the Alexandria Experts Bureau requesting an earlier date in light of the severe delays we had to face so far. The petition was accepted …"

23.5.2005: The Presidency presented a two-page memorandum of defence and the hearing was adjourned to 29.5.2005.

Another big gap in my documentation during which the firm of Matouk and Bassiouny joined the DLA Piper Group.

10.11.2005: "…The hearing of 25.10.2005 is adjourned to 27.11.2005 because the experts committee was incomplete." From Laila El Shentanawi, Junior Associate DLA Matouk Bassiouny. The last hearing took place on 18.5.2006: report from Laila el Shentanawi and Aliaa Salah El Din:

The Tripartite Committee held an inspection of the properties.

1. The representatives of the Egyptian Presidency claimed that the Egyptian Government had compensated the British Government for all the nationalised properties according to the agreement dated March 16, 1959.

2. The above was answered as follows:

3. The above-mentioned agreement did not include these properties. The Smouha family did not receive compensation from the

Egyptian Government for these properties. There are no documents confirming any compensation.

4.The Court requested a report giving the surface area of the properties. The response was that we are unable to do this as it was not permitted to enter in said area as it is restricted by the Egyptian Presidency.

5. We emphasized that the Egyptian Presidency and Government representatives are hindering, obstructing and delaying the procedures of the case.

The Court requested the following documents for the next hearing:

1. Documents proving the ownership of the properties (i.e. the lease contract with the insurance company) to be submitted by the representative of the Egyptian Presidency

2. The area maps of the properties from the concerned authority at Alexandria – by us. Do you mean?

Then yet another long period where we had great difficulty obtaining even a connection with anyone either by telephone or by email. We have many email requests and notes thereof.

5.1.2007: "Relitigation Update Reference to court case No. 42 for the year 200 Judicial … against the Presidency of the Arab Republic of Egypt … development report …"

1. The case was reviewed by the court and was referred to the Experts Commission of the Ministry of Justice at Alexandria.

2. We have attended 13 expert hearings in Alexandria due to the change in the composition of the experts panel as previously outlined.

3. We then conducted a field visit to the Presidential Rest House in view to examine the real property thoroughly along with the appointed expert and the government lawyers.

4. During the field visit, we found that the real subject was composed of two buildings, one owned by the Ministry of Finance and the other by the National Insurance Company and leased to the Presidency by virtue of a lease contract.

5. Subsequently we requested the Presidency to submit evidence that the Smouha family had been compensated for the said buildings.

The Presidency submitted a number of treaties signed between the UK and Egypt …

6. We responded … not collected any compensation and challenged the Presidency to submit any documentation …

7. As the respondent failed to provide any documentation … the government argued that the case was subject to the statutes of limitations due to the elapse of fifteen years.

However we argued back that the inheritors were residents outside … and the matter of statutes of limitation is not within the competence of the expert.

The appointed expert is expected to supply the court with the case file for a review of the report on 3.2.2007.

9.1.2007: Dear Richard, I would like to apologize for the delay in sending you the written update as previously promised. However I was under the impression that one of our associates had already sent it to you ….

On an informal level I have been in contact with a senior ranking official at the Presidency to attempt to resolve the matter on an amicable basis and he recently informed me that the Senior Legal Counsel to the Presidency is against any amicable settlement. He further informed me to expect pressure on the court from the said gentlemen to dismiss the case. I informed him that any such action could prejudice the image of the Egyptian judiciary before international investors …

Then another very long period when we received no news other than that the experts were at work. Then early May I had a conversation with Omar's brother who told me that the experts claimed that we had been compensated, in addition to which there appeared to be a new rule against bringing a court action against the Presidency, and that in any case the action should have been brought in another court.

Finally, and we have presumed that this is a judgment on "the facts", an email from Laila el Shentanawi dated 12.11.2007 and entitled status report.

"…The confiscation included the family house as it is considered as part of the land. We claimed before that the house is not covered under the Compensation Treaty" … because the treaty stipulates that the compensation is made only for certain types of properties (i.e. agricultural land). However, the respondents claimed that the criterion mentioned in the treaty included the house. The court adopted this interpretation. Consequently the court ruled that the house was confiscated according to the Martial decision and compensation was given according to the treaty.

An email from my brother dated 21.11.2007:
"We question how the court could take a decision based on a treaty that they had not seen. Please would you send us a copy of the treaty, which says that the house and the land of the house are included. For your information the main property sequestrated was in the name of an entity called Smouha Family Estates whilst Joseph Smouha personally held the house and its contents. No mention has been made of the valuable contents of the house such as art, valuable furniture, rare carpets and personal jewellery, which should have been returned to Joseph Smouha or his family. If no copy of the treaty is forthcoming please make an appeal on the grounds that the respondent has not shown that it has any right to deprive us of our house property and personal possessions. Also we have been informed that there was a decree issued which specifically gives the rights to owners of houses to repossess them or to make a claim."

I must add one or two comments of my own – based on an email of 29.12.2001 from my much regretted and respected friend Salah

Bassiouny:

1. The Compensation Agreement of 28 February 1959 (not 1956) did not include the house as it only specified agricultural land. However the judge adopted the argument of the respondents claiming that the 1959 agreement included the house. Why does our document say Martial decision No. 5 of year 1956? Why then would it be necessary to sequestrate the house in 1961?

2. The house was sequestrated by No. 140 of 1961 without compensation.

3. Therefore the sale contract of 1964 saying the house is state property because of the compensation agreement is wrong.

4. The High Constitutional Court ruled that all laws which gave the Government the right to sell property under sequestration are unconstitutional.

5. Therefore the sale of the property to the National Insurance Company (as well as the one to the Ministry of Finance) should be considered as null and void.

6. Further confusion is due to the fact that Smouha City belonged to Smouha Family Estates (13 beneficiaries) while the house belonged to Joseph Smouha personally (with two beneficiaries, namely Richard Smouha and Brian Smouha).

We decide that there was too much pressure from the Presidency for it to be worthwhile carrying on.

Then everything was turned upside down with the disappearance of Moubarak from the scene followed by the cancellation, as I understand it, of the Court of Ethics and all its judgements. We are back in the fray.

Cristina Pallini

Annexes

- The Competition Programme
- Report of the Jury
- Correspondence between J. Smouha and L.L. Secchi
- Documents from the Musée Social, Paris
- References for Smouha City: Welwyn and Heliopolis
- Two maps of Smouha City
- Members of the "Race-horse Owners' Association"
- List of British claims in Egypt
- Bibliographical note
- List of newspaper cuttings in R. Smouha's archive

The Competition Programme

Secchi-Tarugi's Archive, Milan.

(typewritten document held at the Secchi Tarugi family archive, Milan, translated from French into English by Richard Smouha)

Concerning the arrangement of a plan of a city -
Sidi Gaber, Suburb of Alexandria

Mr. Joseph Smouha herewith initiates a competition with the object of collating ideas for a plan of arrangement of a limited area of land shown on the attached plan 1:5000 by a red border and projected for a new town as a suburb of the city of Alexandria.

This modern city is to be built on the land of his property situated between the village of Hadra, the public gardens of Nouzha, the promenade along the Mahmoudieh Canal, the State railway network including the Hadra and Sidi Gaber railway stations.

Each candidate is completely free to draw on his own original ideas but in the detail of his project he must not neglect the imposed requirements of aesthetics, technical and health as well as the social and economic requirements, he should even respect them and agree them strictly with the psychic aspects which have priority and which point the way artistically in the construction of a new modern city. The creators must, to a large extent, avoid too strict a line, and avoid giving too little weight artistically, leading to too much regularity and which then results in little variation and too much monotony overall reducing its outstanding aesthetic characteristics without the advantages of the basic requirements of speculation and circulation.

The competitors must seek the means to show from different points of view the various elements of their plan of edility such as the private and public buildings, the apartment blocks to be constructed, the roads, the alleys for horseback riding, the crossroads, the parks, the squares and intersections, the watering places, the plantations, the level crossings, the transit across the railway lines, the tramways, the lighting, and all other accessories including the essential graphic examples, and taking into account all the best work of recent years in England, France, Germany, Austria, Belgium, and more recently in Italy.

As Camille Sitte and Buls say, and with reason, we are still far from the ideal of these former examples but we should digest what has been done in the recent past, now that this America, the creator of these tiresome chessboard-type cities with their unaesthetic houses in the shape of boxes, and the examples of which make us regret.

Our competitors will have to provide in the competition:
1. A main plan at the scale of 1:5000 carrying indications of the dimensions of the roads and squares, configuration of the crossroads and places with traffic and circulation, the areas for public buildings, the system of the living quarters with their outhouses and their courtyards wide and open to the main roads and

circulation and traffic, graceful areas for sports and recreation, squares and gardens, creation of blocks for individual citizens' housing, both isolated and in series, with or without front lawns, and those destined to be luxury homes; disposition of the labourers' city in accordance with the requirements of the new hygienic regulations. The situation of the buildings, in relation to the rest of the city must be chosen in such a way that they are easily identified: and in such a way as to create an aesthetic impression and not isolated but in relation with the road network and avoid creating situations which interfere with the general traffic circulation.

The public buildings will include a mosque, a synagogue, an orthodox church (sic), a Catholic church and a Protestant temple, two schools, two police stations, post and telegraph offices, a fire station, public assistance, a theatre, two cinemas, one or two markets and finally everything necessary for the development of the new town.

2. As an example, a plan of the allotments of one part of the blocks of each category that is to say: outhouses, private buildings, villas and labourers housing on a scale of 1:2000.

3. A detailed plan of these parts emphasizing the artistic and traffic aspects on a scale of 1:1000.

4. Illustration in perspective of specific points that the author feels the need to submit.

5. A bird's-eye view of the whole.

6. Several profiles of the main roads and avenues on a scale of 1:50.

7. A summary statement of the surfaces of the roads, boulevards, squares etc. in relation with the total area of the blocks to be built.

8. A report explaining and describing the project as a whole.

9. A variant covering the arrangement of a sports club with a racecourse, without affecting the overall plan in any way. The total surface of the racecourse must not exceed approximately 500,000 square metres.

This competition will be open only to architects and engineers invited by letter from Mr. Smouha.

The competitors must present their project by midday on 1st October 1925 at the address of Mr. Smouha in Alexandria, rue Port Est, Building Heikal, in a double envelope, with the inside envelope carrying the inscription "PROJECT FOR THE NEW CITY AT SIDI GABER".

Each project and all the accompanying documents must carry a distinctive sign or mention reproduced on a sealed envelope in which there is a bulletin showing the name and address of the competitor. Any attempt to show the identity of a competitor before and during the judgment will entail his disqualification.

The projects presented after the 1st October will definitely be refused and their authors will no longer have the right to take part in the competition. After the judgment, Mr. Smouha reserves the right to exhibit the winning projects for a period of fifteen days.

The non-winning projects and any which are not withdrawn two months after the judgment, Mr. Smouha will have the right to open the sealed envelope, discover the nationality of the competitor and deposit these projects with the competent authorities. At the risk for the authors, and if these authorities refuse to accept them, they will remain as the property of Mr. Smouha and the authors will not have the right to recover them nor to receive any remuneration for them. The jury will be composed of Mr. Smouha, as owner. Mr. Antonio Lasciac Bey, formerly Chief Architect of the Khedivial Palaces, and Mr. Paul Conin Pastour, General Manager at the Ministry of Public Works. Mr. J. Smouha will put at the disposal of the jury the sum of one thousand Egyptian pounds - LEg 1000 allocated for the prizes.

The prizes will be:

LEg 500 for the first

LEg 200 for the second

LEg 100 for the third

If the jury should believe it necessary, it may require the prizewinning authors to provide Mr. Smouha with a general plan of allotments for all the blocks (see Art. 2 where it gives an example of allotment to allotment) for a price of 1Eg.500. - five hundred Egyptian pounds. For this reason Mr. Smouha will retain the half of the prize money until receipt of the requested details.

Mr. Smouha will retain the right to give this order for a period of three months. The complement of details requested must be carried out within a period of three months and be subject to the approval of the jury for it to be accepted.

If the Jury, after the allocation of the prizes, discovers other projects worthy of an honourable mention, Mr. Smouha may offer the authors in question a purchase price which must not exceed LEg 50 - Fifty Egyptian pounds, and the owner of the prize payments is free to carry out or not carry out the projects of works, as also if carried out he will be entirely free to use either completely or partially the ideas of the prizewinning competitors in order to establish a new overall plan, and this without the cooperation of one or other of the other prizewinners.

Signed by   *Daniel Delbourgo, Mr. Smouha's General Manager*

Report of the Jury
Secchi-Tarugi's Archive, Milan.

(Transcription of the handwritten copy enclosed with a letter by J. Smouha to L. Secchi of 29 December 1925)

L'an mil neuf cent vingt-cinq (1925) et le vingt-et-un décembre à neuf heures du matin.

Aux Bureaux de Mr. Joseph Smouha, à Alexandrie, rue Cherif Pacha. Se sont réunis:

Messers: Joseph Smouha, Paul Conin Pastour, Antonio Lasciac formant le jury prévu dans le programme du concours pour l'aménagement du plan de la ville de Sidi Gaber banlieue d'Alexandrie. Monsieur A. Lasciac Bey fait son rapport sur les projets qui sont soumis par le concurrentes au nombre de onze.

Le jury procède à l'examen de chacun de ces projets pour décerner les trois prix promis, le jury écarté de sa décisions pour ces pris, sept projets correspondant le moins aux conditions du concours.

L'attention du jury est retenue par quatre projets, à savoir: "Urbs", "Three Stars", "Ars", "Vox Populi."

Après délibération entre les nombres de jury, il été décidé à l'unanimité ;
- Pour le premier prix : aucun projet n'ayant répondu d'une façon complète aux conditions du concours, le jury a décidé qu'il n'y a pas lieu de décerner ce prix aux concurrents ;
- Le deuxième prix est décerne à l'auteur de projet "Urbs";
- Quant au troisième prix, bien que fixé à la seule somme de LEg 100, le jury décide, également à l'unanimité, de décerner pareille somme de LEg 100 à chacun des trois projets, à savoir: "Three Stars", "Ars", "Vox Populi;"
- Quant aux sept projets ci-dessus, le jury décide de leur décerner à chacun la somme de LEg 50 à titre de mention honorable et a charge par les concurrents de faire abandon de leurs plans à Mr. Smouha, conformément aux dispositions du concours.

Les décisions ainsi prises, le jury procède à l'ouverture des plis contenant les noms des concurrents et constate que:
- l'auteur du projet "Urbs" est Maurice Clauzier, 5 Bd. de la République, Reims;
- l'auteur du projet "Three Stars" MM. Azéma, Edrei e Hardy, 5, Rue Eglise Debbane, Alexandrie;
- l'auteur du projet "Ars" MM. Enrico Cas. [Casiraghi] et Luigi Lorenzo Secchi, Via Vigna n. 3 Milano;
- l'auteur du projet "Vox Populi" MM. Brandon Raoul, Brandon Daniel et Brandon Lionel, 1, Rue Juysmans, Paris;
- l'auteur du projet "Spes" M. Georges Niedermann, 52, Rieterstrasse, Zurich 2;
- l'auteur du projet "Lotus", S.T. de Sain et E. Marchettini, rue Emad El Din, Imm. Davies Bryan, Cairo;
- l'auteur du projet "Urbe" D. Limongelli, 13 Rue El Nemr, Cairo;

- l'auteur du projet "Z." G.A. Loria, 17, Rue Cherif Pacha, Alexandrie;
- l'auteur du projet "Utile Dulci" J. Bossard, Jaulgonne (Aisne) France;
- l'auteur du projet "Roma", Marcel Portevin, 4, Rue de la Terrasse, Paris;
- l'auteur du projet "LYS" René Prud'homme, 4, Rue Nicolas Charlet, Paris XV.

Clos et signé à 2 heures 30' p.m.

Signé   *Joseph Smouha, Paul Conin Pastour, Antonio Lasciac*

Correspondence between J. Smouha and L.L. Secchi

J. Smouha to L.L. Secchi 9.7.1925

Hadra – Sidi Gaber & Nouzha Estates
Joseph Smouha

Alexandria, le 9 Juillet 1925

Monsieur Luigi Secchi
3 Via Vigna
Milan (8)

Monsieur,

En réponse à votre lettre, je vous remets ci-inclus une carte de l'ancienne et de la nouvelle ville d'Alexandrie, ainsi qu'une copie des conditions du concours pour l'aménagement d'une nouvelle ville sur mes propriétés de Hadra, Sidi Gaber, etc.

D'autre part, je vous envoie par même courrier, un plan côté de mes dites propriétés.

Veuillez m'accuser réception de ces documents et agréer, Monsieur, mes salutations distinguées

p.p. J. Smouha
[signed by Daniel Delbourgo]

J. Smouha to L.L. Secchi 21.7.1925

Hadra – Sidi Gaber & Nouzha Estates
Joseph Smouha

Alexandria, le 21 Juillet 1925

Monsieur Luigi Secchi
3 Via Vigna
Milan

Monsieur,

En réponse à votre lettre du 15 courant, je vous informe que je vous adresse sous pli séparé et par même courrier, un plan un plan côté de mes domaines de Hadra, Sidi Gaber, etc.

Je regrette de n'avoir des photographies ou vues des lieux pour vous en envoyer.

Veuillez agréer, Monsieur, mes salutations distinguées

p.p. J. Smouha
[signed by Daniel Delbourgo]

J. Smouha to L.L. Secchi 13.10.1925

Hadra – Sidi Gaber & Nouzha Estates
Joseph Smouha

Alexandria, le 13 Octobre 1925

Monsieur Luigi Secchi
Ingénieur
Via Vigna N° 3
Milan (8)

Monsieur,

J'ai l'honneur d'accuser réception de votre lettre du 7 courant et vous
informe que votre projet a été dûment reçu.

Répondant à votre demande relativement En réponse au résultat du
concours, je regrette de vous informer que le Jury ne s'est pas encore
prononce à ce sujet

Veuillez agréer, Monsieur, mes salutations distinguées

p.p. J. Smouha
[signed by Daniel Delbourgo]

J. Smouha to L.L. Secchi 29.12.1925

(handwritten draft, followed by a copy of the report by the jury)

Hadra – Sidi Gaber & Nouzha Estates
Joseph Smouha

Alexandria, 29 December 1925

Messrs. Enrico Casiraghi et Luigi Lorenzo Secchi
Via Vigna n.3
Milano

Monsieur

J'ai l'avantage de vous remettre ci-joint la copie de procés verbal ré-
digé par le jury qui a procédé à l'examen des projets présentés pour le
plan d'aménagement de la ville de Sidi Gaber, banlieue d'Alexandrie.
Je vous remercie d'avoir voulu prendre part au concours et vous prie
de m'indiquer le façon que vous préférez pour la remise de votre
prime.

Veuillez agréer, Monsieur, mes salutations distinguées

J. Smouha

L.L. Secchi to J. Smouha 7.1.1926

(typewritten draft)

Mr. Joseph Smouha
Rue Cherif –Pacha
Alexandrie

Monsieur,

J'ai le plaisir de vous exprimer, avant tout, ma grande reconnaissance pour la bienveillance avec laquelle vous avez, ainsi que les autres Messieurs composant la Jurie, jugé mon projet pour la construction de la nouvelle ville de Sidi-Gaber.

Je regrette seulement une chose et c'est que la manque de temps ne m'a pas permis de développer mon projet, dans toutes ces lignes harmoniques que mon esprit avait projetées.

Si vous vouliez cependant me soumettre n'importe quelle étude ou projet constructif à complément des lignes générales, je serais bien charmé de l'exécuter car j'ai la direction d'un excellent bureau technique, avec la relative et très importante entreprise de construction et je serais même disposé a me rendre en Alexandrie.

Cela me déplaît de vous déranger, mais, comptant sur votre exquise amabilité, je vous demande le titre et les numéros des journaux et revues locaux qu'on a écrits au sujet du concours que vous avez banni, car je désirerais vivement les avoir.

Quant au moyen de m'envoyer la somme qui représente le 3me prix que j'ai vaincu (LEgyp. 100) vous pourriez m'en faire envoi moyennant un chèque de Leg. 100 sur la Banque Italo-Egiziana de v/Ville payable auprès du Banco di Roma de Milano.

En vous remerciant bien sincèrement, je vous présente, Monsieur, l'expression de mes sentiments très distingués.

Ing. Luigi Secchi
Milano 7 Janvier 1926

J. Smouha to L.L. Secchi 17.1.1926

Hadra – Sidi Gaber & Nouzha Estates
Joseph Smouha

Alexandria, 17 January 1926
Mr. Lorenzo Luigi Secchi
Via Vigna 3, Milan

Dear Sir,

I have pleasure in enclosing cheque to your order, on Lloyds Bank, for the sum of LEg. 100 (One Hundred pounds only), being the amount fixed as the third prize, for the project and per condition of the competition.

Kindly acknowledge receipt and oblige
Yours faithfully
p.p. J. Smouha

[signed by Daniel Delbourgo]

Enclosure.
Cheque No. 12960

L.L. Secchi to J. Smouha 27.1.1926
(handwritten draft)

Milan, January 27th, 1926

Mr. Joseph Smouha
P.O.B 1692 Alessandria

Dear Sir,
Your letter of the 17th inst. to hand together with check on London enclosed therein.
Thanking you very much for your courtesy
I remain
Yours faithfully

Documents from the Musée Social, Paris

The President of the Musée Social to M. Clauzier, 15.1.1926

15 Janvier

Monsieur,

M. Agache vient de me faire connaître que vous seriez disposé à présenter votre plan de la ville d'Alexandrie devant la Section d'hygiène urbaine et rurale et de prévoyance sociale du Musée Social.

Vous serait-il possible de donner cette communication le vendredi 26 février, à 5 heures ?

Je vous serais reconnaissant de vouloir bien me donner une réponse le plus tôt possible pour préparer cette réunion.

Veuillez agréer, Monsieur, l'expression de mes sentiments les plus distingués

Le Président

M. Clauzier to the President, 20.1.1926

Maurice Clauzier
Architecte A.D. Sociétaire des Artistes Français, Urbaniste S.F.U. Diplômé Ec. Hautes Etudes Urb.
Rodolphe Mériaux
Ingénieur-A Architecte Diplômé Ec. Travaux Publics
Successeurs de C. Ouvière Architecte
Reims, le 15 Février 1926
5, Bd de la République

> Monsieur le Président
> du Musée Social
> Commission d'Hygiène
> 5 Rue Las Casas
> Paris

Très Honoré Monsieur,

J'ai l'honneur de vous accuser réception de votre lettre du 15 courant. Je suis particulièrement honoré de votre demande.

Communication du projet peut être faite pour le Vendredi 26 Février à 5 Heures, sur plans à vue ou par projections 9/12 si la Salle dispose d'un appareil.

Titre de l'Espose : Extension d'Alexandrie : Création de la Cité de Luxe de Sidi Gaber.

A votre disposition pour tous renseignements complémentaire

Veuillez croire, Monsieur le Président, à l'expression de mes sentiments les plus distingués

M. Clauzier

The President of the Musée Social to M. Clauzier, 22.1.1926
(draft)

22 Janvier

Monsieur,
J'ai bien reçu votre lettre du 20 Ct par laquelle vous me faites connaître que vous pourrez donner votre communication sur l'Extension d'Alexandrie: Création de la Cité de Luxe de Sidi Gaber, le vendredi 26 Février à 5 heures.
Je me permets de compter sur vous de manière absolument certaine sans nouvelle indication.
Veuillez agréer, Monsieur, l'assurance de mes sentiments les plus distingués
Le Président

The President of the Musée Social to M. Clauzier, 12.2.1926
(draft)

12 Février

Monsieur,
Je vous remets ci-joint le texte de la convocation pour la prochaine réunion de la Section d'hygiène urbaine et rurale et de prévoyance sociale, qui aura lieu le 26 février, et au cours de laquelle vous devez présenter votre plan d'Alexandrie.
Je vous prie de bien vouloir me faire connaître si vous ne voyez pas de modification à apporter à ce texte.
Veuillez agréer, Monsieur, l'expression de mes sentiments les plus distingués

The President of the Musée Social to M. Clauzier , 15.2.1926

Maurice Clauzier
Architecte A.D. Sociétaire des Artistes Français, Urbaniste S.F.U. Diplômé Ec. Hautes Etudes Urb.
Rodolphe Mériaux
Ingénieur-A Architecte Diplômé Ec. Travaux Publics
Successeurs de C. Ouvière Architecte
Reims, le 15 Février 1926
5, Bd de la République

Monsieur le Président
du Musée Social
5 Rue Las Casas
Paris

Très Honoré Président,
J'ai l'honneur de vous accuser réception de votre estimée du 12 courant.
Convenu pour le Vendredi 26 Février à 4 h. ½ .
Veuillez agréer, Monsieur le Président, l'expression de mes sentiments les plus distingués

M. Clauzier

References for Smouha City: Welwyn and Heliopolis

Welwyn was founded in 1920 by Ebenezer Howard following his previous experiment of Letchworth. Being the second garden city and one of the first new towns in England, Welwyn exemplified the physical, social and cultural planning ideals of the time. Garden cities were to combine the benefits of the city and the countryside while avoiding the disadvantages of both. Surrounded by a rural belt, garden cities had to combine a healthy living and industry at the same favouring "a full measure of social life". Welwyn's urban structure featured a central a scenic parkway, almost a mile long, and tree-lined boulevards.

Heliopolis was founded in 1905 by the Belgian entrepreneur Baron Edouard Empain (1852-1929), who laid the first stone of the new town in 1906.
The original idea was that of a new town following the latest town-planning principles while meeting the health standards required by the many Europeans then living in Egypt. The new town was to grow in the NE suburbs of Cairo, on a plateau rising from 30 to 180 m above the Nile Valley, with no water nor vegetation. The site corresponded approximately to ancient Heliopolis, one of the oldest cities in Egypt.
A 3700-km long avenue and electric tramway connected Heliopolis to Cairo; a second tramway linked the new town to the nearest station of the Egyptian Railways.
Designed as a "city of luxury and leisure", with broad avenues and all modern conveniences, Heliopolis was characterised by an eclectic architectural style, featuring some monumental buildings: the Heliopolis Palace Hotel, Baron Empain's Hindu-style palace, some private villas. By the mid-twenties Heliopolis had almost reached completion. In 1929, the new town had 29,000 inhabitants; statistics on death and birth rates bore evidence to its healthy climate.
Comparing the layout of Heliopolis with the Competition Programme for Smouha City, we may find many correspondences, e.g. the decisive presence of modern transport infrastructure, the many religious buildings. Comparing Heliopolis with the actual layout of Smouha City, a common feature is certainly the imposing presence of areas for sport and leisure.

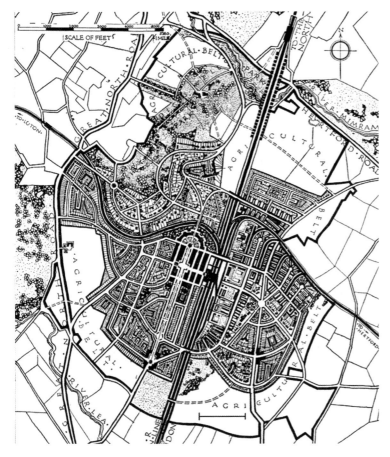

Early map of Welwyn

Map of Heliopolis (drawing by C. Pallini based on "Carte des fonctions" in R. Ilbert, Heliopolis, Editions du CNRS, Paris 1981, p. 51)

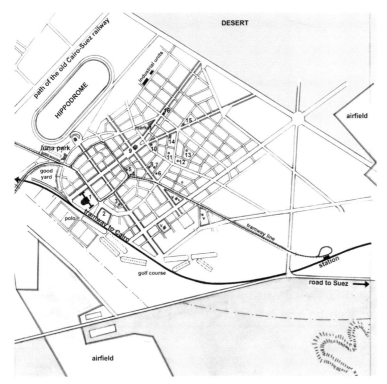

Legend.
1. Heliopolis Palace Hotel
2. Football ground
3. Anglican church
4. Greek Catholic church
5. Synagogue
6. American Mission
7. African Mission and archibishopric
8. Governmental school
9. Cathedral
10. Maronite church
11. Italian school
12. Coptic Orthodox church
13. Armenian church
14. École des Freres
15. Greek Orthodox church
16. Mosque
v. Villas

The area of Smouha City in the maps from
the Survey of Egypt 1941-1943

pp. 200-201
Smouha City (scale 1:2500), 31 March
1955, revised on 1.1.1957, R. Smouha's
Archive.

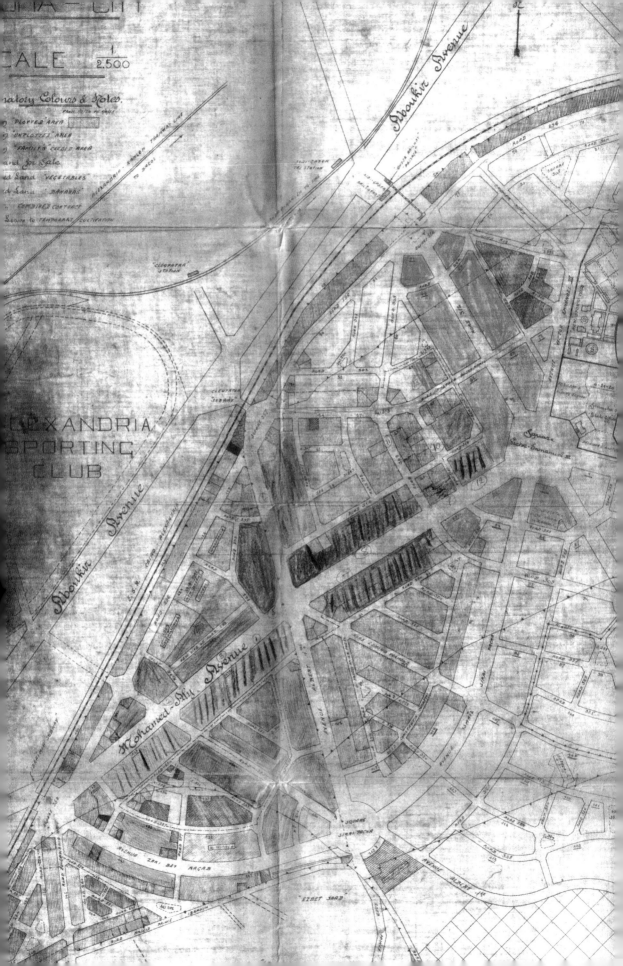

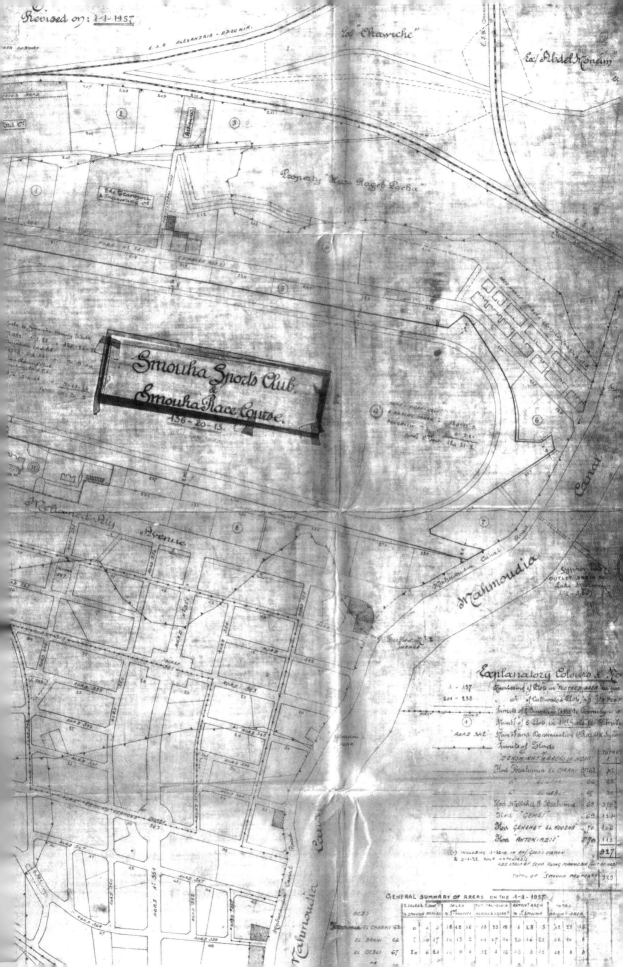

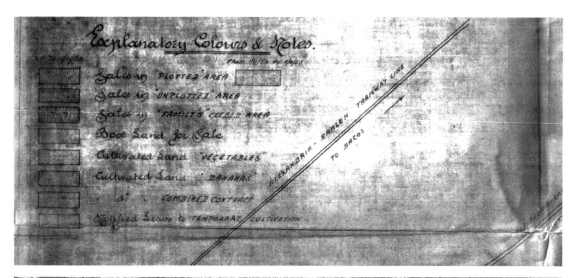

Explanatory Colours & Notes.

Sales in PLOTTED AREA
Sales in UNPLOTTED AREA
Sales in "FAMILY" CEDED AREA
Boor Land for Sale
Cultivated Land "VEGETABLES"
Cultivated Land "BANANAS"
" d° " COMBINED CONTRACT
Modified Leases to TEMPORARY CULTIVATION

ALEXANDRIA – RAMLEH TRAMWAY LINE
TO BACOS

Explanatory Colours & Notes.

1 – 157   Numbering of Plots in "PLOTTED AREA" as per "Deeded Plans"
201 – 238   " d° of Cultivated Plots in "UNPLOTTED AREA"

FIRST   SECOND   Limits of Donations (1955) to Family · AREA
(1)   Numb.of 8 Plots in 1st Sale to Family AREA
"ROAD 542"   Numb.and Denomination of Roads & Squares, as per Surveys
Limits of Hods

Yamani's PUMP.

"DENOMINAT.& AREAS OF HODS"

		TOTAL AREA			AR.TO J.SMOUHA		
		F	K	S	F	K	S
Hod Ibrahimia EL CHARKI N°62		42	22	15	42	22	15
d° " EL BAHRI	66	62	10	8	62	10	8
d° " EL QEBLI	67	99	18	13	68	8	
Hod Mellahet & Ibrahimia	68	375	1	13	370	8	22
Hod "GEMEI"	69	124	8	10	123	22	9
Hod GENENET EL NOUZHA	70	106	1	17	34	14	22 (1)
Hod "ANTONIADIS"	71	112	8	8	65	3	3
(1) INCLUDING 1-22-6 IN EX/ GOODS STATION		927	3	8	768	4	11
& 0-1-22 PUMP ANTONIADIS							
ADD STRIP OF 1000 ALONG MAHMUDIA (OUT OF HOD)					1	19	4
TOTAL OF "SMOUHA PROPERTY		929	8	10	769	28	6

GENERAL SUMMARY OF AREAS ON THE 1-1-1957

HOD'S		SALES & DON.S to SMOUHA FAMILIES			SALES to 3rd PARTIES			TOT: SALI:DON: & ROADS & SQUAR'S			REMAIN.G AREA to J.SMOUHA			TOTAL ORIGIN.L AREA			ROADS,S & SQUARES (3)		
Ibrahimia EL CHARKI	62	0	0	0	18	48	18	33	23	12	8	23	3	42	22	15	15	4	14
EL BAHRI	66	7	10	17	14	13	2	44	17	10	20	16	22	62	10	8	40	13	15
EL QEBLI	67	20	6	14	14	9	4	52	1	16	16	6	12	68	8	8	17	9	15
MELLAHET EL-IBR MIA	68	266	12	14	34	17	15	347	22	7	22	10	15	370	8	22	66	13	2
HOD "GEMEI"	69	72	3	20	4	20	15	113	19	16	10	1	17	123	22	9	36	17	5
GENENET EL NOUZHA	70	22	10	6	2	2	1	34	7	9	0	14	13	34	21	22	4	18	
HOD ANTONIADIS	71	41	8	19	1	0	9	60	7	7	4	19	20	65	3	3	17	22	
OUT OF HOD									19	2					19	4		19	2
GENERAL TOTALS		409	19	1	90	6	16	685	20	7	83	0	6	769	20	13	185	18	13
		(1)			(2)			(4) = 1+2+3			(5)			(6) 4+5					

PREPARED BY
REVISED ON 1/2/1955

204

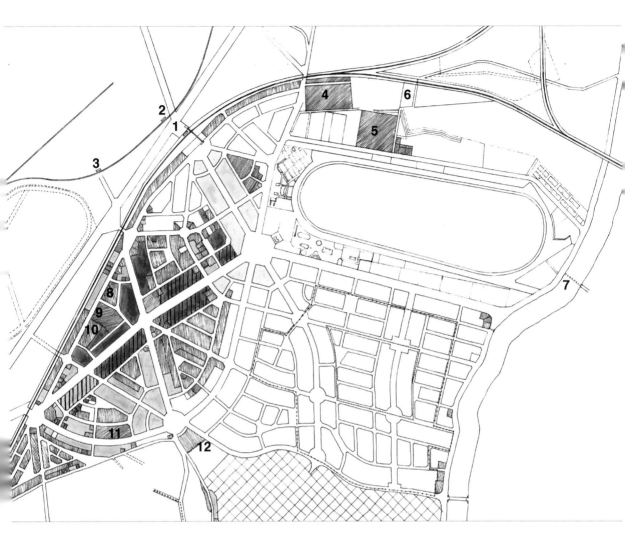

 Sales in plotted area

 Sales in unplotted area

 Limits of donation to Family (1st)

 Limits of donation to Family (2nd)

Smouha City, 31 March 1955, revised on 1.1.1957 (redrawn by C. Pallini): 1. Sidi Gaber Railway Station; 2. Sidi Gaber Station; 3. Cleopatra Station; 4. Ford Co.; 5. The Transport & Engineering Co.; 6. Artisans; 7. Syphon and outlet drain to Lake Maryut; 8. Terrasanta; 9. New Gov. School (1955); 10. Gov. School (1953); 11. Eg. Testing H.; 12. Gov. University

opposite
Smouha City, 31 March 1955, revised on 1.1.1957, detail of the explanatory notes written on the map.

Members of the "Race-horse Owners' Association"

From *La Gazette d'Orient* 24. 4. 1934

- Joseph A. Addà
- Clément N. Adès
- Elie N. Adès
- S.E. Ahmed Ábboud Pacha
- Aboul Fettouh
- Charles Baehler
- Parissi Belleni
- Mme E. Chester Beatty
- Théodore P. Cozzika
- Th. Th. Cozzika
- Baron Jean Empain
- Vittorio Giannotti
- George K. Haddad
- Willie B. Hanna
- Jacques O. Matossian
- Mohamed Sultan
- Ibrahim Rolo
- Robert S. Rolo
- Fernand Rossano
- Ambroise Sevastopoulos
- Shoukri G. Wissa

List of British claims in Egypt for assets over 1 million Eg. pounds, 1957

The Smouha family was the biggest private claimant

From Itamar Levin, *Locked doors,* Praeger, West port, Conn. 2001, p.231.

January 28, 1959.

ASSETS OF OVER £E 1 MILLION

(1) SEQUESTRATED

(All figures in £E..)

1.	Anglo-Egyptian Oilfields	45,887,000	
	Shell Petroleum Co.	1,753,442	
	Shell Co. of Egypt	7,874,000	
	Shell Chemicals Distributing Co of Egypt	158,000	55,672,442
2.	Joseph SMOUHA and family		14,313,674
3.	David Ades & Son (It has been reported by the Swiss, but not by the Egyptians, that this firm has now been Egyptianised.)		1,469,457

Total   71,455,573

Balance of Seq. Assets   61,945,752

GRAND TOTAL   133,402,325 .

(2) EGYPTIANISED

1.	Myddleton Investment Co. (Eastern Co. S.A.E.) Including Dividends		17,200,314
2.	British Banks:-		
	(I) Barclays Bank, D.C.O.	2,322,087	
	(II) Ottoman Bank	2,129,392	
	(III) Ionian Bank	176,070	4,627,549
3.	Tunnel Portland Cement Co. (Helwan Portland Cement Co.) Cumberland Ecldings Limited		4,202,348
4.	Bradford Dyers Association Limited (Beida Dyers S.A.E.)		3,218,046
5.	Peel & Co. Limited		2,059,699
6.	British schools (8 plus British Council Institutes Alexandria and Cairo)		1,798,904
7.	Cable and Wireless Limited (Eastern Telegraph Co. Marconi Radio Telegraph Co.)		1,629,621
8.	Egyptian Phosphate Co. Limited		1,348,236
9.	Calico Printers Association (Société Egyptienne des Industries Textiles)		1,060,475
10.	60 British Insurance Firms, (including (Prudential Insurance Co. £E.1,939,703.)		4,291,699

This does not include Tractor and Engineering Co. and Sinai Mining Co. Ltd. who have concluded a "side-deal".

Total   41,436,891

Balance of Eg. Assets   3,931,521

GRAND TOTAL   45,368,412

CONFIDENTIAL

LE DESSÈCHEMENT DU LAC HADRA

On est en train de réaliser, à Alexandrie, un projet grandiose. Il s'agit du dessèchement du lac Hadra et de la construction, sur les terrains ainsi obtenus, d'une cité ouvrière, et, peut-être, d'une « nouvelle Alexandrie „.

Ce projet avait été plusieurs fois étudié par la Municipalité sans que l'on eût abouti à des réalisations. C'est grâce à l'initiative d'une personnalité en vue dans le monde des affaires et de la finance, Monsieur Joseph Smouha, que nous sommes à la veille de voir le lac Hadra complètement desséché.

Le 21 octobre, en effet, a été inaugurée l'installation de drainage qui déversera les eaux du lac Hadra dans le lac Mariout.

Notre correspondant à Alexandrie est allé trouver Monsieur Delbourgo, le distingué directeur de la maison Smouha, qui a

A HUGE SUCCESS

The First Race Meeting At The Alexandria Racing Club

UN GROS SUCCÈS

Les premières réunions hippiques à l'Alexandria Racing Club

Ce qu'est le nouvel hippodrome

Un nouveau champ de courses, cela ne peut pas, ne doit pas passer inaperçu.

Et lorsque la nouvelle enceinte où l'hippisme doit fleurir et se développer est un chef-d'œuvre du genre, possédant non seulement le nécessaire, mais aussi le superflu, son ouverture prend des proportions d'événement,

افتتح نادي السباق الإسكندري

... (Arabic text) ...

L'inaugurazione del nuovo campo di corse a Hadra

Cinquemila persone affollano l'ippodromo - Il pubblico entusiasta della modernità e dell'eleganza che adornano la costruzione

La prochaine inauguration de l'Alexandria Racing Club

الرياضة الاسبوعية

نحن لا نزعم أننا قد أفرغنا على (الرياضة الاسبوعية) ثوبا جديداً لم يكن لها به
سابق عهد وإنما في هذا الثوب الجديد قد قطعت مرحلة من مراحل النجاح في عالم الصحافة
فهذا الثوب الذي ظهرت به (الرياضة) أخيراً كان نوما الذي بدأت به الظهور في
عالم الصحافة وتنشقت فيه أرج الحياة الصحفية وتدرجت في أكنافها حيناً من الدهر ثم
خلعته لترتدى ثوبا آخر دونه اتساعا ورونقاً ثم الجأها الى ارتدائه الضرورة الملحة . ضرورة
النقص الطبيعي الذي به هذا البلد وكم جهدنا وتحايلنا على سد ذلك النقص فلم نفلح
وقامت في طريقنا عقبات كثيرة .
وأخيراً تهيأت الظروف التي وافتنا يوم خلقت هذه الجديدة في عالم الصحف فاغتنمناها

ALEXANDRIE NOUVELLE

L'hippodrome Smouha

THE ALEXANDRIA RACING CLUB

Accompanied by Mr. M. Monakis, Secretary of the Alexandria Racing Club, we step through a large and impressive gate in the new hippodrome at the "Cité Smouha". This gate, is to be reserved for H. M. the King and for guests of Honour. The public will be admitted through the other gates, thus discarding the idea of any possible confusion.

We first visit the Grand Stand which is of the same style as that of Heliopolis. There is seating accomodation for over 1000 spectators, who are well protected from the sun at all times in the afternoon.

There is perfect visibility of the whole track, which is a magnificent view of green all around. This track running 1 3/4 miles round, has a straight of 5 furlongs, which is about 400 yards longer than that of Heliopolis and it has a width of 30 yards thus allowing 35 horses to

xpress man-on-the-spot Kilian ooks at that Smouha brouhaha

ECAYING 'LOST CITY' HOLDS UP PACT

From Cairo yesterday came the news that once again Egypt refuses to negotiate further with Britain over Suez war claims because of the deadlock over compensation to be paid to the Smouha family. From Smouha City comes this vivid report by RICHARD KILIAN

ALEXANDRIA, Sunday.

NDERED over the land called Smouha City today. is land, freckled with banana trees, villas, and heaps, has held up the signing of the agreement.

Britain and Egypt the other has been of cheating—Egypt dervaluing Smouha's hich it seized in 1956 itain for trying to ne £27,500,000 com- n figure after it had reed upon.

nouha brouhaha is not g matter.

re the figures for these , two and a half miles centre of Alexandria. a's evaluation: 00.

nofficial Egyptian dele- valuation is £500,000 to Highly placed officials' evaluation:).

st one seems closest to

Build-up

approach Smouha City laying roads you see a announcing "Joseph Estates."

s an unmistakable air of a project party com- d now fallen to the and to poor farmers jerrican huts.

eph Smouha turned up ndria in 1918 from t is said.

was, I am told, not socially acceptable to his fellow-members of the British community.

His first holding was 430 acres bought from Prince Toussoun. By clever buying he built this up to around 1.20 0acres.

He built his own golf club and racecourse in obvious competition with Alexandria's snooty Sporting Club.

If Whitehall is confused over the Smouha claim it is not to be blamed although one wonders how the amazing situation was permitted to arise.

The price

The facts as I have gleaned them are:—

Land holdings—290 acres of agricultural holdings, all Egyptianised at the legal rate of £420 an acre;

Racecourse and golf club rented by Smouha Estates to operators for £8,000 a year;

Wasteland—50 acres.

Agricultural land used for market gardening near Alexandria is sold for £1,200 an acre.

Thus the Egyptian price is well below the real price.

Building-site land on the Smouha property has been selling from £3,360 to £4,200 an acre.

At the highest evaluation

PT INSISTS SMOUHA ND "AGRICULTURAL"

From Our Own Correspondent

CAIRO, Feb. 12.

Kaissouny, Egyptian Minister of Economy, said to-day nancial agreement with Britain initialled on January 17 that the Egyptian authorities had seized all lands belong- ish nationals. Payment forthcoming from the which represented ion for all Egptian- rty, he added.

nister said the British ed to consider the d as building lots to be om the provisions of the reement.

uny said the United Arab s "determined to adhere hat the Smouha land was The Government's documents and relevant e property showed, he between 1952 and 1955 made over to his wife ast areas" of land classi- cultural and valued at per feddan (A feddan acres.)

ore the agreement was y had shown the British nts on British land which Egyptianised, and these all the land concerned ral.

A REVIEWED

able information" on the erty was reviewed to-day g presided over by Dr. The spokesman said this would be communicated , president of the World d requested it during a onversation with Dr. st night.

o-day says the authorities 988,000 to the Misrair ne as compensation for losses and damages caused during the Suez intervention. Yesterday Misrair was given a £E500,000 loan by the Government, and this sum will be deducted from the above figure.

TALKS WITH EGYPTIANS BREAK DOWN

MR. BLACK TO TRY AGAIN

SMOUHA ESTATE WRANGLE

From DOUGLAS BROWN, Daily Telegraph Special Correspondent

CAIRO, Thursday.

Direct negotiations between Britain and Egypt for signature of the financial agreement initialled nearly three weeks ago have broken down. Mr. Black, chairman of the World Bank, has resumed by cable from Washington the mediation he thought he had brought to a successful conclusion on Jan. 16.

The situation looks unpromising. Mr. Kaissouni, the United Arab Republic's Minister of Economy, who initialled the agreement for Egypt, asked to-day what Britain's purpose was in "delaying" her signature.

Speaking to reporters, he said: "The British first raised the question of diplomatic relations. Now they raise the question of the value of Smouha property in Alexandria. What are they up to?"

Mr. Kaissouni said Mr. Black had asked for information about the Smouha property. It had been sent to him in Washington to-day.

"NOT BUILDING LAND"

The Minister declared roundly that the Smouha estate was agricultural and not building land. "We have documents to prove it," he said. It is believed he was referring to tax receipts.

The semi-official Al-Shaab said Mr. Kaissouni's reply to Mr. Black was that his Government felt itself bound by every clause in the initialled agreement, which Britain had "thoroughly and exhaustively studied before initialling." The paper quoted an official source as saying Cairo would not budge from this position.

"The only solution is that Britain should give up her attitude and respect the terms of the agreement as initialled by Sir Denis Rickett." The exchanges are now out of the hands of Mr. Colin Crowe, the Foreign Office official in charge of the mission here.

He has seen no Egyptian official since Friday and is merely awaiting a report from London on the results of Mr. Black's new mediation.

It seems clear that the British negotiators imagined that the greater part of the Smouha estate would be returned as sequestrated property.

FAMILY MAKE £12½m CLAIM OVER "SMOUHA CITY"

EXPROPRIATED EGYPT ASSETS

DAILY TELEGRAPH REPORTER

A BRITISH family whose lands in Egypt were expropriated by the Egyptian Government during the Suez affair in 1956, sought £12½ million compensation yesterday. The claim was made in London before the Foreign Claims Commission, which investigates claims and evaluates property involved.

Compensation, paid out of the £27½ million which the Egyptian Government handed over to Britain in respect of all such claims by British nationals, is on a percentage basis.

This is on a sliding scale, so that as the amount of money involved increases the percentage paid in compensation decreases. Yesterday's claim was made by Mr. ELLIS

12 Daily Telegraph and Morning Post, Saturday, August 12, 196

£1m INTERIM PAYMENT FOR 'SMOUHA CITY'

14 WILL GET SHARES

DAILY TELEGRAPH REPORTER

A CASH payment of about £1 million will be made to the Smouha family as interim compensation for the loss of "Smouha City," expropriated by the Egyptian Government in the 1956 Suez affair.

The payment will be shared by 14 members of the family. Their dependants number more than 50.

The £1 million is based on the compensation assessment of the Foreign Compensation Commission of £3,106,516. The family had claimed £12½ million compensation for their lands, an area of more than 400 acres forming about a sixth of the total area of Alexandria.

Although the £3 million assessment is the highest yet awarded for expropriated assets in Egypt, the amounts paid to the individuals concerned in the claim will be no means the highest.

LARGEST AMOUNT

Separate Awards

A Commission official said yesterday that a separate award would be made to each member of the family. By far the largest claim is that of Mr. Joseph Smouha, 83, former Manchester textile merchant who bought and developed the Alexandria estate after the first world war. His share of the £3 million is more than £500,000.

Payment, made from the £27½ million provided by Egypt to meet compensation claims, is based on a table. For losses assessed at more than £500,000, it is £138,500 and 20 per cent. of the balance of

(Continued on Back Page, Col. 5)

"SMOUHA CITY"

(Continued from P.1, Col. 6)

the amount. Mr. Smouha's pay ment will be assessed on this basi

Scales of payment for othe members of the family range fro 70 per cent. of the amour assessed where this does not excee £5,000. For assessments of £5,0C to £50,000 the scale is £3,500 an 50 per cent. of the balance ove £5,000, and for £50,000 to £500,0C assessments it is £26,000 and 2 per cent. of the balance ove £50,000.

The cash payment, which wi probably be made within the ne three to four weeks, is subject deduction of any loans made t the Anglo-Egyptian Advisor Board. After Suez the Smouh family shared some £80,000 advances for living expenses.

VARIABLE SCALES

Already Amended

All payments by the Commissio are regarded as interim compens tion. Further amounts could b paid in the future if the Govern ment should decide to increase th rate of compensation from th Fund. It has already bee amended once, to give increase since the scale was first set in 195

News of the award was give yesterday to Mr. Joseph Smouh at his Paris home by his son, M Ellis Smouha, a London barriste who submitted the claim for th family at the Commission's hearir last month.

The Alexandria estate was de veloped to include a racecourse, garden village and planned as "city." Income collected from th property has not been returned t the family since 1956.

Because of this the family wa said yesterday to be "hardly likel to be over pleased" by an assess ment of only a quarter of the valu of its claim. But the interim pay ment is expected to help som branches who have had difficulty i re-establishing themselves in fresh start.

Out of the £27½ million con pensation fund, nearly £7 millior has already been paid. But mor than a dozen claims for sums c over £½ million compensation ar still to be heard among some 6,00 to 7,000 claims outstanding. It likely to be two to three year before all claims are formulate and assessed.

EGYPTIANS REFUSE ARBITRATION OVER SMOUHA ESTATES

From Our Correspondent

CAIRO, Feb. 8

Dr. Kaissouny, Minister of Economy, is quoted to-day as saying that the United Arab Republic would not accept any dividing up of the financial agreement with Britain, "which is an integral and inseparable whole." This was his reply to the reported suggestion that the two parties might sign an accord, agreeing to leave the question of the disputed Smouha property for settlement later, perhaps through arbitration.

The Minister said that Egypt had already refused to accept arbitration on the total sum payable as compensation, and the figure reached had been agreed by both sides.

DETAILS WITHHELD

Moussu Arafa, Minister of Public Works, and formerly sequestrator of British property, said the reasons for the difference could only be that "either the British have, as they imagine, been deluded when they accepted the agreement, or they are attempting to disengage themselves. . . ." They had estimated the value of the Egyptianized British property on several occasions during the long negotiations, and the U.A.R. had "taken these talks to the limit."

The Egyptians are reported to ha refused throughout to let the Briti negotiators see lists giving details their valuation of the Smouha lanc which are about three miles from t centre of Alexandria. Their value—eve as market gardens—would perhaps b three times the £420 an acre stipulate in the agrarian reform law. Estimat of their value as building sites could b far higher. Part of the acreage is occ pied as a racecourse and a golf cours

VARYING ESTIMATES

Estimates of the properties' total valu vary widely, and it can only be assume that the reason for the deadlock is tha after initialling the agreement, th British found the division of the pr perty between Egyptianized and seque trated portions was not what, on th basis of all the available evidence, the had believed it to be. Newspapers he are now saying that all Mr. Smouha lands are in the former category.

DEFENCE WHITE PAPER

The Defence White Paper, which wa finally approved by the Cabinet la week, is expected to be published ear this week, probably to-morrow.

Bibliographical note

Sources on the site of Smouha City in antiquity (by M.-C. Bruwier):
-Ashton, S.A., "Egyptian Archeology," *Bulletin of the Egypt Exploration Society*, 27, 2005, pp.30-32.
- Betz, R., "A Ptolemaic Bust in Mariemont Museum: The Detective Story," *Ancient Egypt – The History, People and Culture of the Nile Valley*, vol. 14, n° 1, issue 79 August/September 2013, pp.44-49.
- Bruwier, M.-C., "Enquête sur l'origine des fragments d'une statue colossale ptolémaïque. Fouilles du Musée royal de Mariemont à Alexandrie," *Revue belge d'Archéologie et d'histoire de l'Art*, LXXXI-2012, Bruxelles, pp.197-198.
- Bruwier, M.-C., "Enquête sur les fragments d'une dyade colossale d'Alexandrie," in *Bulletin de la société française d'égyptologie*, 179, Mars 2011, pp.29-40.
- Bruwier, M.-C., "À la recherche du temple de Cléopâtre," Fouilles du Musée royal de Mariemont à Alexandrie, in *Ceci n'est pas une pyramide... Un siècle de recherche archéologique belge en Égypte*, Leuven-Paris, Peeters, 2012, pp.178-187.
- Bruwier, M.-C., "The Smouha Excavations," *Ancient Egypt – The History, People and Culture of the Nile Valley*, vol. 14, n° 3, issue 81 December 2013/January 2014, pp.28-33.
- Pococke, R., *Description of the East and some other Countries I. Observations in Egypt*, London, 1743, p.12.
- Van den Bercken, B., "Excavation Smouha, Alexandria," in *Eternal Egypt*, ed. by B. Van den Bercken and W. Van Haarlem, Amsterdam, Allard Pierson Museum, 2013, pp.126-127.

Sources and/or references about Sidi Gaber and Smouha City (alphabetical order):
- Awad, M. F., and Youakim, R.S., "Nouvel Ordre Urbain et Nouvelles dynamiques 1958-2005," *ROMM* 45, 1987-4, pp.187-194.
- Awad, M. F., and Pallini, C., "The Italianisation of Alexandria: an Analogy of Practice," in *Caire–Alexandrie architectures européennes*, ed. by M. Volait, Cairo, IFAO-CEDEJ, 2001, pp.89-98.
- Awad, M. F., *Italy in Alexandria*, Alexandria Presevation Trust, 2008, pp.190-191.
- Breccia, E., "Ramleh," in *Alexandrea ad Ægyptum*, Bergamo, Istituto italiano d'arti grafiche, 1914, pp.10-15.
- Forster, E. M., *Alexandria. A History and a Guide* (1922), New York, Overlook Press,1974.
- Ilbert, R., *Alexandrie 1830-1930*, Cairo, IFAO, 1996.
- Lackany, R., *Quelques notes de toponymie Alexandrine*, Alexandrie, 1976.
- *Les Enduits Decoratifs en Égypte*, published by the Cement Marketing Co. Ltd., London (no date).
- Levin, I., *Locked doors: the seizure of Jewish property in Arab Countries*, Prae-

ger, West port, Conn. 2001, pp.121-125, 231.

- Mansel, P., *Levant*, New Haven and London, Yale University Press, pp. 246, 262, 285.

- McLean, W. H., *City of Alexandria Town Planning Scheme*, Cairo, Imprimerie Nationale, 1921.

- Pecnik, C., *Ramleh, La Riviera Eleusinienne et Alexandrie (Egypt)*, Manuals de voyage Woerl, Liepzig, Léon Woerl, 1901.

- Pallini, C., and Scaramuzzi, A., "Italian projects for the new city of Sidi Gaber, Alexandria," in *Italian Architects and Engineers in Egypt from the Nineteenth to the Twentyfirst Century*, eds E. Godoli, M. Giacomelli, Florence, Maschietto, 2008, pp.152-159.

- Pallini, C., "La costruzione di Alessandria Moderna", in *Alessandria d'Egitto oltre il mito*, eds. L. Ferro and C. Pallini. ArabaFenice, Boves, 2009, pp.76-103.

- Shaalan, Cécile, "Essai de localisation du lieu de découverte des statues colossales dans le quartier de Smouha (Alexandrie)," *Cahiers de Mariemont*, Musée royal de Mariemont, Morlanwelz, in preparation.

- Spitaleri, G., *Costruttori Italiani in Egitto. Filippo Cartareggia*, Alexandria, Tipografia A. Procaccia 1933, pp.25-34.

- Susani, E., "Il concorso di Sidi Gaber," in *Milano dietro le quinte, Luigi Lorenzo Secchi*, ed. E. Susani, Milan, Electa, 1999, pp.30-35.

- Tehemar, S., *Livre d'or - Vingt-cinq ans d'hippisme*, Alexandrie, Procaccia, 1947.

- Torella di Romagnano, T., *Villa Jela*, Garzanti, Milano, 1948.

Journal articles published at the time of the competition (chronological order):
- Competition announcement, *La Construction Moderne*, XL, 37, 14 June 1925, p. 444.

- "Sistemazione di una località nei pressi di Alessandria d'Egitto," *Ingegneria*, IV, 9, September 1925, p.346.

- Competition results, *La Construction Moderne*, XLI, 16, 17 January 1926, p.191.

- "La nuova città di Sidi Gaber in Egitto", *Ingegneria*, V, 4, April 1926, p.148.

- Lepol, G., "Le Salons de 1926" (Plan by M. Clauzier at the Salon des Arts décoratifs, Paris), *La Construction Moderne*, XLI, 40, 4 July 1926, pp.469-473.

- Lafollye, P., "Extension d'Alexandrie. Création de «Sidi Gaber», cité de luxe," *L'Architecture*, XXXIX, 12, 1926, pp.155-157.

- "L'Urbanisme aux Colonies," *La Construction Moderne*, 26 June 1927, pp.446-449.

- "Il Piano Regolatore della nuova città-giardino di Smouha (Cairo)," *Architettura e Arti Decorative*, VI, 1926-27, p.132.

- "Communication de M. Maurice Clauzier, architect urbaniste : Présentation du plan d'extension d'Alexandrie : création de la cité de luxe de Sidi Gaber," *Le Musée Social*, March 1927, pp.71-73.

List of newspaper cuttings held in Richard Smouha's archive

- "Draining Hadra Lake," *The Egyptian Gazette*, 10.8.1925
- "Il prosciugamento del Lago di Hadra," *Messaggero Egiziano*, 22.10.1925
- "Le dessèchement du Lac Hadra," *Le Magazine Egyptien*, 1.11.1925
- *Le Stade*, 9.4.1929
- "L'avenir de l'hippisme a Alexandrie. Le Sporting Club pourra déménager. Le possibilités de Siouf," *La Reforme*, 1.3.1930
- *L`Echo Sportif*, 9.4.1930
- "Le nouvel hippodrome," *La Cloche*, 22.5.1930
- "Les terrains de Hadra offrent de réels avantages nous déclare une haute personnalité", *La Cloche*, 29.5.1930
- "Le nouvel hippodrome", *Sporting*, 4.6.1930
- "A propos du transfert éventuel de l'hippodrome de Sporting. Après l'Assemblée Générale et le vote d'ajournement. Le dessous des cartes - un vilain son de La Cloche," *L'Echo Sportif*, 6.6.1930
- "Le nouvel hippodrome Siouf ou Hadra?", *Le Phare Egyptien*, 8.6.1930
- "Le nouvel hippodrome," *La Cloche*, 12.6.1930
- "Me Gaby Maksud change en faveur de Sioufisme," *Le Phare Egyptien*, 22.6.1930
- "Le nouvel hippodrome... Le transfert à Siouf est de nature à comprometter très gravement l'avenir du sport hippique en Egypte," *La Cloche*, 26.6.1930
- "A la Commission Municipale. Une question d'échange de terrain provoque une discussion passionnée e deux incidents," *La Reforme*, 19.3.1931
- "A la Commission Municipale - Des discussions de principe qui durent des heures," *La Bourse Egyptienne*, 19.3.1931
- "Trois heures de discussions sans aborder à l'ordre du jour ...," *La Cloche*, 19.3.1931
- "Chinoiseries Municipales - A propos d'un échange de terrains," *La Reforme*, 20.3.1931
- "Affaires Municipales - Un éxchange des terrain à Hadra provoque 2 heures de discussion," *L'Informateur*, 20.3.1931
- "Alexandria Municipal Commission. An exchange of land - a heated debate," *The Egyptian Gazette*, 20.3.1931
- "L'affaire de l'échange des terrains de Hadra," *La Reforme*, 21.3.1931
- "Le gâchis municipal - Du bromure pour Orabi Bey," *Le Phare Egyptien*, 22.3.1931
- "Mr. Smouha and the Municipality," *Akbar Al Eskanderia*, 23.3.1931 [in Arabic, also published in *Al Masria* and *Al Shaab*]
- "The issue of the exchange of Land," *Eskanderia Ambar*, 26.3.1931 [in Arabic]
- "The Exchange of Land," *Al Attchar*, 26.3.1931 [in Arabic]
- "False news," *Eskanderia Ambar*, 28.3.1931 [in Arabic]
- "Storm in a teacup," *Al Masr*, 31.3.1931 [in Arabic]

- "Exchange of Smouha Land," *Al Ahram*, 31.3.1931 [in Arabic]
- "Alexandria Municipal Commission - Heavy agenda - Mr. Toriel's 'Summer Resort' Scheme," *The Egyptian Gazette*, 1.4.1931
- "Commission of Alexandria Municipality," *Al Ahram*, 2.4.1931 [in Arabic]
- "A la Commission Municipale - Dans une atmosphère chargé… d'électricité on s'occupe… du gaz, de l'eau, de terrains etc…," *La Reforme*, 2.4.1931
- "Smouha land and Municipality," *Al Dia*, 2.4.1931 [in Arabic]
- "A la Commission Municipale - L'échange des terrains avec M. Smouha est approuvé," *La Bourse Egyptienne*, 2.4.1931
- "Alexandria Municipal Commission - Exchange of land question - Settled after long discussion," *The Egyptian Gazette*, 3.4.1931
- "Session of the Municipality," *Al Dia*, 3.4.1931 [in Arabic]
- "Municipal Commission," *Wadi el Nil*, 3.4.1931 [in Arabic]
- "Session of Municipal Commission," *Al Ahram*, 3.4.1931 [in Arabic]
- "Session of Commission," *Al Shaab*, 3.4.1931 [in Arabic]
- "La dernière séance de la Commission Municipale d'Alexandrie," *La Liberte*, 3.4.1931
- "Sharia Mohamed Ali," *Al Bahrir*, 26.12.1933 [in Arabic]
- "Smouha problem with the Municipal Committee," *Wadi el Nil*, 24.12.1933 [in Arabic]
- "Smouha – Alexandria interest discussed in Parliament," *Al Balar*, 26.12.1933 [in Arabic]
- "Two Parliamentary questions," *Al Shaab*, 26.12.1933 [in Arabic]
- "The problem of Sharia Mohamed Ali," *Al Maktam*, 26.12.1933 [in Arabic]
- "La 'route des choux' - Des questions à la Délégation Municipale," *La Bourse Egyptienne*, 2.1.1934
- "The Mohamed Aly road - Councillor's question to delegation," *Egyptian Mail*, 4.1.1934
- "L'enquête sur l'affaire de la Corniche", *La Reforme*, 20.1.1934
- "Another inquiry into municipal affairs? - The building of Mohamed Aly road", *Egyptian Mail*, 21.1.1934
- "Bus service to the new racecourse," *The Egyptian Gazette*, 22.1.1934
- "A propos du nouveau champ de courses," *La Reforme*, 24.1.1934
- "Une excellente initiative - Le nouvel hippodrome du Domaine Smouha," *La Gazette d'Orient*, 27.1.1934
- "Alexandrie Nouvelle. L'hippodrome Smouha," *La Gazette d'Orient*, 3.2.1934
- "The Mohamed Aly road inquiry," *Egyptian Mail*, 7.2.1934
- "Les Couses d'Alexandrie en 1934," *Le Favori*, 19.2.1934
- "L'Hippodrome de l'Alexandria Racing Club," *Le Favori*, 19.2.1934
- "The Alexandria racing season," *The Egyptian Gazette*, 9.3.1934
- "Notre visite à l'Alexandria Racing Club," *Le Favori*, 12.3.1934
- "The Alexandria racing season - The two clubs – ARC's position," *The Egyptian Gazette*, 17.3.1934
- "Le Nouvel Hippodrome," *Le Dimanche Illustré*, 4.3.1934
- Crow's Nest, "The Alexandria racing season - Jockey Club takes action – Explanation of Arrajas running not satisfactory," *The Egyptian Gazette*, 21.3.1934
- "La prochaine inauguration de l'Alexandria Racing Club," *La Gazette d'Orient*, 24.3.1934
- "Alexandria racing season - Jockey Club notice," *The Egyptian Gazette*, 20.3.1934
- "Alexandria City Police - Guard Company win cross-country race," *The Egyptian*

Gazette, 3.4.1934
- "The Alexandria Racing Club," *The Sprinter*, 6.4.1934
- "Announcement of the inauguration and of the Alexandria Gold Cup and of the Smouha Cup," *La Gazette d'Orient*, 7.4.1934
- "Notre nouveau champ des courses," *La Gazette d'Orient*, 7.4.1934
- "Inauguration de l'Alexandria Racing Club," *Le Favori*, 10.4.1934
- "L'Alexandria Racing Club ouvre ses portes cette semaine," *L'Echo Sportif*, 13.4.1934
- "Alexandria Racing Club," *Jocker*, 13.4.1934
- *Al-Riadah*, weekly sports paper, 13.4.1934 [in Arabic]
- Said Téhémar, "Sul l'emplacement d'un ancien lac - Les organisateurs de la Cité Smouha recevont demain une nombreuse et grouillante clientèle," *Le Turf*, 13.4.1934
- "Le nouvel hippodrome," *Le Phare Egyptien*, 15.4.1934
- "L'inaugurazione del nuovo campo di corse a Hadra. Cinquemila persone affollano l'ippodromo. Il pubblico entusiasta della modernità e dell'eleganza che adornano la costruzione," *Il Giornale d'Oriente*, 15.4.1934
- "Un gros succès - Les premières réunions hippiques à l'Alexandria Racing Club," *La Bourse Egyptienne*, 16.4.1934
- "A Hadra. Les premières réunions hippiques à l'Alexandria Racing Club, Ce qu'est le nouvel hippodrome," *La Bourse Egyptienne*, 16.4.1934
- "Panache s'adjuge la Gold Cup. Churbara enlève le beau trophée offert par M. J. Smouha. Johnny Michaelidis à l'honneur," *Le Favori*, 16.4.1934
- *El-Safir*, 17.4.1934 [in Arabic]
- "A huge success - The First Race Meetings at the Alexandria Racing Club," *Egyptian Mail*, 17.4.1934
- "Notes du jour," *Le Stade*, 17.4.1934
- "De semaine en semaine," *Sporting*, 18.4.1934
- Crow's Nest, "The Smouha City Racecourse - Opens new era for Egyptian turf. Minor modification necessary, Panache staying power in gold cup race," *The Egyptian Gazette*, 19.4.1934
- *Al-Riadah*, 19.4.1934 [weekly sports paper in Arabic]
- *L'Echo Sportif*, 19.4.1934
- "Vue d'ensemble du nouvel hippodrome," *Jocker*, 20.4.1934
- Said Téhémar, "L'évènement de 1934 - Un hippodrome est né sur l'emplacement d'un ancien lac - Une fête du sport et d'élégance," *Le Turf*, 20.4.1934
- "Through my field-glasses. Record Crowd attends opening meeting. Panache Churbara carry off Big Races Johnny Michailidis' fine winners," *The Sprinter*, 20.4.1934
- "Racing - Opening of the new Alexandria Course - Unprecedented Crowd in Attendance," *The Sphinx*, 21.4.1934
- "La Semaine," *La Reforme Illustrée*, 22.4.1934
- *Sporting*, 25.4.1934
- *Jocker*, 27.4.1934
- "A l'Alexandria Racing Club - Le second gala hippique - Le Président du conseil y assiste," *La Bourse Egyptienne*, 30.4.1934
- *Le Stade*, 30.4.1934
- "A l'Alexandria Racing Club," *La Bourse Egyptienne*, 1.5.1934
- "Le 'Premier' à l'Alexandria Racing Club," *Le Phare Egyptien*, 1.5.1934
- "Alexandria Racing Club," *La Gazette d'Orient*, 5.5.1934
- *La Reforme Illustrée*, 6.5.1934

- "Vers l'accord ? - Une éclaircie à l'horizon," *Le Turf*, 18.5.1934
- "Reports and rumours," *The Egyptian Gazette*, 25.5.1934
- "The irrigation scandal - Combating Favouritism and Arbitrariness - How water is distributed in the provinces," *Egyptian Mail*, 28.11.1934
- "Alexandria's new games centre - Smouha City Sports Club - Attractive premises," *The Egyptian Gazette*, 19.12.1934
- "New Sports Club - Une exquise oasis à Smouha City," *La Gazette d'Orient*, 20.12.1934
- "Le Développement d'Alexandrie. La Cité Smouha," *Le Dimanche Illustré*, 23.12.1934
- "The New Sports Club - Smouha City -Conditions of Membership," *Egyptian Mail*, 23.12.1934
- "NSC conditions of membership," *Al Bahar*, 23.12.1934 [in Arabic]
- *Al Jihad*, 24.12.1934 [in Arabic]
- "Smouha – extension of 9-metre canal drainage tunnel," *Al Ahram*, 25.12.1934 [in Arabic]
- "The New Sports Club - Cité Smouha - Les conditions requises pour l'inscription des membres," *La Reforme*, 26.12.1934
- "Cité Smouha. The New Sports Club," *Efimeris*, 28.12.1934 [in Greek]
- "Le New Sports Club au 'Smouha City'," *Le Phare Egyptienne*, 29.12.1934
- *Al Ahram*, 29.12.1934 [in Arabic]
- "The New Sports Club. Cité Smouha. Le condizioni richieste per l'iscrizione dei soci," *Il Giornale d'Oriente*, 30.12.1934
- Photo of the new Club House, *Egyptian Mail*, 30.12.1934
- "Alexandria Municipality. Administrative Organization. Minister of Interior issues regulations," *The Egyptian Gazette*, 7.1.1935
- "Sante, vigueur, divertissement. Le New Sports Club à la Cité Smouha offre ces trois avantages," *La Bourse Egyptienne*, 9.1.1935
- "Communications with Smouha City. New omnibus services," *The Egyptian Gazette*, 22.2.1935
- "The new bus connections with Smouha City," *Anatoli*, 22.2.1935 [in Greek]
- *Al Ahram*, 4.3.1935

The available newspaper articles from 19.12.1935 to 28.10.1937 indicate the routine running of the New Sporting Club and the increasing number and importance of the competitions of both golf and tennis as well as the social life of the club. The following articles instead concern the sequestration of Smouha City and negotiations over compensation by the British and the Arab Republic of Egypt.

- *Daily Telegraph and Morning Post*, 17.11.1958
- "Britons stood to lose millions on Suez pact," *Daily Mail*, 3.2.1959
- *Daily Telegraph and Morning Post*, 3.2.1959
- *Daily Telegraph and Morning Post*, 6.2.1959
- Richard Kilian, "Decaying 'lost city' holds up pact," *Daily Express*, 9.2.1959
- "Egypt insists Smouha land 'agricultural'," *The Financial Times*, 13.2.1959
- "Not so agricultural," *The Times*, 13.2.1959
- *Daily Telegraph and Morning Post*, 14.2.1959
- Douglas Brown, "Smouha Estate wrangle," *The Times*, 16.2.1959
- Wilson Broadbent, "Mediators Black flies to end Suez Pact deadlock," *Daily Mail*, 20.2.1959

- Joe Alex Morris Jr., "British Jarred by report of Black's trip," *New York Herald Tribune*, 21.2.1959
- "Mr. Black for Cairo," *Daily Mail*, 21.2.1959
- Joe Alex Morris Jr., "Black Expected to mediate last U.K.-U.A.R. differences," *New York Herald Tribune*, 23.2.1959
- "At last, Egypt pact is ready, *Daily Express*, 27.2.1959
- "The Smouha Affair," *The Illustrated London News*, 28.2.1959
- "Shorn in Egypt," *The Sunday Times*, 1.3.1959
- "Egypt pact a sell-out, says Britons' leader," *Daily Telegraph and Morning Post*, 7.3.1959
- "Reluctant approval to Egypt agreement," *Daily Telegraph and Morning Post*, 20.3.1959
- "Family make £12½m claim over 'Smouha City'," *Daily Telegraph and Morning Post*, 25.7.1961
- "Family wins Nasser millions," *Daily Express*, 11.8.1961
- "£1m interim payment for 'Smouha City'," *Daily Telegraph and Morning Post*, 12.8.1961
- "Egypt fund tax," *Daily Telegraph*, 30.9.1961
- "Rich Egyptians' wealth seized," *The Financial Times*, 23.10.1961
- "Higher payment from Egypt fund," *The Times*, 21.11.1961
- "Cairo claims a 'new confession'," *Daily Telegraph and Morning Post*, 4.12.1961

Acknowledgements

Pride of place in my thanks goes to Alan Macgregor who spent 25 years in Alexandria as the journalist representing *The Times*. In his later years, living in Geneva, he did extensive research on the history of my family and much of my contribution to this book stems directly or indirectly from interviews he made with members of my family and other connections. His son, John, has kindly given his approval to Alan's wish that one day, this book would appear.

Yun joined me at a time when, administratively I had lost my way on this project. She has taken it over and a load off my back. I am eternally grateful for the pleasant and efficient contact she has had with myself and all who she have been in contact with, and for the enthusiasm she had put into bringing it to its conclusion.

Among the many people to whom I owe thanks are Sandro Manzoni with his AAHA group for the many openings he has provided; Bob Nagger for his advice and assistance on the computer; my cousin Jean and her son David Nagger of Amazon for information on changes in the publishing scenario; Maura Atwater of Amazon; Omar Bassiouny, my friend and lawyer for his help and feedback; Joe Boulad and many others who have kept me up to date on the changes of the situation in Alexandria, Jean-Louis McGregor; Serge Kaplun Tricorne; Olivier Guignard; Chewikar Abdelaziz; Freddy Martell; Adam Chapman and Emily Carter; Michael Haag.

I am also grateful for the moral support and advice of my brother, Brian Smouha and many of my cousins.

As for Marie-Cecile and Cristina, I have enjoyed their enthusiasm and our relationship. And last but not least, my wife Sylvia, who has had to put up with a lot.

Richard Smouha

Firstly, I wish to thank Sandro Manzoni and his wife Anne-Marie, who first welcomed me in Geneva in June 2008 and put me in touch with Richard and Sylvia Smouha. I was then writing a paper about the Sidi Gaber competition with my dear friend and colleague Armando Scaramuzzi, who has done a lot of work at the initial stage of the project.

My warmest thanks also go to Rodolfo Loria who, in the late 1990s, handed to me what was left of his father's archive, and to Luisa Secchi Tarugi, who also managed to find in her family records whatever was left of her father's project for the Sidi Gaber competition.

My friend Margarita Sakka kindly allowed me to use some rare iconographic material, without which we would have had some difficulties in showing how Smouha City looked like in its heyday. Cécile Shaalan from CEAlex has always been a reliable support whenever I needed consult on "Alexandrian matters". Among the many people to whom I owe thanks are certainly Anna Caccia-Dominioni, Mohamed Awad, Mercedes Volait, Claudine Piaton, Juliette Hueber, Dorothy Vivien Sinnott Smith, Francesca Bonfante, Luca Monica and Giorgio Fiorese.

As always, my friend and colleague Annalisa Scaccabarozzi has joined this project with enthusiasm, competence and dedication. Yun Zhang John has been a priceless support to complete the book.

I have very much enjoyed Richard's insights on the Alexandria society of his grandfather and father's times, as well as Marie-Cécile's knowledge of the site in antiquity.

Finally, I wish thank Sylvia for her exquisite hospitality, who made every trip to Geneva a nice break from Milan's daily toil.

Cristina Pallini

Biographical note

Richard Smouha was born in 1932. Educated at Harrow School and Magdalene College, Cambridge, he took a degree in Economics and Law after two years national service in the RAF. He was called to the Bar in 1959 and then obtained a degree in French Law from Paris University.
After serving as a company lawyer in Geneva, he was employed in Swiss banking before setting up as an independent investment adviser and bond fund manager.
He and his wife Sylvia have three children, each of whom has three children.

Cristina Pallini was born in Milan in 1964. She took a degree in Architecture from Milan Politecnico, where she is currently employed in teaching and research activities. She holds a Phd in Architectural Composition from Venice University of Architecture (2001). Her research on Alexandria has been funded by the Italian Research Council (CNR) and by the Aga Khan Program at MIT.

Marie-Cécile Bruwier is an archaeologist and art historian. She specializesed in Egyptology and initiated the archaeological research in Smouha (Alexandria) from 2009-2012. The author of over 50 publications, she was the recipient of the The Bologna Lemaire Prize in 2010. Presently she is the Scientific Director of the Royal Museum of Mariemont and lectures at the Catholic University of Louvain.